Palgrave Studies in Classical Liberalism

Series Editors

David F. Hardwick, Department of Pathology and Laboratory Medicine, The University of British Columbia, Vancouver, BC, Canada

Leslie Marsh, Department of Economics, Philosophy and Political Science, The University of British Columbia, Okanagan, BC, Canada

This series offers a forum to writers concerned that the central presuppositions of the liberal tradition have been severely corroded, neglected, or misappropriated by overly rationalistic and constructivist approaches.

The hardest-won achievement of the liberal tradition has been the wrestling of epistemic independence from overwhelming concentrations of power, monopolies and capricious zealotries. The very precondition of knowledge is the exploitation of the epistemic virtues accorded by society's situated and distributed manifold of spontaneous orders, the DNA of the modern civil condition.

With the confluence of interest in situated and distributed liberalism emanating from the Scottish tradition, Austrian and behavioral economics, non-Cartesian philosophy and moral psychology, the editors are soliciting proposals that speak to this multidisciplinary constituency. Sole or joint authorship submissions are welcome as are edited collections, broadly theoretical or topical in nature.

David Gordon · Wanjiru Njoya

Redressing Historical Injustice

Self-Ownership, Property Rights and Economic Equality

palgrave
macmillan

David Gordon
Ludwig von Mises Institute
Auburn, AL, USA

Wanjiru Njoya
Law School
University of Exeter
Exeter, UK

ISSN 2662-6470 ISSN 2662-6489 (electronic)
Palgrave Studies in Classical Liberalism
ISBN 978-3-031-26583-9 ISBN 978-3-031-26584-6 (eBook)
https://doi.org/10.1007/978-3-031-26584-6

This Palgrave Macmillan imprint is published by the registered company Springer Nature Switzerland AG
The registered company address is: Gewerbestrasse 11, 6330 Cham, Switzerland

To Kiara Maria Njoya
and to the memory of my Father and Mother, Hyman and Sybil Gordon

Preface

I first encountered Dr. Wanjiru Njoya in June 2021, when she sent me the first chapter of her outstanding book *Economic Freedom and Social Justice* (Palgrave Macmillan, 2021) and, to my surprise and delight, asked me to write a foreword to it. In the time since then, she has become a very dear friend and, in our many Zoom meetings and hundreds of emails, I have been impressed with her commitment to liberty, philosophical acuity and immense knowledge of law.

Now, she has honoured me even more by asking me to be the co-author of her new book, and I was once more delighted to accept, though with a sense of guilt also, as she is responsible for the text of the book, and my contribution to it does not approach what would standardly be expected of a co-author. She has been kind enough to tell me, though, that she has been influenced by my work, and for that reason I have accepted my undeserved place as her collaborator.

Demands for "social justice" and reparations to members of groups deemed disadvantaged are everywhere on the rise, but these strident calls for action ignore a fundamental question. What is justice? Classically, justice is to give each person what is due to him, and contrary to much modern dogma, this does not require enforced equality of outcomes but is inconsistent with it. Even worse are proposals to grant members of certain groups privileges far beyond what others receive.

Through a detailed analysis of these proposals, we show that they not only violate the classical concept of justice, essential to a free society, but raise insurmountable legal problems when it is attempted to put them into practice. We do not deny that various minorities have suffered unjust harms in the past through slavery and imperialism, but the historical record shows, contrary to fashionable propaganda, that the social and economic problems facing these minorities today do not primarily stem from ancestral injuries. The way to help minorities is clear, and it is the way to help everyone. We must establish and maintain a complete free market, resting on libertarian rights.

Our stance is out of favour but we believe that the perennial wisdom we have endeavoured to articulate remains true for our time. "Great is truth, and mighty above all things." (1 Esdras 4: 41, KJV).

Auburn, Alabama — David Gordon
Exeter, England — Wanjiru Njoya

Acknowledgements

I wish to express my gratitude to Dr. David Gordon for collaborating with me on this project, for his generosity in scheduling Zoom meetings despite the time difference between us, for sharing his encyclopaedic knowledge of philosophy, history, law and economics, and most of all for his wisdom, friendship and inimitable sense of humour.

In this book we develop further some of the themes arising in the interplay between individual liberty and economic inequality which have inspired our earlier work, in particular *An Austro-Libertarian View: Essays by David Gordon* Volumes I, II and III (Ludwig von Mises Institute, 2017) and *Economic Freedom and Social Justice: The Classical Ideal of Equality in Contexts of Racial Diversity* (Palgrave Macmillan, 2021). Our aim in writing this book is to evaluate the racial justice debates from the perspective of the natural law tradition in which objective truth can be ascertained through reason and through an understanding of human nature.

We owe an intellectual debt of gratitude to Murray Rothbard's *Ethics of Liberty* (Humanities Press, 1982) and to all the Lockean philosophers, radical in the truest sense, who have endeavoured to explicate the meaning of human liberty.

We are also grateful to Leslie Marsh and David Hardwick, editors of the *Palgrave Studies in Classical Liberalism*, for their enthusiastic support for this project and to Ellie Duncan, Lynnie Sharon and the editorial team at Palgrave Macmillan for their helpfulness and professionalism.

Above all, we acknowledge the love and support of our families. This book is dedicated to Kiara Maria Njoya, and to the memory of Hyman and Sybil Gordon.

Auburn, Alabama
Exeter, England
December 2022

David Gordon
Wanjiru Njoya

Contents

1
Introduction

The concept of self-ownership lies at the heart of individual liberty. No legal system can rightly be said to uphold the ideal of liberty if it undermines self-ownership and property rights. Yet in recent years the concept of self-ownership has increasingly come under attack from proponents of restorative justice who seek to reallocate private property between different racial or ethnic groups in a bid to redress historical injustice. Wealth redistribution is favoured as a means of eradicating economic inequality between different racial groups, and resources are therefore transferred from one group to another without regard to the implications for property rights and equality before the law. The dominant view seems to be that wealth redistribution in favour of marginalised racial groups takes priority over the protection of property rights. This book defends the idea of self-ownership in the context of proposals to pay reparations for colonialism and slavery. We argue that the notion of distributive justice undermines the idea of self-ownership, and reparations based on redistributive schemes, therefore, attempt to achieve justice through unjust methods. The analysis focuses on three issues: wealth redistribution schemes designed to redress historical injustice, the

D. Gordon and W. Njoya, *Redressing Historical Injustice*, Palgrave Studies in Classical Liberalism,
https://doi.org/10.1007/978-3-031-26584-6_1

implications of such schemes for self-ownership and property rights, and the role of private property in defending liberty and justice.

The central question addressed by the book is: why not redistribute property in accordance with people's demands for compensation based on historical grievances? These demands are based on allegations of historical crimes which are said to have left a legacy of economic inequality manifested in a racial wealth gap. Satisfying these demands would be consistent with many people's belief in distributive justice and collective guilt, so a politically compelling case could be made that wealth ought to be redistributed unless there are good reasons not to do so. Many people feel that paying for historical injustice is self-evidently moral, especially if they feel in a vague sense morally tainted by historical events and would therefore be willing to make amends to shake off those feelings: "people often feel shame, and are stigmatized by others, as a result of their association with the wrongful conduct. Though the shame and stigma seem irrational from a moral point of view, they are psychological and social facts, which have behavioral consequences."[1] Many would therefore support paying reparations as a way of atoning for past events that cast a shadow over contemporary race relations.

To address that question the book draws upon Lockean theories of natural rights. The basic principle is that "no one ought to harm another in his life, health, liberty, or possessions."[2] Philosophers writing in the Lockean tradition such as Rothbard and Nozick defend property rights by reference to principles of natural justice, and would therefore agree that property must be justly acquired and transferred.[3] As Nozick explains, "justice in holdings is historical; it depends upon what actually has happened."[4] As will be discussed in Chapter 3 of this book, it

[1] Posner, E. A. and Vermeule, A. (2003). Reparations for Slavery and Other Historical Injustices. *Columbia Law Review*, 103, pp 689, 709.

[2] Locke, J. (1980). *Second Treatise of Government* (C. B. Macpherson, Ed.). Hackett Publishing, Section 4.

[3] Rothbard, M. N. (2002). *The Ethics of Liberty*. New York University Press; Rothbard, M. N. (1995). *An Austrian Perspective on the History of Economic Thought*. Volumes I & II, Edward Elgar; Olsthoorn, J. (2019). Self-Ownership and Despotism: Locke on Property in the Person, Divine Dominium of Human Life, and Rights-Forfeiture. *Social Philosophy and Policy*, 36(2), p 242; Nozick, R. (1974). *Anarchy, State and Utopia*. Blackwell Publishing.

[4] Nozick, *Anarchy, State and Utopia*, p 152.

is sometimes impossible to ascertain exactly what happened when the details of the original acquisition are lost in the mists of time. But the principle is clear, that any property which is unjustly acquired or seized must be returned to its rightful owner if justice is to be served. Nozick frames the relevant philosophical questions as follows:

> If past injustice has shaped present holdings in various ways, some identifiable and some not, what now, if anything, ought to be done to rectify those injustices?...How, if at all, do things change if the beneficiaries and those made worse off are not the direct parties in the act of injustice, but, for example, their descendants?...How far back must one go in wiping clean the historical slate of injustices? What may victims of injustice permissibly do in order to rectify the injustices being done to them, including the many injustices done by persons acting through their government?[5]

Waldron identifies the essential reason why many people support the payment of reparations in answer to those questions: "individual men and women are mortal; but groups are not" and therefore it seems to many people that the groups which suffered historical injustice "are still there, even if their individual membership has changed."[6] It then seems to follow that the case should not be treated as historical at all: based on notions of group claims and group liability the present members of the group that suffered can demand reparation, and present members of the group that perpetrated the injustice are liable to satisfy the demand. Waldron argues that a just system of property rights must take historical injustice into account partly because that injustice is not really "historical" in the sense that it lies in the past. Rather, the historical injustice experienced by a group endures through time even if the individual members of the group may have changed through the generations.

Waldron's point is that just as the police should not say "let bygones be bygones" to anyone reporting the theft of his property, so we ought not to say let bygones be bygones to a group whose land was stolen in ages

5 Ibid., p 27.

6 Waldron, J. (2002). Redressing Historic Injustice. *The University of Toronto Law Journal*, 52(1), pp 135, 146.

past. But from a classical liberal perspective rights and liabilities do not vest in groups. As will be detailed in Chapter 4 of this book in discussing the importance of individual liberty for the rule of law, it does not make sense to say that "we" suffered from slavery and "we" have been waiting for our slavery reparations for 400 years. *We* were not there at the time of those events. Group identity is deeply meaningful to many people in a cultural, family, community or religious sense, but in allocating legal liability and making people pay for past crimes nobody can be held responsible for wrongs committed by someone else, whether present or past. An important implication of formal equality and individual liberty is that liability is individual, not collective. Collectivist interpretations of guilt, responsibility and retribution are therefore incompatible with the rule of law. Nor can anyone seek vindication of a claim that vests in someone else. If no valid claim vests in any individual member of a group, then that group of individuals as a collective unit cannot have a valid group claim.

To substantiate these arguments the discussion draws upon the idea of justice as a set of principles denoting something more than majority opinion or popular vote based for example on the number of people who believe that a scheme would be just. Instead, an attempt is made to evaluate whether, and if so in what sense, the proposals in question are described as just, and the precise grounds on which the claim to justice is made. We do not argue that all must agree on a precise definition of justice, but rather that each justice-based argument should aim for precision in identifying the grounds for its conception of justice. Clarity of definitions and ideological positions is essential to enable coherent debate between different political and philosophical perspectives. A clearer and more explicit consideration of what is meant by justice is also essential to avoid the tyranny of a majority that might result if all ethical questions are decided by a democratic show of hands.

We define justice as a system of liberty based on self-ownership and property rights, which means that we consider a defence of property rights to be essential in meeting the demands of justice. Restorative justice in the context of the reparations debates refers to notions of corrective justice or reversing historical injustice.[7] Restorative justice in that context expresses ideas of social justice which seek to reconcile different groups and create social peace and harmony, focusing on "building connections and enhancing communication between perpetrators and those they victimized, and forging ties across the community."[8] That concept of restorative justice often invokes the rhetoric of property, for example through "stolen land" acknowledgments, proprietary restitution for slavery, honouring historical promises to transfer property to freed slaves upon emancipation, or claims that the wealth of former colonial powers "rightfully belongs" to those exploited by colonialism. By invoking the language of justice to seek the restoration of property to its rightful owner, or to seek financial restitution in lieu of property transfers to victimised groups, these interpretations of restorative justice call into question the classical foundations of property rights. They seek to reconceptualise property rights in a way that overrides classical interpretations of property rights in order better to reflect the distributive goals of restorative justice. To that extent Lockean ideals including the concept of self-ownership, just acquisition of property through homesteading, the prerogative of a property owner to exclude others for any reason or indeed no reason, and the right to resist the compulsory seizure of one's property, all of which are essential components of private property, are fundamentally irreconcilable with the wealth redistribution claims made under the aegis of restorative justice.

Yet many people consider the desire to redress historic injustice to be so morally compelling that they would be likely to support wealth redistribution proposals that are framed as a necessary response to injustice. The reparations debate is heavy with emotional arguments invoking the grievance of racial exploitation and cruelty. The scholarly literature is dominated by egalitarian and socialist perspectives which see racial justice as a basis for wealth redistribution and do not question the underlying rationale of the case. Posner and Vermeule argue that "the literature is often tendentious and rhetorical (in the pejorative sense) rather than

[7] The idea is that "corrective justice is the relevant or primary category for reparations involving groups or large numbers of individual victims of injustice": Walker, M. U. (2006). Restorative Justice and Reparations. *Journal of Social Philosophy*, 37(3), p 377.

[8] Ibid.

analytical" and that where it is analytical it does not address normative debates.[9] They are also critical of those who minimise the merits of reparations claims: "Opponents of reparations, on the other hand, minimize the relevant injustices and portray reparations proposals as outlandish or even unprecedented, overlooking that federal and state governments have often paid reparations in one form or another."[10] From a natural law perspective, the fact that governments have paid such claims in the past does not mean that the claims are presumptively just; on the contrary, our discussion emphasises the extent to which governments themselves undermine property rights and thereby perpetrate new injustices.

While our discussion considers some of the practical difficulties that may arise in paying reparations, the main aim of the book is to address the normative implications for theories of property rights. Understanding the moral and ethical implications of reframing the concept of property rights may not directly influence political decision-making on whether to pay reparations, which tends to proceed based on a cost–benefit analysis, but may nevertheless be of interest to any policymakers who might care about the moral and ethical considerations of different policy choices. Policy analysis tends to focus on the costs and benefits of particular decisions and to overlook the ethical considerations: "To some social scientists, an ethical or philosophical critique of any political programme may seem idle, because political actors are not driven by moral theories. But people's ideas at least partly explain their behaviour, and those ideas include their notions of what is right and wrong, just and unjust."[11] In addition, the moral case is central to evaluating the legitimacy of state power which is invoked to raise taxes and spend social welfare funds on paying reparations. As Nozick argues, "moral philosophy sets the background for, and boundaries of, political philosophy. What persons may and may not do to one another limits what they may

[9] Posner and Vermeule, *Reparations for Slavery and Other Historical Injustices*, p 690.

[10] Ibid.

[11] Shaw, W. H. (2003). They Stole Our Land: Debating the Expropriation of White Farms in Zimbabwe. *The Journal of Modern African Studies*, 41(1), p 75.

do through the apparatus of a state, or do to establish such an apparatus. The moral prohibitions it is permissible to enforce are the source of whatever legitimacy the state's fundamental coercive power has."[12]

This book therefore conducts a normative evaluation of the implications of the reparations debates for individual liberty and property rights. While we draw upon historical, political and philosophical perspectives, the discussion focuses on the implications for the legal framework and the rule of law. It is increasingly the case that property rights are so heavily regulated in the public interest that little is left in the contemporary discourse of the classical foundations of property rights. The concept of self-ownership seems in that sense an unlikely theoretical and normative lens through which to evaluate the historical injustice debates. But regulatory attacks on the foundations of private property, for example through eminent domain or compulsory acquisition, do not eliminate the need to consider carefully the normative foundations of property rights and the importance of such rights for our concept of justice; on the contrary the attempt to erode private property rights only emphasises the need to understand better the importance of property rights and how such rights relate to prevailing theories of justice. Given that reparations payments are claims on public funds, and that public resources are ultimately dependent on resources that the state derives from its citizens, the implications of the reparations debate for property rights and the rule of law merit more careful analysis.

1.1 Classical Liberalism and Natural-Rights Libertarianism

The book draws upon classical liberal theories in which individual liberty, self-ownership and private property are interdependent in the sense that encroachment on one of these rights undermines the others. In this

[12] Nozick, *Anarchy, State and Utopia*, p 6.

tradition, property rights are conceptualised as human rights.[13] Our argument relies in particular upon theories of property rights as conceptualised in the Lockean tradition, treating principles of natural law as a normative standard by which to evaluate the various demands advanced under the banner of "justice." The aim of our discussion is not to outline a complete theory of property rights or to evaluate all the theoretical debates surrounding Lockean principles of justice which are well canvassed in the literature.[14] Rather, the aim is to address new questions arising in the context of reparations demands currently being debated in liberal democracies and in particular the UK, the USA and Canada.

To that end the book treats natural law principles of self-ownership and property rights as "a guidepost for shaping and reshaping whatever positive law may be in existence" and establishing, in a normative sense, what should be the rules of positive law.[15] The natural-rights philosophy of rights aims to delineate the nature and content of property rights as rights governing legal and social systems, and the book focuses in particular on implications for the rule of law and public policy. The discussion is therefore not concerned with theories of private morality which aim to advise people on how they should behave in their private lives: "What may be the moral or immoral ways of exercising [property rights] is a question of personal ethics rather than of political philosophy—which is concerned solely with matters of right, and of the proper exercise of physical violence in human relations."[16] The analytical distinction between natural law principles of justice and private morality is important in understanding the basic nature of property rights. For example, the right to exclude, which is central to the definition of ownership and private property, does not mean that individuals are advised to exclude (or indeed not to exclude) others from their homes or lives. This point may seem self-evident, but it is often forgotten in critiques of property

[13] Alchian, A. A. (2007). Private Property. In Henderson, D. R. *The Concise Encyclopedia of Economics*. Liberty Fund: "Inequality exists in any society. But the purported conflict between property rights and human rights is a mirage—property rights are human rights."

[14] For a critique of Lockean theory see Waldron, J. (2012). *The Rule of Law and the Measure of Property*. Cambridge University Press; Waldron, J. (2002). *God, Locke and Equality: Christian Foundations of John Locke's Political Thought*. Cambridge University Press.

[15] Rothbard, *Ethics of Liberty*, p 17.

[16] Ibid., p 24.

rights. Thus we see Bauer's analysis of economic development, in which he highlights the importance of property rights for economic progress, being criticised as "scarcely a tenable position for those who are called to love their neighbour as themselves."[17] For purposes of analytical clarity economic analysis ought to be distinguished from personal morality, and on that basis, this book examines the conceptual nature of self-ownership and private property as foundational ideas in legal and political thought.

The book draws upon a variety of examples from different jurisdictions to illustrate the argument. Wealth redistribution efforts are increasingly extended beyond the borders of nation states through ideas of global justice which seek to redistribute wealth between countries. Traditionally this was mainly done through foreign aid, but redistributive schemes are increasingly framed as reparations for historical events such as slavery and colonialism that transcend national borders. For example in recent debates about industrialised nations owing reparations for climate change to less developed countries, the idea of reparations for historical events (which in the case of the environment is expressed as a way to atone for the impact of the Industrial Revolution) has acquired increasing influence in global debates about fairness between richer and poorer nations.[18] In referring to these developments we do not suggest that the demands of justice are best defined or met at the global level, nor that the demands of justice vary from the national to the global level. On the contrary, justice derived from self-ownership is justice based on individual liberty. Nevertheless, the global context of the wealth redistribution debate means that the underlying concerns cannot fully be understood within the confines of a single jurisdiction.

Although our analysis is philosophically rooted in natural-rights libertarian thought, we also discuss a wide range of other classical liberal perspectives which treat self-ownership as the conceptual foundation for liberty and property. This approach requires to be justified at the outset, as there are several important issues on which proponents of these

[17] Hay, D. (1984). Equality, the Third World and Economic Delusion. *Transformation*, 1(2), p 27.

[18] Mayer, B. (2017). Climate Change Reparations and the Law and Practice of State Responsibility. *Asian Journal of International Law*, 7, p 185.

different philosophical positions would disagree. For example, natural-rights libertarians and utilitarians differ in some of their foundational philosophical constructs.[19] Although all classical liberals accord high priority to individual liberty and property rights, many natural-rights libertarians would treat property rights as absolute while many classical liberals would regard property rights as presumptively important but not absolute. In the context of redressing historical injustice, utilitarians might frame the issues as a purely practical set of questions, rather than invoking notions of justice. For example, Posner and Vermeule argue that the legal and institutional considerations are as important as considerations of justice:

> the question of whether reparations should be paid turns crucially on choices about the form of payment, the identity of the beneficiaries, the identity of the parties who will bear the costs of payment, and so forth. The prudential and institutional issues surrounding reparations schemes, in other words, are as important as the high-level questions about justice and injustice that are usually the focus of reparations debates.[20]

It will be seen in Chapter 2, in discussing the importance of property rights in classical liberalism, that some theorists defend property rights on utilitarian grounds while others defend such rights as natural rights. The concept of self-ownership may therefore be defended, as an idea worthy of explication in its own right, by drawing upon these different traditions. That is not to say that scholars writing in different classical traditions would necessarily agree with each other's arguments, or indeed with the arguments we advance in this book. In referring to different perspectives as "classical liberal" it is not intended to suggest that all classical liberals agree on all points concerning the scope and parameters of liberty and property. Nor is any attempt made in this book to reconcile

---

[19] For example, "Rothbard's approach is normative, based strictly on natural law justice principles rather than economic efficiency. Mises, by contrast, is a strong critic of natural law. His "rule utilitarianism" views markets as a form of social cooperation, and seeks rules of conduct which encourage such cooperation for land disputes": Deist, J. (2021, June 3). A Libertarian Approach to Disputed Land Titles. *Mises Wire*. https://mises.org/wire/libertarian-approach-disputed-land-titles.

[20] Posner and Vermeule, *Reparations for Slavery and Other Historical Injustices*, p 689.

the different perspectives with each other—an impossible and unnecessary task, as they all merit consideration in their own right. But these interpretative differences do not mean that nothing can be learned from considering a variety of perspectives on the role of property rights in classical liberal thought. The relevance of each theory for our analysis lies in the priority each theory accords to the concept of self-ownership, and in the extent to which each theory helps to explain why property rights matter for liberty and justice.

In drawing upon classical liberal perspectives we do not suggest that these are the only valid ways to understand justice, nor that all other ways of understanding justice in connection with property rights are invalid. We disagree with egalitarians, but we do not suggest that egalitarian views are somehow invalid; instead, we outline the basis on which we disagree.[21] Similarly, egalitarians are able to contribute to the debate without suggesting that their view of justice precludes any different understanding of justice. For example, Harris, who like most modern theorists follows Rawls, observes that "there is no etymological or conceptual warrant for insisting that the term 'justice' must be deployed in only one sense."[22] For purposes of our analysis, it is necessary only to acknowledge that justice may be understood in different ways and that it is not necessary, for peaceful coexistence, for everyone to arrive at a unanimous consensus on what is meant by "justice" or what a theory of justice must entail. Nor should debate on the meaning of justice be stifled in an attempt to create the impression of a consensus on matters that are in fact deeply contested. Our aim is to highlight the specific tenets of classical liberal thought which illuminate the debates on redressing historical injustice. Therefore, the aim is not to delineate the nature and boundaries of the property in a general sense, nor to reconcile different philosophical perspectives on property rights, but specifically to address contemporary demands for restorative justice.

---

[21] For a more detailed discussion of the different interpretations of justice in the context of the social justice debates see Njoya, W. (2021). *Economic Freedom and Social Justice: The Classical Ideal of Equality in Contexts of Racial Diversity*. Palgrave Macmillan.

[22] Harris, J. W. (1996). *Property and Justice*. Oxford University Press.

The book argues that any popular demand labelled "property rights" which inherently contradicts and dismantles the classical liberal conception of property cannot meaningfully be described as property rights, nor can the conclusion be avoided that such demands are destructive of the concept of private property. A theory that aims to dismantle property rights cannot simply be described as "redefining" property rights. Instead, clarity of discourse requires such a theory to acknowledge that by setting out to dismantle property rights it signals that it considers property to be of little importance in a theory of justice. The premise of the rule of law, which includes the ideal of governance according to clear principles decided in advance, requires that concepts used to express principles of justice and individual rights must have a readily identifiable meaning.

The concepts of liberty, equality and property have of course long been highly contested. For example, some liberal perspectives defend self-ownership but deny that property rights in land and other natural resources are a necessary condition of freedom.[23] It is neither feasible nor desirable to tackle all philosophical questions that may arise concerning the meaning of these terms within the confines of one book, and we do not attempt to do so. Given the broad scope of the economic inequality and economic development debates with which the book is concerned, each chapter carefully delineates the limits of our inquiry. The aim is not to seek comprehensive solutions to all questions of economic inequality that may arise, but to highlight the implications for property rights of attempting to advance equality in a manner which encroaches upon, and in some cases goes so far as to extinguish, property rights.

We ask important questions about the justice of the case for reparations and about the legitimacy of the role played by the state in reallocating wealth based on race. In doing so we draw upon theories of natural law that highlight the normative implications of racial wealth redistribution. At the end of the book, we call into question the legitimacy of the state in so far as it violates the core principles of property rights. We do not suggest that we have thereby formulated a complete theory of justice, but we suggest that we have offered an alternative

---

[23] Steiner, H. (1994). *An Essay on Rights*. Oxford University Press; George, H. (1881). *Progress and Poverty*. D. Appelton & Co.

starting point for understanding the applicable principles of justice, an alternative that better meets the demands of justice than Rawlsian redistributive justice.[24]

To that end, we conceptualise a free-market society as one which rests on a system of private property rights, and the key policy implication of our approach to the reparations debate is that prioritising free markets requires a legal system which robustly protects the right to private property. Justice in turn depends on upholding the key tenets of the rule of law including the protection of property rights. We argue that questions of economic development inevitably raise a further set of related and interconnected questions about the meaning of equality, liberty and justice. Pulling on the thread of private property, by dismantling property rights in a bid to equalise wealth, risks unravelling the entire tapestry of classical liberalism, individual liberty, and the economic prosperity associated with market societies. The book, therefore, highlights the connections between the different conceptual pillars of a free society, connections which are often overlooked in the attempt to resolve pressing social and economic problems.

1.2 The Question of Racial Justice

In evaluating claims based on historic injustice, the reparations debates are further complicated by concerns about racial inequality. Much attention is devoted in these debates to the wealth "gaps" between racial groups. The presumption is that wealth inequalities between racial groups must be *caused* by racial discrimination. Questions of causation thus arise frequently throughout our discussion. There is a further presumption that frames the debates, namely that we have arrived at a general consensus about the need to close the racial wealth gap by redistributing wealth. The racial justice debate, therefore, concerns itself

[24] "What more does one need or can one have, in order to begin progressing toward a better theory, than a sketch of a plausible alternative view, which from its very perspective highlights the inadequacies of the best existing well-worked-out theory?": Nozick. *Anarchy, State and Utopia*, p 230.

not with the causes of inequality, but with the quickest and most effective ways of redistributing wealth. Classifying economic inequality as an injustice without regard to the causes of that inequality implies that wealth redistribution is the appropriate, or at any rate the quickest solution to redress that injustice. Thus there is a widespread view that some form of race-based reparations ought to be paid and it is simply a matter of ascertaining the appropriate limits, mechanisms and boundaries of such payments. For example, Moller identifies "important limits to reparations claims" based for example on the passage of time since the claims are said to have arisen.[25] He defends a "burden-shifting" approach to evaluating such claims, which places moral limits on the extent to which we "transfer our misfortunes to others," but he emphasises that property rights are not absolute and therefore accepts that in principle reparations for slavery and colonialism which fall within the moral limits he identifies would be justified.

In arguing that we can identify appropriate limits to reparations claims Moller aims to shed light on the "underlying logic of the claims," but he is concerned with establishing the moral bounds of an expansive welfare state rather than with questioning or challenging the essential validity of redistributive claims.[26] Darity and Mullen go further in arguing that the wealth gap can be closed through reparations by making financial payments to individuals from disadvantaged races.[27] The underlying presumptions, namely that wealth gaps justify non-voluntary forms of redistribution, go unchallenged, and little attempt is made in the racial justice literature to address the questions posed by Williams concerning the lack of any causal connection between discrimination and poverty.[28]

In addition to seeing wealth redistribution as the solution to racial inequality, disregarding the causes of inequality leads to the perception that tackling racism will resolve the racial wealth gap. For example, Perry depicts economic inequality as a racial discrimination problem and

---

[25] Moller, D. (2019). *Governing Least: A New England Libertarianism.* Oxford University Press.

[26] Ibid.

[27] Darity, W. A. and Mullen, K. (2020). *From Here to Equality: Reparations for Black Americans in the 21st Century.* University of North Carolina Press.

[28] Williams, W. E. (2011). *Race and Economics: How Much Can Be Blamed on Discrimination?* Hoover Institution Press.

argues that the prosperity gap can be resolved by tackling racism.[29] The idea that economic inequality is caused by racism is taken as self-evident. But if the causal links between these three factors—historical events, ongoing race discrimination and wealth distribution—are unclear then the case for regarding unequal economic outcomes or patterns of wealth distribution as an injustice rests on unsound foundations.

If the problem of economic inequality is described simply as a "gap" between the rich and the poor, and racial inequality is depicted as a gap between the wealth of white people and that of other races, it is easy to see why the solution is thought to lie in simply closing the gap through wealth transfers. But in the long run wealth redistribution designed to close gaps amounts to nothing more than a levelling-down scheme of wealth destruction and equally shared poverty. This would not only be absurd but would also violate the difference principle of Rawlsian redistributive justice which takes inequality as presumptive evidence of injustice only if these inequalities are not to the advantage of the least well-off class. Even Rawls did not presume the mere existence of a wealth gap to be conclusive evidence of injustice. If increased wealth and prosperity in society are valuable to all members of society, and if all members of society derive a benefit from living in a prosperous economy through the availability of more resources than would be available in a poor economy, then the question is not how to redistribute wealth but how to weigh competing values against each other. Rather than pursuing forms of redistribution that are inimical to productivity, economic equality instead depends upon the property rights that fuel economic progress.

In evaluating the debates about the most effective way to promote racial justice and economic equality the book highlights the importance of property rights for economic growth and prosperity. The book evaluates not only the specific claims made in relation to racial justice but also the symbolism reflected by the terminology of justice. Restorative justice

[29] Perry, A. (2020). *Know Your Price: Valuing Black Lives and Property in America's Black Cities*. Brookings Institution Press.

debates, to the extent that they question the validity of private property rights, often have as much to do with political power positioning and ideological opposition to capitalism as with claims for financial restitution. The book aims to highlight the importance of self-ownership and private property in the moral defence of capitalism, in defending individual liberty and in incentivising sustainable economic progress. We consider not only the conditions under which property should be returned to its rightful owners, but we also evaluate claims rooted in the wider and more amorphous claims based on reversing racial exploitation. In doing so we conceptualise property rights as essential not only for advancing economic equality and prosperity but also for safeguarding liberty.

1.3 Key Concerns in Redressing Historical Injustice

The book addresses three key concerns. First, the need for effective responses to global poverty. This is the key concern of economic development efforts. We argue that the preoccupation with colonial exploitation and legacies of racial discrimination masks the true causes of economic inequality and obscures the importance of free markets and voluntary exchange in alleviating poverty and advancing economic equality.

The second concern relates to how markets interact with theories of justice. The dominant perspectives of distributive justice not only fail to resolve economic inequality but also exacerbate inequality by diverting attention away from the real causes of poverty and encouraging people to be preoccupied with historical grievances as an explanation for their material conditions. While many economists have shown that distributive justice does not work, it is important to go further to address the moral case advanced by proponents of wealth redistribution and to offer a moral defence of capitalism. A moral defence offers an important perspective because the overriding concerns of those who see financial reparations and financial equity as the best response to historical injustice are framed as moral concerns rather than being efficiency related. Those who view reparations as the path to justice would therefore argue that it is always worth trying to address concerns about inequality even if the measures adopted prove to be ineffective. The moral case must therefore be squarely addressed. After all, those whose concerns are primarily influenced by moral considerations, such as compassion, could respond to the evidence of various causal factors driving poverty (such as poor levels of health and education) by saying that perhaps these are just further examples of the residual harms of historical exploitation. Moreover, when it is proved that wealth redistribution does not work, the Marxists who view society as a system of structural exploitation may simply retort that if redistribution does not seem to work the solution is to implement even *more* wealth redistribution. The evidence that wealth transfers do not work has long been clear, and has long failed to deter socialists from their path:

> President Johnson's "war on poverty" was intended, at least in substantial part, to redress the horrors of slavery and its aftermath. Furthermore, in the name of ameliorating the effects of our past aggression against Native Americans, we now offer them various forms of public assistance. Not only have these efforts failed to narrow the substantial wealth gap that has existed for many generations between whites and members of these communities, but there is ample evidence that because of the perverse incentives that were built into these programs, they have actually done more harm than good. Such long-term governmental largess promotes dependency and social isolation, and thus the kindest policy that we could implement for the victims of past wrongs is to wean them off such aid.[30]

For these reasons the appeal to utilitarian principles normally preferred by defenders of property rights is unlikely, by itself, to sway the historical injustice debates. The reasons for implementing wealth transfers in the first place are emotionally driven and appeals to the unworkability of the efforts therefore fail to persuade. An ethical defence of self-ownership and property rights is required. As Rothbard observes, "Neither can

[30] Friedman, M. D. (2015). *Libertarian Philosophy in the Real World: The Politics of Natural Rights*. Bloomsbury Academic, pp 19, 20.

Marxist views be rebutted by utilitarian paeans to the virtues of 'social peace.' Social peace is all very well, but true peace is essentially the quiet, unmolested enjoyment of one's legitimate property."[31]

In addressing both the causes of inequality and the morality of capitalism we aim to show that history and economic inequality are not causally connected, except perhaps in the general sense that everything in life, being part of the same world, is connected in a cosmic sense. As Sowell has argued, this general cosmic approach cannot serve as a blueprint for justice. Justice in the classical liberal ideal is not coterminous with economic or material equality. Justice, as we depict it in this book, is a system of liberty based on a set of natural rights including rights of self-ownership and property. It is often said that this view of justice is unhelpful in understanding historical injustice as it fails to equalise the fortunes of those who suffered historical exploitation. The question then arises whether a theory of justice must encompass the idea of wealth redistribution.

The notion of distribution is of course regarded by critics of classical liberalism as central to a theory of justice. For example, Seidman depicts the distributional challenge as emblematic of the failure of classical liberalism to promote justice.[32] All this means is that classical liberalism fails to achieve egalitarian goals, which is no more than a way of saying that classical liberalism reflects a different worldview from the egalitarian worldview. Where people pursue different priorities, it is unhelpful to say that one has failed to meet the goals of the other. By describing his critique of classical liberalism as a failure of *justice* Seidman presumes the meaning of justice to be self-evident or at least reflective of a consensus on the idea that wealth redistribution is necessary to meet the demands of justice. Such critiques bypass altogether the meaning of justice in the classical philosophy of liberalism, and are also wrong to suppose that poverty is of no concern for classical liberalism. The contentious issue does not concern the importance of poverty alleviation, racial harmony,

---

[31] Rothbard, *Ethics of Liberty*, p 53.

[32] Seidman, L. (2018). Seven Problems for Classical Liberals. In Henderson, M. T. (Ed.). *The Cambridge Handbook of Classical Liberal Thought*. Cambridge University Press, p 270.

or the desire to assist the vulnerable, but rather the respective roles of private charity, voluntary market exchange, government interventions and state coercion in achieving these goals. Liberalism in the classical tradition directs its focus to improve material conditions, as the best and more assured means of alleviating poverty and abolishing want and misery. As Mises explains:

> That there is want and misery in the world is not, as the average newspaper reader, in his dullness, is only too prone to believe, an argument against liberalism. It is precisely want and misery that liberalism seeks to abolish, and it considers the means that it proposes the only suitable ones for the achievement of this end.[33]

The book evaluates the coherence of the case for redressing historical injustice by identifying the underlying theories of justice on which that case claims to be based. Rather than proceeding on the basis of Rawlsian distributive justice wherein equality and fairness are essential to a theory of justice, the discussion treats self-ownership, property rights and liberty as the overriding principles of justice. Our analysis of the social justice arguments is based in part on ethical grounds, and in part on the interaction between property rights and concern for the welfare of others in the context of development economics. It may appear, superficially, that the owner's right to exclude is incompatible with concern for the welfare of others. Concern for others implies inclusion, not exclusion. But it does not follow if one is concerned about the plight of others, that the solution is to dismantle property rights. Including others may seem superficially to be the solution to social problems, but in the longer term inclusion is in itself neither productive or beneficial.

In that light the book treats property rights as essential to justice, as well as to peace, prosperity and liberty. These values are in turn preconditions for the third concern of our book: economic equality. We argue that people are more equal in peaceful societies which uphold individual liberty. Dismantling peace and prosperity in an attempt to

[33] Mises, L. v. (2005). *Liberalism: The Classical Tradition* (B.B. Greaves, Ed.). Liberty Fund, p xxiv.

achieve equality does not advance equality. On the contrary, it undermines social cohesion and renders equality meaningless. It is true that a defence of private property rights does not promise to yield equal distribution of wealth and fortune, which would be impossible in a world of diverse humanity, but we do not regard an identikit world of make-believe equality (to use Sowell's terminology)[34] as an ideal to which we ought to aspire.

1.4 Outline of the Book

The book is structured as follows. Chapter 2 highlights different philosophical justifications for self-ownership and property rights, including utilitarian and natural-rights perspectives. The chapter highlights the central role played by property rights in economic progress. Chapter 3 evaluates the case for redressing historical injustice through reparations. The chapter argues that the moral foundations of the case for reparations are unsound, and suggests that a better approach in pursuit of economic equality would be to address the true causes of inequality and poverty. Chapter 4 discusses the ideals of liberty, equality and the rule of law. The argument is that redefining property rights in a manner that violates the principles of private property is not only inimical to individual liberty but also violates core tenets of the rule of law. Chapter 5 focuses on markets and development economics, showing that economic development cannot be achieved through wealth transfers. Chapter 6 concludes by highlighting the implications of the historical injustice debates for how we understand the role of the state in liberal market democracies.

---

[34] Sowell, T. (2013). *Intellectuals and Race*. Basic Books, p 138: "Many people who advocate what they think of as equality promote what is in fact make-believe 'equality'. In economic terms, taking what others have produced and giving it to those who have not produced as much (or at all, in some cases) is make-believe equality."

References

Alchian, A. A. (2007). Private Property. In D. R. Henderson (Ed.), *The Concise Encyclopedia of Economics*. Liberty Fund.

Darity, W. A., Jr., & Mullen, A. K. (2020). *From Here to Equality: Reparations for Black Americans in the 21st Century*. University of North Carolina Press.

Deist, J. (2021, June 3). *A Libertarian Approach to Disputed Land Titles*. https://mises.org/wire/libertarian-approach-disputed-land-titles

Friedman, M. D. (2015). *Libertarian Philosophy in the Real World: The Politics of Natural Rights*. Bloomsbury Academic.

George, H. (1881). *Progress and Poverty*. D. Appelton & Co.

Harris, J. W. (1996). *Property and Justice*. Oxford University Press.

Hay, D. (1984). Equality, the Third World and Economic Delusion. *Transformation, 1*(2), 27.

Locke, J. (1980). *Second Treatise of Government*. (C. B. Macpherson, Ed.). Hackett Publishing.

Mayer, B. (2017). Climate Change Reparations and the Law and Practice of State Responsibility. *Asian Journal of International Law, 7*, 185.

Mises, L. v. (2005). *Liberalism: The Classical Tradition* (B. B. Greaves, Ed.). Liberty Fund. (Original work published 1927).

Moller, D. (2019). *Governing Least: A New England Libertarianism*. Oxford University Press.

Njoya, W. (2021). *Economic Freedom and Social Justice: The Classical Ideal of Equality in Contexts of Racial Diversity*. Palgrave Macmillan.

Nozick, R. (1974). *Anarchy, State and Utopia*. Blackwell Publishing.

Olsthoorn, J. (2019). Self-Ownership and Despotism: Locke on Property in the Person, Divine Dominium of Human Life, and Rights-Forfeiture. *Social Philosophy and Policy, 36*(2), 242–263. https://doi.org/10.1017/S0265052519000438

Perry, A. (2020). *Know Your Price: Valuing Black Lives and Property in America's Black Cities*. Brookings Institution Press.

Posner, E. A., & Vermeule, A. (2003). Reparations for Slavery and Other Historical Injustices. *Columbia Law Review, 103*, 689.

Rothbard, M. N. (1995). *An Austrian Perspective on the History of Economic Thought* (Vols. I & II). Edward Elgar.

Rothbard, M. N. (2002). *The Ethics of Liberty*. New York University Press (original publication 1982).

Seidman, L. (2018). *Seven Problems for Classical Liberals*. In M. T. Henderson (Ed.), *The Cambridge Handbook of Classical Liberal Thought* (p. 270). Cambridge University Press.

Shaw, W. H. (2003). They Stole Our Land: Debating the Expropriation of White Farms in Zimbabwe. *The Journal of Modern African Studies, 41*(1), 75.

Sowell, T. (1999). *The Quest for Cosmic Justice*. Touchstone.

Sowell, T. (2013). *Intellectuals and Race*. Basic Books.

Steiner, H. (1994). *An Essay on Rights*. Oxford University Press.

Waldron, J. (2002). *God, Locke and Equality: Christian Foundations of John Locke's Political Thought*. Cambridge University Press.

Waldron, J. (2012). *The Rule of Law and the Measure of Property*. Cambridge University Press.

Walker, M. U. (2006). Restorative Justice and Reparations. *Journal of Social Philosophy, 37*(3), 377.

Williams, W. E. (2011). *Race and Economics: How Much Can Be Blamed on Discrimination?* Hoover Institution Press.

2

Self-Ownership and Property Rights

Over the centuries philosophers have defined property rights in different ways. In recent years it has been proposed that the conceptual foundations of property rights should be redefined to meet the demands of distributive justice, in particular, to redress injustices relating to historical exploitation and conquest. This chapter explores two distinct lines of inquiry into the theoretical foundations of property rights in these debates: first in relation to claims for reparations to compensate for property that was historically stolen or expropriated from marginalised racial groups; and second in relation to non-voluntary wealth redistribution designed to redress the legacies of such historical events. The chapter offers a normative justification for private property rights in the context of racial economic disparities, arguing that the egalitarian concern with disparities does not justify undermining the classical concepts of self-ownership and property rights.

The classical interpretation of property rights, as it has evolved in the English common law tradition, is feared to be unsuited to the

D. Gordon and W. Njoya, *Redressing Historical Injustice*, Palgrave Studies in Classical Liberalism, https://doi.org/10.1007/978-3-031-26584-6_2

goals of distributive justice because it does not require that the prerogatives of ownership be subordinated to the "public interest" or "public policy." While it is possible in all common law jurisdictions to regulate the use of property in such a way as to promote the public interest, this is done through legislative interventions rather than through the conceptual framework of common law property rights. For example, taxation, eminent domain, compulsory acquisition, and other forms of regulation which are generally understood to be an encroachment on property rights, albeit said to be justifiable, are defined by statute. In most countries, such regulation is explicitly permitted by the constitution. Compensation is generally payable where regulation amounts to a "taking" or an expropriation.

More intrusive regulation of property, and in particular a redefinition of common law concepts of private property, is now sought in order to justify and validate further encroachments that are deemed necessary to eradicate economic inequality. Such interventions are said to be required to respond to pressing social welfare and racial justice concerns. The argument is that redressing the historical legacies of specific racial groups does not fall within the established parameters of land use regulation and therefore new ways of thinking about property distribution are necessary. As Posner and Vermeule have observed, reparations claims do not distinguish between claims that fall within the parameters of the law and those which call for new forms of political redress: "there are no clear conceptual boundaries that demarcate reparations from ordinary legal remedies, on the one hand, and other large-scale governmental transfer programs, on the other."[1] In this chapter we are concerned with the types of reparations claims that seek wealth transfers that would not ordinarily be legally available; in other words claims constructed on the premise that the existing legal framework does not offer sufficient redress and new forms of entitlement are required to redress historical injustice.

[1] Posner, E. A. and Vermeule, A. (2003). Reparations for Slavery and Other Historical Injustices. *Columbia Law Review*, 103, 689, p. 691.

We evaluate these claims within the theoretical framework described by Zwolinski and Ferguson as the "property-based approach to liberty."[2] In this libertarian tradition "liberty is *defined* in terms of respect for individuals' fundamental rights to self-ownership and justly-acquired external property."[3] Libertarianism treats private property not only as desirable, or even strongly desirable, but indispensable. The point here is not simply that property rights are important in libertarian theory, as it could be argued that property rights are important in many different political theories. Most philosophical theories would accord *some* importance to property rights, and thus the issue often debated is not whether property rights are important but rather the content and limits of property rights. As Zwolinski and Ferguson observe, "Of course, many non-libertarians support the institution of private property as well. But what makes libertarians distinctive is the *scope* and *weight* that they assign to this right…For many libertarians, property rights (especially the individual right of self-ownership) play a foundational role, undergirding most if not all of the other libertarian commitments, such as the right to free speech, or the right to own and use weapons for self-defense."[4] The aim of this discussion is to explore the implications of treating property rights as foundational in that sense.

2.1 The Concept of Self-Ownership

The idea of self-ownership is expressed in the principles of individual liberty and the inalienable rights that vest in all human beings. Self-ownership delineates the boundaries beyond which state power and majority rule ought not to encroach upon the rights of the individual. The classic principle of self-ownership is stated by Locke: "every man has a property in his own person; this nobody has any right to but himself.

[2] Zwolinski, M. and Ferguson, B. (2022). Introduction. In Zwolinski, M. and Ferguson, B. (Eds.). (2022). *The Routledge Companion to Libertarianism.* Routledge, p. 5.

[3] Ibid. (emphasis in original).

[4] Ibid., p. 3 (emphasis in original).

The labour of his body and the work of his hands we may say are properly his".[5] As Kurrild-Klitgaard explains, self-ownership in this sense is more than a technical concept about the right to control specific things with which one has mixed his labour. It also expresses the essential nature of humanity:

> The concept of self-ownership conceptualizes the unity and "wholeness" of the individual, the idea that one cannot, in terms of morality, separate an individual's personality from his reason, from his body, from his earthly life. In this sense, the concept denotes a sphere of autonomy within which an individual may act in a self-directed way without interference from others.[6]

Therefore self-ownership is much more than a right to ownership of one's own body, or "body ownership rhetoric" as Harris puts it.[7] It is not limited to protests couched in the language of "my body my choice," and Harris rightly observes that courts do not explicitly rely on the language of self-ownership in enforcing laws against crimes such as assault or murder. For purposes of such crimes the principle that violence is prohibited would suffice, and the moral justifications for prohibiting murder, assault, and theft are too deeply rooted in the common law for any judge to need to ask *why* they are prohibited. These prohibitions—do not commit murder, do not steal—originate in natural law concepts and principles of ethics and morality that reflect the concept of self-ownership. But the idea of self-ownership goes beyond ownership of one's body to invoke free will and freedom of choice in relation to economic activity, including the freedom to choose how to direct one's own labour and resources and to exercise control of the fruits of one's labour.

Individual liberty, therefore, rests on a defence of self-ownership, and cannot fully be defended without defending self-ownership. This point was expressed as follows by Overton in 1646:

---

[5] Locke, J. (1980). *Second Treatise of Government*. (C. B. Macpherson, Ed.). Hackett Publishing.

[6] Kurrild-Klitgaard, P. (2000). Self-Ownership and Consent. *Journal of Libertarian Studies*, 15(1), 43.

[7] Harris, J.W. (1996). *Property and Justice*. Oxford University Press, p. 184.

> To every Individuall in nature, is given an individuall property by nature, not to be invaded or usurped by any: for every one as he is himselfe, so he hath a selfe propriety, else could he not be himselfe, and on this no second may presume to deprive any of, without manifest violation and affront to the very principles of nature, and of the Rules of equity and justice between man and man.[8]

Overton sees the ideas of life, liberty and property as intrinsically linked to one another: "Liberty of conscience in matters of Faith, and divine worship; Liberty of the Person, and liberty of Estate: which consists properly in the propriety of their goods, and a disposing power of their possessions."[9] This is the essential reason why self-ownership matters in the defence of liberty. It explains why slavery and any form of domination or control by the state of individual citizens is unjust. As expressed by Fichte in 1793, "Man can neither be inherited, sold, nor be made the object of a gift; he can be no one else's property because he is his own property."[10] It is certainly ironic that it is now proposed, in the name of redressing the harm caused by slavery, to unravel the very concept that explains why slavery is unjust from a legal and moral perspective. The idea that no man can own another—as expressed in the abolitionist slogan *Am I not a man and a brother*?—is the normative basis of asserting that formal laws which legalised slavery were unjust, as they purported to define human beings as chattels owned by other human beings.

Within the libertarian tradition which regards self-ownership and property rights as foundational there are still philosophical points of divergence. For example, as mentioned in chapter one, natural-rights libertarians and utilitarians differ in their philosophical explication of

---

[8] An Arrow [Against All Tyrants and Tyrany, shot from the Prison of Newgate into the Prerogative Bowels of the Arbitrary House of Lords, and all other Usurpers and Tyrants whatsoever], October 12, 1646, reprinted in Gerald E. Aylmer, ed., The Levellers in the English Revolution (Ithaca, N.Y.: Cornell University Press, 1975), p. 3; discussed in Kurrild-Klitgaard, Self-Ownership and Consent.

[9] Kurrild-Klitgaard, Self-Ownership and Consent, p. 59.

[10] Johann Gottlieb Fichte, in Schmidt, J. (Ed.). (1996). *What is Enlightenment? Eighteenth-Century Answers and Twentieth-Century Questions*. University of California Press.

property rights.[11] Although it could be said that natural law also has utilitarian foundations, a key point of distinction between these perspectives concerns the relevance or importance of moral or ethical ideas within the framework of understanding property rights.[12] Utilitarian arguments are essential in explaining the role of property rights as the basis of economic progress and prosperity, as well as human liberty and happiness, but they do not directly address the moral concerns of the social justice debates. The next part of the discussion outlines utilitarian perspectives before moving on to consider the natural law perspectives which address the ethical concerns of those who seek to eradicate economic inequality.

2.2 Utilitarian Perspectives

Property rights may be defended on grounds that property is essential to prosperity, and all members of society are better off when society becomes more prosperous. The appropriate comparison for those concerned with social justice should not be how much better off each group in society is compared to other groups (that is, focusing on the gap between groups) but rather how much better off each group is compared to the previous position of that same group. It would then become apparent that it is more important to improve the living and material conditions of all groups than to erase the gap between different groups. Property rights help to achieve that goal. Dismantling property rights would leave society much worse off. In that sense, the value of property rights may be understood by reference to their function. Property rights may also be defended as human rights. As Alchian explains,

[11] "Rothbard's approach is normative, based strictly on natural law justice principles rather than economic efficiency. Mises, by contrast, is a strong critic of natural law. His "rule utilitarianism" views markets as a form of social cooperation, and seeks rules of conduct which encourage such cooperation for land disputes": Deist, J. (2021, June 3). A Libertarian Approach to Disputed Land Titles. *Mises Wire*. https://mises.org/wire/libertarian-approach-disputed-land-titles.

[12] Epstein, R.A. (1989). The Utilitarian Foundations of Natural Law. *Harvard Journal of Law and Public Policy* 12, 711.

> Private property rights do not conflict with human rights. They are human rights. Private property rights are the rights of humans to use specified goods and to exchange them…That is a fundamental reason for preference of a system of strong private property rights: private property rights protect individual liberty.[13]

This definition of property rights highlights their role as a foundation for human cooperation, productivity, peaceful coexistence, prosperity and human progress.[14]

This however does not directly address the moral claims advanced by social justice proponents because while Alchian's defence of property rights acknowledges that such rights are human rights, it does not incorporate moral or political arguments that might help to resolve conflicts between different human rights. This exclusion of moral or political arguments is by design. Mises, for example, excludes moral considerations from his economic analysis, arguing that moral questions are to be addressed outside the framework of economics. He explains: "there is another aspect from which human action might be viewed than that of good and bad, of fair and unfair, of just and unjust. In the course of social events there prevails a regularity of phenomena to which man must adjust his action if he wishes to succeed."[15] Mises's approach reflects "a science of given relations" rather than "a normative discipline of things that ought to be."[16] This approach is not concerned with normative ideals: "Science never tells a man how he should act; it merely shows how a man must act if he wants to attain definite ends."[17]

Utilitarian perspectives offer a powerful perspective from which to understand and defend classical liberal ideals by showing the centrality

---

[13] Alchian, A. A. (2007). Private Property. In Henderson, D.R. *The Concise Encyclopedia of Economics*.

[14] Mises, L. v. (2005). *Liberalism: The Classical Tradition* (B.B. Greaves, Ed.). Liberty Fund.

[15] Mises, L. v. (2012). *Human Action: A Treatise on Economics*. Martino Publishing, p. 2.

[16] Ibid. It is not claimed that this science produces perfect outcomes. "There is no such thing as perfection in human knowledge, nor for that matter in any other human achievement. Omniscience is denied to man": Ibid., p. 7.

[17] Ibid., p. 10.

of property rights in meeting desired goals. They also offer a valuable basis on which to evaluate reparations claims. It could for example be argued that there are practical impediments to reversing historical injustice so the means we select to achieve that goal are unlikely to lead us to the desired end. This is certainly the case in relation to contemporary proposals for payment of reparations, which raise several questions that have proved difficult to resolve.[18] For example, it is unclear how liability for payment would be apportioned, and many commentators have pointed out the injustice of making everyone, including recent immigrants to a country, pay taxes to fund reparations for historic crimes. There is no easy way to make only some people pay reparations while others do not. Yet the crimes occurred decades or even centuries ago so nobody present in the relevant jurisdiction today can be held personally accountable to atone for those crimes. Moreover, many different states participated in activities such as the slave trade, and not all of these states are facing demands for reparations. For example, some commentators argue that liability for reparations ought fairly to fall upon modern African nation states, to pay reparations to the descendants of slaves in the Americas for rounding up their own kin and selling them off in the first place.[19] While these difficulties in apportioning liability are not by themselves a conclusive argument against reparations, they illustrate the practical difficulties that must be overcome if the system is to work in a manner that is perceived to be fair.

A similar practical difficulty arises in identifying the victims of historical injustices. Much has been said in the reparations debates about the

[18] "Senate majority leader Mitch McConnell stated: "I don't think reparations for something that happened 150 years ago for whom none of us currently living are responsible is a good idea … We've tried to deal with our original sin of slavery by fighting a civil war, by passing landmark civil rights legislation. We elected an African American president." Senator McConnell is not alone in his position. Critics of reparations for slavery and its effects have historically argued that the challenges of pragmatism, causation, and time make reparations improper and infeasible:" Kim, J. (2019). Black Reparations for Twentieth Century Federal Housing Discrimination: The Construction of White Wealth and the Effects of Denied Black Homeownership (December 1, 2019). *Boston University Public Interest Law Journal*, 29(135).

[19] Muhammad, P. M. (2020). The Trans-Atlantic Slave Trade's African Elephant in the International Courtroom: African Nations Owe Blacks of the Diaspora Reparations. *UC Davis Journal of International Law & Policy* 27(1), 81.

unlikelihood of ascertaining who is entitled to be paid reparations, especially when claims are said to be based on genealogical lineage, blood lines and DNA testing.[20] As Waldron observes, "If the individuals whose entitlements were violated were still alive, then we could deal with the matter by way of direct restitution and compensation. But of course they are not. Many generations have passed since the injustice complained of took place."[21] It is difficult, perhaps impossible, fairly to allocate liability for historical events that are shrouded in complexity let alone to quantify the sum of money that would right the historical wrong. Epstein has also argued that among other difficulties with reparations claims there is the fact that historic suffering applies to many groups in society based on many different grounds other than race, and no explanation is given by those demanding reparations for "why certain kinds of mistreatment deserve reparations but not others."[22] Further, the expansive scope of reparations based on race is unprecedented and likely also to be a

[20] "The group bases the legitimacy of its claims upon genealogy. It states that it has moral authority because it has "done DNA testing" to identify the extent of Nigerian slave ancestry among Caribbean peoples and African-Americans and that these people ought to be considered "co-owners" of the [Benin] bronzes": Samuel, J. (2022, August 27). The Case of the Benin Bronzes, or How the Woke Monster is Eating Itself: we should reject any claim that revives, for political purposes, the use of bloodlines as a legal instrument. *The Telegraph*. https://www.telegraph.co.uk/news/2022/08/27/case-benin-bronzes-how-woke-monster-eating/; See also her argument that "I have read more than 100 pages of history and it ended here, with a pool of blood money whose rightful recipient its donor can't even identify. No wonder it can't: the victims of these crimes are long dead...If money could buy redemption, would $100 million – 0.18 per cent of Harvard's endowment – even be enough? Why not more?" Samuel, J. (2022, April 30). Nothing Can Give the Victims of Slavery Justice – and Certainly Not Money: We could just wind up Harvard University and donate its wealth to Liberia. It still wouldn't change the past. *The Telegraph*. https://www.telegraph.co.uk/news/2022/04/30/nothing-can-give-victims-slavery-justice-certainly-not-money/.

[21] Waldron, J. (2002). Redressing Historic Injustice. *The University of Toronto Law Journal*, 52(1), 135, p. 143.

[22] Other difficult questions arise: "the report favors the establishment of a "genealogy branch," but does not set out the criteria needed to determine eligibility. Do recent African-American immigrants to the state receive full or partial benefits? What about African-American citizens who were raised in California but who moved to other states? What about persons with mixed parentage? Will children yet to be born receive anything if their parents have already been compensated? Should these new programs be integrated with existing tax and business programs?" Epstein, R.A. (2022, June 22). California's Reparations Overreach. *Defining Ideas*. https://www.hoover.org/research/californias-reparations-overreach.

breach of constitutional prohibitions on racial discrimination.[23] Posner and Vermeule pose several other difficult questions:

> Is the guilt of whites affected by the participation of Arabs and Africans in the slave trade? Is the relevant comparison the standard of living of Africans and African Americans (and which ones?) prior to slavery and during slavery, or prior to slavery and today? And what is the relevant measure - mortality rates, population size, satisfaction of basic needs, wage differentials, or something else? Are the sacrifices by (Northern) whites during the Civil War to be taken into consideration?[24]

The fact that the reparations movement remains undeterred by these questions shows that there are limits to the persuasive reach of these types of practical arguments in the context of social justice disputes. First, those who promote reparations as a path to social justice are in any case impervious to merely practical concerns. If the challenges faced by their proposals are purely of a practical nature they would simply seek ways to work around the challenges or failing that just proceed as intended *despite* the practical difficulties. Further, it must be recalled that they follow critical race theories in which objective reasoning is said to be "infused with systemic racism."[25] So objective reasons by themselves will not dissuade those who regard reparations as necessary to meet the demands of social justice. Many would be prepared to overlook elements of unfairness in the allocation of liability if the scheme as a whole seemed to be the second-best way to address historical grievances. For example, Waldron, who is in principle sympathetic to the reparations claims, suggests that "the best hope of reparation is to make some sort of adjustment in the present circumstances of those descended from

---

[23] Epstein contrasts the "carefully calibrated reparations plan in the Civil Liberties Act 1988 [which] granted redress of $20,000 and a formal presidential apology to every surviving US citizen or legal resident immigrant of Japanese ancestry incarcerated during World War II.": Ibid.

[24] Posner and Vermeule. Reparations for Slavery and Other Historical Injustices, p. 708.

[25] "We must confront the institutional barriers to justice for Black people in academia and beyond, challenge the notion of the meritocracy whereby "objective and neutral" criteria infused with systemic racism are used to exclude Black people from physics and other academic disciplines, and rebuild our institutions and collaborations in a way that is just and equitable." (2020, June 10). A Strike For Black Lives. https://www.particlesforjustice.org.

the persons who suffered injustice (and also of anyone else whose present position has been affected by these past events)."[26]

This means that utilitarian arguments against reparations can take us only so far in defending property rights. Epstein also reveals the philosophical limits of the utilitarian case when he argues that some forms of property "takings" without consent may be justified: "The issue, rather, is whether or not the distinction between consent and coercion is so absolute that one would say that whenever there is consent, the transaction ought to be blessed, and that whenever there is coercion, the transaction ought to be damned."[27] Epstein asks:

> What is the difference between the strong or radical libertarian such as Walter [Block], and the more moderate or restrained classical liberal such as myself? It is that we classical liberals believe that there is a very strong presumption in favor of consent over coercion, but we do not believe that this is an absolute. The question is, What counts as a reason for the exceptions, and how is it that we can implement them and put them into practice?[28]

In other words, there may be an element of coercion and expropriation involved in wealth redistribution, but on this interpretation of utilitarian reasoning redistribution may be justified if it would serve a beneficial social purpose that makes it worth the encroachment on liberty. The same reasoning applies to reparations.

2.3 Natural Law Perspectives

There are serious practical hurdles that cast doubt on the feasibility of paying reparations for historical grievances. But even if a way were to be found to resolve those issues, such wealth transfers would still constitute an unjustified encroachment on property rights. Therefore the ethical

---

[26] Waldron, Redressing Historic Injustice, pp. 143, 144.

[27] Block, W. and Epstein, R. A. (2005). Debate on Eminent Domain. *NYU Journal of Law & Liberty*, 1(3), 1148, p. 1148.

[28] Ibid., p. 1149.

arguments cannot be avoided and it is necessary to evaluate the underlying considerations of ethics, morality and justice. Further, a debate based on practical difficulties strikes social justice claimants as unmeritorious. It appears to amount to an implicit acceptance of the justice of their demands: it appears to concede that the claim is just, but practical difficulties stand in the way of implementing it. If that were the case it would appear that the only thing left to do is find a workable way to satisfy the claim or, more likely, to proceed with the scheme despite any anticipated practical setbacks. For these reasons we must ultimately evaluate the case for reparations on grounds other than simply that it would not work.

Nor does it suffice to argue that would be unconstitutional, given that the proponents of expropriation without compensation tend increasingly to regard appeals to the constitution as "hiding behind the constitution."[29] They argue that if the constitution conflicts with the evolving "liberal democratic consensus" on the demands of justice then perhaps it means only that it is time to amend the constitution. After all, constitutions have been amended before and thus they can in principle be amended again. Such arguments have been heard in various jurisdictions in the context of the homelessness crisis, where the focus is on finding a sound legal basis on which to implement proposals to use private property for social purposes.[30]

In that light, it can be seen why Rothbard is critical of the potential for utilitarianism to overlook the unjust acquisition of property. He argues that it is not sufficient to defend property entitlements based on identifying the owner without considering the ethical basis of the acquisition: "For if we do so, we are in grave danger of defending the 'property right'

[29] For example in the Irish debate on amending the constitution to limit property rights it was argued: "I think it is class interest that is at play here. That class interest is reflected in the kind of Constitution that we have but the Government hides behind it:" Deputy Richard Boyd Barrett. Thirty-ninth Amendment of the Constitution (Right to Housing) Bill 2020: Second Stage [Private Members] https://www.oireachtas.ie/en/debates/debate/dail/2021-06-03/46/.

[30] See for example California, where the case for seizing empty hotel rooms to house homeless people have been put to a legislative vote, with arguments surrounding questions of convenience and safety rather than property rights: Wick, J. (2022, August 5). L.A. voters to decide whether hotels must rent vacant rooms to homeless people. *Los Angeles Times*. https://www.latimes.com/california/story/2022-08-05/initiative-would-require-l-a-hotels-to-provide-rooms-to-homeless-people.

of a criminal aggressor—in fact, we logically must do so. We may therefore only speak of just property or legitimate property or perhaps 'natural property'."[31] This applies to a first acquisition as well as any subsequent acquisition. Rothbard argues further: "Thus, we cannot simply say that the great axiomatic moral rule of the libertarian society is the protection of property rights, period…we must modify or rather clarify the basic rule of the libertarian society to say that no one has the right to aggress against the legitimate or just property of another."[32]

Rothbard points out that utilitarian perspectives leave unanswered important questions of justice: "For the utilitarian, who has *no conception*, let alone theory, of justice, must fall back on the pragmatic, ad hoc view that all titles to private property currently existing at any time or place *must* be treated as valid and accepted as worthy of defense against violation…This is an ethic that is blind to all considerations of justice, and, pushed to its logical conclusion, must also defend every criminal in the property that he has managed to expropriate."[33]

It is certainly the case that the relativity of common law title would defend anyone in possession of property regardless of how he came to be in possession, against all but the real owner. A squatter who breaks into a property is entitled to possession against a subsequent squatter and indeed against all the world except the true owner of the property. From a utilitarian perspective adverse possession would settle disputed claims to land after many years of quiet and peaceful possession. The law of adverse possession may also be compatible with natural law principles, subject to the caveat that this would only apply in cases where the original acquisition cannot be proved to be unjust: "if Green comes upon land that has obviously never been transformed by anyone, he can move onto it at once and with impunity, for in the libertarian society no one can have a valid title to land that has never been transformed."[34] The idea of land "that has obviously never been transformed by anyone" is reflected in

[31] Rothbard, *Ethics of Liberty*, p. 52.

[32] Ibid., pp. 51, 52.

[33] Ibid., p. 52.

[34] Rothbard, *Ethics of Liberty*, p. 65.

the common law principle that for possession to give rise to title possession must be maintained by the interloper "openly, notoriously, adversely, exclusively and continuously for the prescribed period."[35]

In libertarian theory title can therefore justly lie where it falls, if it relates to previously unowned land, if no prior ownership claim can be ascertained or proved, or if the perpetrator or victim of the original unjust dispossession cannot be identified. Rothbard explains:

> Suppose that a title to property is clearly identifiable as criminal, does this necessarily mean that the current possessor must give it up? No, not necessarily. For that depends on two considerations: (a) whether the victim (the property owner originally aggressed against) or his heirs are clearly identifiable and can now be found; or (b) whether or not the current possessor is himself the criminal who stole the property.[36]

This accords with the English common law position, which applies the principle of relativity of title to such a case: the person who now owns the land has a title good against all the world *except the original owner*. True homesteading cases, where there is a claim based on original acquisition, may therefore be regarded as straightforward cases that would be vindicable based on established legal principles. In some cases practical difficulties may arise in ascertaining whether a "theft" in fact occurred, where hundreds of years have passed since the time of the acquisition. The important point for purposes of establishing a legal entitlement to ownership of disputed resources is that the claim to original ownership itself requires to be substantiated, not merely asserted based on the historical presence of a specified tribe on the lands in question. But this is simply a point about the evidentiary burden. Although with the passage of time it is increasingly unlikely that titles lost in the mists of time can be traced, nevertheless it is clear that in cases where the title can indeed be traced to the original owner whose descendants have presented

---

35 Thomas, D. A. (1996). Adverse Possession: Acquiring Title to Stolen Personal Property. 10 *Probate & Property* 12, p. 12.

36 Rothbard, *Ethics of Liberty*, p. 57.

their claim, that title can be vindicated without the need to "redistribute" property. This is illustrated by cases such as this recent one in California:

> Bruce's Beach was purchased in 1912 to create a beach resort for black people at a time of racial segregation in southern California. Located in the desirable city of Manhattan Beach, it was forcibly taken by the local council [under eminent domain laws] in 1924. But on Tuesday, Los Angeles officials voted to return the land to the family.[37]

Restoring property to its rightful owner in such cases does not undermine the integrity or priority of property rights and does not pose difficulties for a theory of justice. If the current owner holds an unjustly acquired title it is not unjust to force him to share with or restore that title to the descendants of the original owner.[38] In cases involving racial injustice, where the reason for the unjust dispossession of the original owner under the government's eminent domain powers was motivated by racial animus, the restitution of the property promotes justice and may also be perceived for that reason as a form of racial justice. As the family in the Bruce case said, "We hope this opens people's eyes to a part of American history that isn't talked about enough, and we think it's a step toward trying to right the wrongs of the past."[39] But the unjust seizure of property through eminent domain should always be corrected regardless of whether or not it involves a racial element. It should be corrected because it is unjust tout court, not because it is *racially* unjust.

From a natural-rights perspective eminent domain power is unjust, in principle, because it amounts to the seizure of property by the state without the owner's consent. Theft is wrongful, even when it is done by the state and even without the racial element. The intervention of the state in the reallocation of property obscures rather than clarifies the question concerning whether property rights are defined in a just manner

[37] Molloy, D. (2022, June 29). Bruce's Beach returned to family nearly a century after seizure. *BBC*. https://www.bbc.co.uk/news/world-us-canada-61981785.

[38] "Indeed, a large part of libertarian punishment theory is predicated upon restitution": Block, W. (2019). *Property Rights: The Argument for Privatization*. Palgrave Macmillan, p. 28.

[39] Ibid.

and how seizing property from an owner without his consent is in principle distinguishable from theft. Nor would describing the seizure as an attempt to redress a historical theft justify a wrongful dispossession of the owner. As Block explains: "If someone stole something from you, having the state steal from someone altogether different does not really solve the problem, does it? And if the state robbed—or more accurately, allowed someone else to pilfer—something from your ancestors, does it make sense for them to now steal something from everyone else and give it to you? Not at all."[40]

In this context "justice" does not form part of the common law test in ascertaining questions of title. The common law of property has little to say in answer to the value-laden ethical language in which the justice debates are couched. The moralistic language of reparations can be seen for example in the claims made for financial reparations to atone for historical injustice, which is framed as an urgent moral imperative and depicted as a way to expiate the "original sin."[41] Reparations claims also make aspirational value-judgements about the kind of society in which we wish to live, our social and political self-concept as people who uphold justice, and how justice should be understood in such a liberal democratic society. None of these ethical considerations forms part of the common law framework. For these reasons we turn to natural law for a normative standard by which to evaluate these claims.

As Rothbard observes, those calling for "expropriation of the expropriators…cannot be successfully countered by the maxims of utilitarian economics or philosophy, but only by dealing forthrightly with the moral problem, with the problem of justice or injustice of various claims to property."[42] The meaning and content of property rights in the social justice debates may be understood by reference to natural law principles of reason: "an objective set of ethical norms by which to gauge human actions at any time or place."[43] As Harris defines it, "'Natural

---

[40] Ibid., p. 168.

[41] Swerling, G. (2021, September 14). Britain should pay reparations for slavery, says Cambridge Dean. *The Telegraph*. https://www.telegraph.co.uk/news/2021/09/14/britain-should-pay-reparations-slavery-says-cambridge-dean/

[42] Rothbard, *Ethics of Liberty*, p. 53.

[43] Ibid., p. 27.

rights' are such rights as follow from the interaction between the formal and substantive requirements of just treatment and the facts of the world."[44] Ethical principles derived from natural law bear the mark of early Thomist influences, but as Waldron observes, natural law principles need not be derived from religion:

> For some, natural law is simply a set of objective moral truths about man and society. Though the idea of moral objectivity has its problems, it need not rest on theological foundations. The secular and theological versions of natural law share a conviction that it is possible for humans to use their reason and their moral insight to work out the best way to live and the best way to order society.[45]

Similarly, Kurrild-Klitgaard observes that while the early natural law theorists were inspired by the Christian religion which was prevalent at the time, their theory was not "justificationally dependent upon theological arguments."[46]

Natural law in this context is not invoked in a bid to formulate a set of principles or tenets that would encompass a comprehensive theory of justice, but rather for a specific and much narrower purpose: "primarily to assist the practical reflections of those concerned to act, whether as judges or as statesmen or as citizens."[47] As Finnis argues, "a theorist cannot give a theoretical description and analysis of social facts unless he also participates in the work of evaluation, of understanding what is really good for human persons, and what is really required by practical reasonableness."[48] An inquiry into the ethics of the property rights debates, and an ethical defence of liberty, becomes necessary. Principles of natural law in that way offer a theoretical framework within which to evaluate the meaning and content of property rights, thereby enabling an evaluation of the moral claims advanced under the banner of social justice.

---

44 Harris, *Property and Justice*, p. 182.

45 Waldron, J. (1990). *The Law*. Routledge, p. 34, 35.

46 Kurrild-Klitgaard, P. Self-Ownership and Consent, p. 49.

47 Finnis, J. (1980). *Natural Law and Natural Rights*. Oxford University Press, p. 18.

48 Ibid., p. 3.

Natural law theories do not claim that all objective truths must be legally enforced and backed by force, nor that objective truth ought never to be questioned. The claim is, instead that the validity of arguments must be evaluated based on reason, rationality and objective evidence. As Maritain explained: "In reality it is through rational means, that is, through persuasion, not through coercion, that the rational animal is bound by his very nature to try to induce his fellow men to share in what he knows or claims to know as true or just."[49] This does not mean that all human beings are, or ought at all times to be, rational. The argument is that the existence of objective truth offers a basis on which to derive objective principles of natural law. The essential principle of natural law in relation to self-ownership is one delineating "the legitimate boundaries of state power."[50] It constrains the state against the use of force against citizens, which includes not only the direct use of force but also the indirect use of force to back any edicts other than those necessary to defend the property rights of others. This principle may also be derived from Kant: "Act in such a way that you always treat humanity, whether in your own person or in the person of any other, never simply as a means, but always at the same time as an end."[51]

2.4 Inequality and the Validity of Property Rights

The first ethical question that arises in the reparations debates is how to justify property rights in conditions of racial wealth inequality. A defence of private property must address the argument that wealth redistribution is needed to resolve the plight of those considered to be vulnerable in the sense that they are said to lack property or the wherewithal to acquire it, and are therefore said to be unable to participate in markets or to share in

[49] Maritain, J. (1961). *On The Use of Philosophy: Three Essays*. Princeton University Press, p. 20.
[50] Friedman, M.D. (2015). *Libertarian Philosophy in the Real World: The Politics of Natural Rights*. Bloomsbury Academic, p. 15.
[51] Ibid., p. 16.

economic progress and prosperity. For example, Cohen rejects the principle of self-ownership in situations where economic inequality persists, and where property rights could therefore be said to undermine distributive justice.[52] He acknowledges that the principle of self-ownership may help in identifying appropriate limits on the power of the state to redistribute resources according to need, for example by identifying personal boundaries which the state should not cross in its redistributive efforts. For example, "to conscript potential eye donors into a lottery whose losers must yield an eye to beneficiaries who would otherwise not be one-eyed but blind" would violate the principle of self-ownership.[53] But although Cohen sees some value in the concept of self-ownership, he is apprehensive that each person's freedom to do as he wishes may prompt the self-owner to adopt a devil-may-care attitude towards the plight of others unless the state intervenes.[54]

Other egalitarian perspectives regard private property, with its core right to exclude, as reflective of selfishness and greed. For example, Roemer argues in support of "the dream of society based on a norm of equality rather than a norm of greed."[55] Since nobody wants to promote greed as the moral foundation of society, that perspective garners support by presenting its egalitarian values as the alternative to greed. In addition, it makes a claim to reflecting a consensus of all reasonable people who should not wish to be greedy: "egalitarianism [is] not simply a value judgment that people might or might not hold according to their taste but [is], rather, a view of what social arrangements [are] right, a view that any rational, honest person [has] to accept."[56] That interpretation implies that anyone who does not endorse egalitarianism is irrational and dishonest. Others go further, arguing that only someone with a

[52] Cohen, G.A. (1995). *Self-Ownership, Freedom, and Equality*. Cambridge University Press. Gordon, D. (1998, April 1). A Reluctant Marxist. Mises Review. https://mises.org/library/self-ownership-freedom-and-equality-ga-cohen.

[53] Ibid., p. 70.

[54] Cohen, *Self-Ownership, Freedom, and Equality*; See also Brenkert, G. G. (1998). Self-Ownership, Freedom, and Autonomy. *The Journal of Ethics*, 2(1), 27.

[55] Roemer, J. (1994). *A Future for Socialism*. Harvard University Press, p. 25. See discussion in Gordon, D. (1995, October 1) A New Socialism? *Mises Review*. https://mises.org/library/future-socialism-john-roemer.

[56] Gordon, D. A New Socialism?

personality disorder would defend individual liberty, capitalism and free markets.[57]

This hostile interpretation of self-ownership underpins the claim that private property rights ought to be subject to the overriding social welfare function of the state. That critique acquires particular political force when wealth inequalities are mapped by reference to race, due to the social harm which it is feared might result if racial wealth inequality is not eradicated. A central egalitarian tenet is that those with more should share their wealth with those who have less. Although such views have intuitive appeal, their reliance on majoritarian democratic endorsement carries the risk of ushering in a tyranny of the majority and the defeat of minority and individual rights. Ultimately, in identifying sound principles of justice it does not suffice for a majority to agree that it would be fair and just to seize property from the minority by force. Injustice cannot be transformed into justice by majority vote. The basic question of justice therefore cannot be avoided. Nor can questions of justice be decided purely by reference to democratic processes.

Self-ownership and property rights stand as a bulwark against coercive wealth transfers. Classical liberalism upholds the rights to life, liberty and property but does not require people to provide goods or services to others for the purpose of equalising wealth, atoning for historic injustice, or any other purpose which, however worthy its goals, is designed to take effect through coercion. In libertarian theory the use of coercion and force can only be justified in self-defence or in defence of one's own property, but cannot justly be deployed to seize the property of others. This does not mean that how an owner uses his or her property may not be criticised. It simply means that critics may not use force to compel the owner to direct his property towards the use preferred by the critics. Even Cohen, himself no defender of theories constructed upon self-ownership, recognises this analytical distinction: "The self-ownership principle says

[57] A representative example is Duggan, L. (2019). *Mean Girl: Ayn Rand and the Culture of Greed*. University of California Press. She argues that the high school drama "Mean Girls" yields insight into the "culture of greed" promoted by "the reign of brutal capitalism" and "persistent zombie neoliberalism": pp. xii, xiii.

that people should be free to do as they please with themselves, not that what they are pleased to do with themselves is beyond criticism."[58]

Some who support distributive justice would disagree with those limits on the use of force, as they would evaluate the just use of force to seize the property of another based on the intention or purpose of the seizure—they would argue that subject to considerations of procedural fairness such as ample warning and an opportunity to reply, compulsory acquisition of property designed to equalise wealth would be justified. This type of procedural fairness is an essential principle of eminent domain. Waldron, following Kant, argues that redistributing property is sometimes necessary in order to live peaceably with others and that if anyone chooses to dissent from this moral consensus (that is to say, the consensus that property may be redistributed within a moral framework of distributive justice) that person may legitimately be forced to do so: "entering into political society with those with whom you are otherwise likely to be in conflict is a matter of natural duty. Indeed, it is something that a person might legitimately be forced to do."[59]

Waldron acknowledges that from a Lockean perspective it would only be morally justified to use force in defence of one's life and property, while from a Kantian perspective (on Waldron's interpretation) it would be morally justified to use force also to defend the redistributive democratic consensus of political society.[60] Waldron argues that force could legitimately be used against dissenters without dishonestly attempting to rationalize that coercion as a form of "tacit consent."[61] The egalitarian rationale for wealth redistribution which violates property rights is not that the property owner has tacitly agreed to it simply by being a member of society, as often claimed by those who declare that dissenters should simply go and live elsewhere (leaving all their property behind, of course). At a deeper level, the rationale is rather that it is justified to seize the owner's property *without* his consent to promote the public good. In

[58] Cohen, Self-ownership, Freedom, and Equality, p. 68.

[59] Waldron, Redressing Historic Injustice, p. 138.

[60] Ibid.: "A theorist like John Locke might argue that people have a choice as to whether to enter into political community with others or not" which follows from the "natural liberty" which inheres in each individual.

[61] Ibid., p. 138.

the debate about self-ownership and private property, we therefore have two opposing views on legitimate use of force.

We also have opposing views on the importance of economic progress. Property rights are essential to economic growth, but by the same token may be viewed as unimportant by those who care more for equality than for prosperity. Property rights underpin free market capitalism, and the essential meaning of capital is linked to property rights: capital is "a bundle of ownership rights—in particular, the right to sell one's property and the right to receive income from that property. When those rights are attenuated, capital is destroyed."[62] Thus it would be inconsistent to purport to be in favour of capitalism while undermining private property. Economic history reveals a clear link between property rights and economic progress. The institutions of private property which enable capital accumulation are a key determinant of economic growth and are essential to a market economy. As Mises explains: "Private ownership of the means of production is the fundamental institution of the market economy. It is the institution the presence of which characterizes the market economy as such. Where it is absent, there is no question of a market economy."[63] The attenuated nature of highly regulated property rights is characteristic of socialist economies, which are distinguishable by the absence of private ownership of the means of production: "all are socialists who consider the socialistic order of society economically and ethically superior to that based on private ownership of the means of production."[64]

The importance of property rights for economic and social prosperity in free market capitalism has been referred to as "the property principle of growth," as the principle that "people who create wealth can keep most of it" is a prerequisite for human progress.[65] As Epstein explains:

---

[62] Dorn, J. Piketty's Plan for Equality Would Reduce Personal Freedom and Undermine Growth. In Delsol, J-P., Lecaussin, N. and Martin, E. (Eds). (2017). *Anti-Piketty: Capital for the 21st Century*. Cato Institute, p. 234.

[63] Mises, L. v. (2012). *Human Action: A Treatise on Economics*. Martino Publishing, p. 678.

[64] Mises, L. v. (1962). *Socialism: An Economic and Sociological Analysis*. Yale University Press, p. 26.

[65] Cooter, R.D. (2006). An Escape from Poverty: Developing Productive Organization. *Southwestern Journal of Law and Trade in the Americas*, XII(2), 186. p. 186.

> Once the rules of self-ownership and property ownership are established, two further rules kick in. The first is the simple proposition that individuals can enter into voluntary transactions for their mutual benefit. In general, their agreements create positive externalities by increasing the transactional opportunities of parties outside the immediate transaction, thereby augmenting the total wealth in society available for further exchange as well as for further investment.[66]

These are not simply theoretical observations that apply to the classification of economic systems, but they explain the practical conduct of daily life in societies where economic freedom pertains. In practice, even the most modest business in a fledgling informal economy requires property rights to prosper. Friedman illustrates this point by reference to the ability to purchase and exchange: "societies that recognize and protect private property are likely to be much more prosperous than those that don't. And, in such communities people will be able to purchase or lease all the raw materials, including land, that they require without the hardship of homesteading. You don't need to own a salt mine to obtain all you want of this mineral at an affordable price."[67] In a similar vein Easterly gives the example of a food stall owner in a developing economy, who needs property rights for the business to succeed and grow:

> Only if I felt secure that I would keep my taco stand would I invest in more sanitary food-processing equipment. I can borrow from a bank to purchase such equipment only if I have title to the property to put down as collateral. Only then will the bank feel secure that I will not abscond with the loan.[68]

Easterly's example is particularly compelling because contrary to popular wisdom the poor need property rights more than the rich, who are able

---

[66] Epstein, R.A. (2018). Meeting the Fundamental Objections to Classical Liberalism. In Henderson, M. T. (Ed.). (2018). *The Cambridge Handbook of Classical Liberal Thought*. Cambridge University Press, p. 280.

[67] Friedman, M.D. (2015). *Libertarian Philosophy in the Real World: The Politics of Natural Rights*. Bloomsbury Academic, p. 18.

[68] Easterly, W. (2006). *The White Man's Burden: Why the West's Efforts to Aid the Rest Have Done So Much Ill and So Little Good*. Oxford University Press, p. 79.

to rely on other mechanisms such as patronage or social connections to secure loans or protect their wealth. The poor lack any such protection and without property rights are more vulnerable to exploitation. Again, Easterly offers a pertinent example from a developing country where people who are unable to defend their property rights are left at the mercy of despots:

> For example, a man in Isla Trinitaria, Ecuador, cut back even on food and clothing to save enough to build up a small shellfish business. But he lost it all when the mayor seized the land.[69]

For these reasons Devine argues that property rights serve the function of safeguarding the most vulnerable in society, and it is quite incorrect for people to suppose that property rights are only of benefit to the wealthy.[70] Historically, legislation such as the Married Women's Property Act of 1882 protected the more vulnerable party, in that case, married women, from the more powerful or dominant party. Property rights are needed, even if they lead to inequality, because without them vulnerable people are unable to safeguard their rights: "Property does lead to inequality…but fair property rights are an economic necessity for those without power. The rich and powerful do not need property rights, since they can protect their own."[71]

2.5 Is Property Merely a Cultural Construct?

In debates about economic development, it is often said that Western capitalist culture should not be imposed on developing countries and that cultures based on communal property ownership should be respected and encouraged to continue following their own communitarian path to economic success. The assumption is that self-ownership and property rights are Western cultural concepts and therefore other

[69] Ibid.

[70] Devine, *The Enduring Tension*, p. 39.

[71] Ibid.

societies with different cultures should neither be expected nor encouraged to embrace private property. Communitarians argue that property rights take different forms in different societies, and that cultural preferences should form part of our understanding of property rights. Since some societies or cultures lack an established classical liberal concept of self-ownership or private property, this would seem to imply that property rights in the classical liberal sense are not universal and ought not to be treated as such.

From that perspective the solution to poverty alleviation or redressing historical grievances in communitarian societies which regard property rights as foreign to their cultural values is said to lie in tailored state interventions which preserve traditionally socialist cultures while at the same time equalising the material conditions of all who adhere to those cultures. The argument is essentially that cultural traditions inimical to market participation, traditions which preclude their members from participating in labour markets in common with other citizens, require state protection of the right to abstain from market participation as well as the right to have the economic consequences of this non-participation mitigated by artificial wealth equalisation schemes. For example, the law in Canada grants financial support to mitigate the effects of unemployment among indigenous communities on the basis that respect for indigenous culture requires protection and mitigation of their choice not to participate in labour markets.[72]

Bauer argues that this is the wrong way to approach economic development. He observes that many impediments to economic progress lie in exactly these types of parallel development or "respect all cultures" schemes, in which it is hoped to uphold communal values antithetical to productivity while redistributing wealth from those whose values are compatible with productivity to those who remain poor due to nothing more than clinging to cultural values which are incompatible with productivity. Bauer observes that the poverty of the third world is often characterised by cultural values which promote neither progress nor prosperity: "in much of the Third World the political, social, and

[72] Widdowson, F. (2019). *Separate but Unequal: How Parallelist Ideology Conceals Indigenous Dependency*. University of Ottawa Press.

personal determinants of economic performance are often uncongenial to economic development. And the policies of many governments plainly obstruct economic achievement and progress. Again, people often refuse to abandon attitudes and mores which obstruct economic performance. They are not prepared to give up their established ways for the sake of greater prosperity. This is a preference which is neither unjustified nor reprehensible."[73]

In saying that this choice to uphold cultural values which impede progress is "neither unjustified nor reprehensible" Bauer recognises that it is of course open to any people, for cultural or any other reasons, to be content to live in a non-industrialised society. This is a free and valid choice and those who exhort that we should "respect all cultures" are correct in that sense—nobody should dictate to any people the culture they ought to embrace. As Mises observes, "the legal concepts of property do not fully take account of the social function of private property"[74] and it is true that legal concepts which are alien to the culture in which they are enforced are unlikely to be effective. Bauer therefore emphasises that anyone is free for moral or cultural reasons to be content with the minimum level of subsistence they can sustain based on communal living.[75] But if they desire further economic progress and the improvement in material conditions that is made possible by wealth, certain further steps must be taken. Certain means must be adopted if specific ends are desired to be achieved. In a similar vein, Mises observes that some may freely choose not to pursue material wealth, and this too is a valid choice: "The very existence of ascetics and of men who renounce material gains for the sake of clinging to their convictions and of preserving their dignity and self-respect is evidence that the striving after more tangible amenities is not inevitable but rather the result of a choice."[76]

The reality is however inescapable that a choice falls to be made. Choosing the ascetic life yields the result of material inequality, as

[73] Bauer, P. (2000). *From Subsistence to Exchange and Other Essays*. Princeton University Press, p. 60.

[74] Mises, *Human Action*, p. 650.

[75] Bauer, *From Subsistence to Exchange* p. 60.

[76] Mises, *Human Action* p. 19.

expressed in the vow of poverty often made by those who choose this lifestyle. But choosing a life of material progress requires an entirely different set of institutional values.

2.6 The Institutional Foundations of Private Property

What then is to be done: is it feasible to persuade socialist societies to embrace private property if they wish not to? Development economists have highlighted the challenges of persuading communitarian societies of the causal connection between private property and economic progress. There is naturally resistance to any concept which is thought to be alien, to go against one's own culture, and to be the culture of the "colonialist." For example Easterly highlights the challenges in introducing formal property rights, such as land titles, in communities which do not recognise private property rights in land and regard natural resources as unowned, freely shared between all members of the community for the use of whoever desires it. Easterly observes, in relation to the implementation of land title systems in Africa, that property rights will not be effective if they are not observed in practice. He highlights instances in which people simply ignore land titles and recognise as the true "owner" the person who happens at the time to be using the land so that the paper title and "real title" do not match.[77] In many such cases, "the system of formal titles gradually lost correspondence with those who the locals knew owned the land. An increasing number of formal titleholders resided in the local graveyard."[78]

It is interesting to note that the ethos behind the colonial era use of legislation to implement land titles was expressed as an expectation that this would help the idea of private property in land to evolve as its benefits became increasingly apparent. As Easterly observes:

---

77 Easterly, *The White Man's Burden.*

78 Ibid., p. 84.

> Lord Lugard, the architect of British colonial rule in Africa, said land tenure follows "a steady evolution, side by side with the evolution of social progress." This "natural evolution" leads to "individual ownership." The Native Land Tenure Rules of 1956 privatized land in Kenya, advertising it as "a normal step in the evolution of a country," under which "energetic or rich Africans will be able to acquire more land.[79]

Easterly is correct to emphasise that for this type of introduction of property rights to work effectively it is critical that there be a reasonably widespread understanding or acceptance of the desirability of private property.

> Alas, property rights are more complicated than the state enforcing them from the top down (and the state itself may be a thief...) Your right to your property is only as strong as those around you are willing to acknowledge.[80]

But it does not follow that societies without an embedded legal framework to protect property rights should not be advised of the merits of doing so *if* they wish to advance economically. Comparison between economically highly developed and less developed nations shows a high correlation between economic progress and the degree to which the institutions of property rights are well established in the country's legal and economic systems. The importance accorded to property rights goes a long way in explaining wealth distribution between nations.[81] The lesson to be drawn from this is not that those who lack property rights should not be encouraged to have them because after all it is not their culture and we should respect all cultures. On the contrary, the lesson is that they *should* be encouraged to do so if they wish to make progress. This does not mean that they should be *forced* to do so with financial whips, sanctions and penalties from the World Bank, but it means that poor

[79] Ibid., p. 83.

[80] Ibid., p. 79.

[81] Kay, J. (2003). *The Truth about Markets—Why Some Nations Are Rich but Most Remain Poor*. Harper Collins.

countries should not be encouraged to rely on foreign aid and "reparations" from the West instead of establishing a robust legal system based on private property.

The difficulties in creating a system of private property are significant, but not insurmountable. Part of the difficulty in the early evolution of the land title system in Africa lay in the lack of a suitable dispute resolution system, as the traditional council of elders proved to be a costly way to resolve title disputes. Easterly recounts situations where the number of goats or cattle required to pay the elders for their service simply seemed not worth it to enforce titles to land.[82] The only cost-effective way to enforce land ownership was the time-honoured method of homesteading the land and remaining in possession of it peacefully and openly. In a situation where one was not in physical possession and had only the land title to back up their claim, the enforcement of that claim often proved not to be worth the effort. But the lack of support from the wider institutional framework does not mean that the system of land title or private property was inherently unsuited to the cultural terrain and ought not to have been introduced. After all, there are cases of disputed land ownership owing to adverse possession in many jurisdictions in the West, where ownership on the ground may have departed over time from the paper title even though there is no suggestion that private property is culturally unknown.

Thus a better way to understand this divergence between property rights in the books and property rights on the ground in African communities is to say that the protection of property rights cannot be understood in an institutional vacuum. The degree to which property rights are upheld depends to a degree on other complementary institutions (whether formal or informal) for the enforcement of rights. This principle is as true for colonial Africa as it was for the "title methods

82 "The system favoured whoever could bring more goats to the feast. Often claimants would not bother with adjudication as the costs of the feast exceeded the value of the property": Easterly, *The White Man's Burden*, p. 84.

on the American frontier" which Easterly describes elsewhere.[83] Easterly suggests that "A more likely way forward for formal law would be building on the customary law rather than contradicting it"[84] but while this may be true, it may yet cause intractable problems if customary law is not well suited to economic development. In the end, property rights are indispensable to economic progress. There is no cultural "other way of knowing" how to achieve economic progress.

It must be acknowledged that there are significant difficulties in respecting private property in cultures where communal instincts are so strong that individuals have no real choice about pursuing their preferences due to their individual preferences being forcibly subsumed within those of the collective. This emerges clearly from Baudin's study of pre-capitalist communities which dehumanise individual members of society by holding their preferences to be irrelevant and subsuming individual life goals within that of the collective.[85] Individual choice and individual action become irrelevant, as the social system determines everyone's life path and life outcomes. Baudin gives a compelling account of "life under a collectivist regime, the spectre of a human animal deprived of his essentially human quality, the power to choose and to act [with] nothing to worry about because their personal fate did not depend on their own behaviour, but was determined by the apparatus of the system."[86]

But it would not be right to say that because a communitarian culture collectively prefers or collectively chooses, to remain mired in poverty therefore individual preferences for progress do not matter in identifying the appropriate policy responses. The value of individual liberty matters even if collectivist societies do not uphold property rights. Those who ask whether a culture recognises or values property rights are therefore wrongly attributing to the collective, to the culture as a generalised whole, a question that is fundamental to individual liberty. It is only

---

83 Ibid., p. 80, where Easterly describes "land chaos" with a "tug of war between squatters' rights and more formal legal titling" as well as "lax enforcement [which] made for inconsistency on the ground.".

84 Ibid., p. 85.

85 Baudin, L. (1962). *A Socialist Empire: The Incas of Peru*. Duke University Press.

86 Mises, L. v. (1962). Foreword. In Baudin, L. (1962). *A Socialist Empire*, p. xi. If such societies are "free", they enjoy only "the freedom that the shepherd grants to his flock.".

by discounting the importance of individual liberty that one might pronounce a "culture" not to value property rights, and conclude that self-ownership within that culture is unimportant. Individuals in such a society are not constrained by their own preferences or choices, as they clearly lack any freedom of choice. They are constrained, as Mises puts it, by "the apparatus of the system."[87] Individual liberty is the antidote to this cultural trap.

The issue then is not whether different cultures are free to reject property rights, but whether upon rejecting property rights they can nevertheless demand that wealth be transferred from those who produce it to those who reject the very foundations of productivity. Even more so the question is whether those who profess to be unconcerned about economic progress may not only claim entitlement to coercive wealth transfers but also act in such a way as to impede others in their productive activities. If non-industrialised societies desire productivity and economic progress then it behoves them to reflect upon the universality of property rights, and especially to consider that reliance on coercive wealth transfers as a path to economic progress undermines the property rights of others. It is wrong to impose private property rights on countries that wish to be socialist, but by the same token it is wrong to impose socialist values on individuals or indeed countries which wish to defend private property. Further, "revising" or "redefining" property rights to make them more socialistic in their nature must answer the criticism levelled by Bauer at those who wish to have their cake and eat it.

Nor can it credibly be said that some cultures do not desire economic progress. As Mises observes, the desire for material progress is exhibited by most human beings: "of course, the immense majority prefer life to death and wealth to poverty."[88] People may disagree on the best means of achieving those ends but in most cases, despite the nihilism that has accompanied the modern environmentalist movement, they cannot credibly deny that those are in fact the ends they seek. As we observed in chapter one, there are certain ways people must act if they wish to attain specific ends, and it is not open to them to choose means which do not

[87] Ibid.

[88] Mises, *Human Action,* p. 19.

produce the desired ends in the sense that if they persist in their chosen means they will not achieve the desired ends. As Mises explains: "The only standard which [the science of human action] applies is whether or not the means chosen are fit for the attainment of the ends aimed at."[89]

Therefore, while a society might choose to forgo both property rights and progress, that choice cannot be made at the same time as demanding wealth transfers from societies that choose to pursue economic progress. We can study the importance of property rights to the goal sought, namely economic progress. But we cannot address, from that perspective, the case of those who do *not* desire economic progress. We may nevertheless deduce from their actions whether their expressed lack of concern for economic progress is credible. After all, anyone who claims to be unconcerned about economic progress but then seeks wealth transfers from the rich shows that he is in fact very much concerned about the fruits of progress, but simply unwilling to be involved in the methods of producing the desired product. What else is the preoccupation with inequality, other than a quest to achieve the same lifestyle and material conditions as those perceived to be wealthier than others?

The question then arises whether or how property rights can vest in an individual if he lives in a culture where the legal system (such as it is) does not define or recognise property rights. The answer lies in the insight that property rights have both legal and moral elements: from a natural law perspective property rights are legal rights as well as moral rights.[90] The fact that a culture does not appear to recognise property rights does not mean that individual people in that society do not wish to exercise and defend such rights. Easterly gives an example from communist China,

---

[89] "the teachings of praxeology and economics are valid for every human action without regard to its underlying motives, causes, and goals. The ultimate judgements of value and the ultimate ends of human action are given for any kind of scientific inquiry; they are not open to any further analysis. Praxeology deals with the ways and means chosen for the attainment of such ultimate ends. Its object is means, not ends…it refrains from passing any value judgments": Mises, *Human Action*, p. 21.

[90] Cf "The conventional nature of property rights is both perfectly obvious and remarkably easy to forget... We cannot start by taking as given... some initial allocation of possessions—what people own, what is theirs, prior to government interference": Murphy, L. and Nagel, T. (2002). *The Myth of Ownership: Taxes and Justice.* Oxford University Press.

where people spontaneously recognised private property even though the state did not:

> The villagers of Xiaogang reached an agreement: they would divide up the land and farm it individually, with each person keeping [his own] output ... Before long, the Communist authorities got wind of the spontaneous outbreak of property rights in the countryside.[91]

The important issue thus concerns the significance that ought to be accorded to property rights in an objective sense, rather than designating which cultures are or are not amenable to the protection of private property. This is particularly important in an era where cultural diversity is considered a priority, and we are exhorted to respect all cultures. Undermining property rights on grounds that such rights are not recognised in the culture of others is difficult to justify given that there are, after all, people in all cultures who find market participation challenging and would prefer to withdraw from society altogether if an appropriate means of material subsistence could be secured. To make such a choice in reliance on charitable or other voluntary donations is a tradition that may be admired, as in the ancient monasteries. For example, it was said of Edward the Confessor that he "scorned money beyond human custom and seemed neither sadder when he lost it, nor more cheerful when he gained it."[92] But to make such a lifestyle choice in reliance on "predation by public officials such as tax collectors, planners, licensing authorities, regulators and politicians"[93] involves a degree of coercive state expropriation that calls for a different type of analysis, where the guiding principle is based not on culture but on objective reason and the reality of human nature.

Not all important questions can be determined by reference to culture. In particular, if it is hoped by a developing country to emulate the

[91] Easterly, *The White Man's Burden,* p. 94.

[92] Aelred of Rievaulx, 1163: 746. Vita S. Edwardi regis et confessoris, PL, 195, col. 746; quoted in Gasper, G.E.M. and Gullbekk, S. H. (Eds.). (2015). *Money and the Church in Medieval Europe, 1000–1200: Practice, Morality and Thought*. Ashgate Publishing.

[93] Cooter, R.D. (2006). An Escape from Poverty: Developing Productive Organization. *Southwestern Journal of Law and Trade in the Americas*, XII(2), 186, p. 186.

economic success of the West, it is important to recognise that the principles on which the West was founded owed more to reason than to "culture" or other idiosyncratic factors. As Mises argues:

> The legal guarantees effectively protecting the individual against expropriation and confiscation were the foundations upon which the unprecedented economic progress of the West came into flower. These laws were not an outgrowth of chance, historical accidents, and geographical environment. They were the product of reason.[94]

Understood in that light, human reason does not vary from one culture or race to another. The capacity for human reason vests in all human beings, regardless of differences in culture, in IQ or in the reasonableness of one belief compared to another. This is the meaning of equality in the classical ideal: not that all human beings and cultures are equally reasonable, but that all human beings have the capacity to exercise reason.

> Locke wrote that all humans are "born to all the same advantages of nature, and the use of the same faculties." ... For example, as humans, we all have the faculty of reason. That does not mean that we are all equally reasonable.[95]

Formal equality, the principle that all people are born equal refers not to their material conditions or their natural endowments such as skills or talents, but to the inherent capacity of human beings to use reason and to choose means that will bring about the ends they desire. As Mises explains, the precepts of human action are therefore true for all people and do not vary by cultural context:

> The categories of human thought and action are neither arbitrary products of the human mind nor conventions...They are instruments in man's struggle for existence and in his endeavors to adjust himself as much as possible to the real state of the universe and to remove uneasiness as

[94] Mises, *Human Action*, p. 497.

[95] Locke, *Two Treatises of Government*.

> much as it is in his power to do so. They are therefore appropriate to the structure of the external world and reflect properties of the world and of reality. They work, and are in this sense true and valid.[96]

The link between material subsistence and economic progress may not always be self-evident in a cultural environment where property rights are not well established, but even in such cases it remains true that economic progress is necessary to improve one's material conditions, and if economic progress is desired the need to protect property rights is inescapable. Reluctance to acknowledge this reality has contributed to many governments in Africa, for example, becoming trapped in the futile loop of desiring material subsistence but lacking the institutional framework necessary to drive economic progress. This is one factor that explains why many African societies were historically far removed from economic success even in contexts where, as in West Africa, they had trading contacts with the outside world. Law explains how they became trapped in this "vicious circle":

> Only governments committed to a more aggressive ideology of economic progress, and therefore ready to incur speculative expenses in the confidence of ultimate economic advantage, could break out of this vicious circle [wheeled transport could not be adopted without improved roads, but the roads would not be improved as long as there was no wheeled transport to use them]; and such governments arrived in West Africa only with the imperialism of the late nineteenth century.[97]

We can therefore conclude not only that property rights are central to the ideology of economic progress, and lend coherence to the desire to create the institutional conditions necessary for such progress, but also that we should not treat culture as a reason not to protect property rights. The priority in the global justice debates should therefore be to defend property rights not as "Western culture" but as natural rights that inhere in all people in virtue of our humanity.

---

[96] Mises, *Human Action* p. 86.

[97] Law, R. (1980). Wheeled Transport in Pre-Colonial West Africa. *Africa: Journal of the International African Institute*, 50(3), 249, p. 258.

2.7 Natural Rights and Individual Liberty

It has been argued so far that property rights are essential because they enable economic progress. But even more importantly, property rights are essential to human liberty. In theory, liberty may be defended without recourse to the idea of private property, for instance in a society that defends individual rights while private property is held in common. But this would omit the vital component of individual liberty reflected in self-ownership which is an essential element of human liberty. As Rothbard argues, property rights are human rights, not only in the sense that "property can only accrue to humans, so that their rights to property are rights that belong to human beings" but more importantly in the sense that "the person's right to his own body, his personal liberty, is a property right in his own person as well as a 'human right'."[98] Further, human rights derive their coherence from property rights:

> For not only are there no human rights which are not also property rights, but the former rights lose their absoluteness and clarity and become fuzzy and vulnerable when property rights are not used as the standard… human rights, when not put in terms of property rights, turn out to be vague and contradictory, causing liberals to weaken those rights on behalf of "public policy" or the "public good."[99]

On that basis Rothbard regards property rights as the basis of all rights. Those who regard rights as the creation of statutes may question why this is so, given that statutes do not define human rights as property rights. Some human rights legislative instruments, such as the Canadian Charter, do not include property rights.[100] Others include so-called socioeconomic rights such as the right to housing, to education or to a job, which may violate the property rights of others. Positive rights of this nature reflect the social and political goals of the society and they are accorded the appellation of "rights" to signify the importance that society

---

[98] Rothbard, *The Ethics of Liberty*, p. 113.

[99] Ibid.

[100] Newman, D.G. and Binnion, L. (2015). The Exclusion of Property Rights from the Charter: Correcting the Historical Record, 52(3) *Alberta Law Review* 543.

attaches to them rather than to reflect their intrinsic conceptual nature. The idea that all rights are property rights rejects the notion of rights as merely the creation of statute or a reflection of political ideals, and conceptualises all rights as natural rights. Therefore to understand the importance of self-ownership we must understand the nature of natural rights. Rothbard defines natural rights as follows:

> the assertion of human rights is not properly a simple emotive one; individuals possess rights *not* because we "feel" that they should, but because of a rational inquiry into the nature of man and the universe. In short, man has rights because they are *natural* rights. They are grounded in the nature of man: the individual man's capacity for conscious choice, the necessity for him to use his mind and energy to adopt goals and values, to find out about the world, to pursue his ends in order to survive and prosper, his capacity and need to communicate and interact with other human beings and to participate in the division of labor.[101]

Natural rights are not invented and defined by legislatures, nor are they an outcome of democratic agreement or some form of "social contract." As Gordon explains:

> Natural rights of the sort that Rothbard favors are prepolitical. In other words, these rights aren't dependent on the state for their existence. Each person is a self-owner and may acquire property in the "state of nature," before there are states and state-created legal systems.[102]

In the natural-rights libertarian theory, therefore, property rights do not emanate from the state or treaties between states such as human rights declarations. Instead natural rights are "ascertained through an inspection of human nature and the essential circumstances of human life."[103]

---

[101] Rothbard, Ethics of Liberty, p. 155.

[102] Gordon, D. (2021, February 19). Are There Any Limits to Natural Rights? *Friday Philosophy*. https://mises.org/library/are-there-any-limits-natural-rights.

[103] Mack, E. Natural Rights. In Zwolinski, M. and Ferguson, B. (Eds.). (2022). *The Routledge Companion to Libertarianism.* Routledge. Natural rights are moral rights in the sense that they arise from moral principles and not state edict, but the converse does not hold: it does not follow that all entitlements people might consider moral are natural rights. See Mack for a

States may protect and defend rights, but such rights are not merely the gift of the state. Natural rights are:

> our baseline, original, moral rights. They are rights that come with being a person because the basis for affirming these rights is some deep feature (or small set of deep features) of all persons. That is why, if there are such rights, all persons possess the same natural rights. The point of saying that our natural rights are *moral* rights is to indicate that these rights are prescriptive rather than descriptive.[104]

Treating property rights as natural rights, a tradition in which the common law is deeply rooted, is sometimes criticised as lending legitimacy to imperial conquest and colonial invasion or, at any rate, failing to condemn such historical activities as immoral or failing to accord the requisite moral weight to historical injustice in contemporary discussions of property rights. The answer to that lies in the distinction between property rights as natural rights, and the types of political "group" rights created by equality legislation. Political group rights are defined in such a way as to reflect social and moral expectations of distributive justice, a good example being antidiscrimination legislation. By contrast, natural rights arise from self-ownership and thus are not artificially constructed in a bid to reflect any political ideology. Rothbard is concerned with natural rights in that sense:

> Rothbard's analysis is based on *individual* cases and *specific* claims, not generalized calls for redistributive justice for past actions. For Rothbard, there is no generalized political justice for slavery, genocide, military land grabs or groups with historical grievances.[105]

Critics of natural rights have argued that the philosophical premise of natural rights is vague and that it fails to settle all the disputed issues on how property is originally acquired in different contexts. Although

discussion of natural rights in the writing of Hugo Grotius, John Locke, Lysander Spooner, Ayn Rand and Robert Nozick.

[104] Ibid.

[105] Deist, J. (2021, June 3). A Libertarian Approach to Disputed Land Titles. *Mises Wire*. https://mises.org/wire/libertarian-approach-disputed-land-titles.

a general defence of natural law is beyond the scope of this discussion, we may observe that it is not necessary to offer a general philosophical defence of natural rights arising in all factual circumstances in order to defend self-ownership from the natural rights perspective. A defence of self-ownership does not depend on showing that all the components of a theory of natural law are precisely delineated. As Gordon explains:

> But suppose that it can't be shown that there is a correct theory of natural rights that settles all important issues and that people in a particular society must rely in part on convention to fix the boundaries of these rights. It hardly follows from this that natural rights are useless and everything important rests on the social practices of a particular society. Suppose that we don't know the exact boundaries of the correct principle of initial acquisition. We do know, though, that people have a natural right to acquire property, so that social conventions that altogether deny people the right to own property are ruled out.[106]

Nor is it necessary, for the purpose of explaining the conceptual nature of property rights, to offer a comprehensive framework of property rights. As Gordon argues:

> A Lockean framework leaves many questions of detail unsettled, true enough; but then people must simply choose what to do within this framework and stick to it, in order to arrive at a stable system of property. Why must a correct theory of property resolve in advance all questions, leaving nothing to be decided by convention?[107]

Moreover, it may be said of other philosophical frameworks that they also do not offer a definitive answer to all criticisms levelled at them. In defending Nozick's theory of natural rights Friedman observes that: "Nozick's argument for natural rights is certainly controversial, but so are all competing political theories, such as those that would promote what is called social (or distributive) justice, egalitarianism, communism, traditionalist values, or theocracy. However, Nozick's theory compares

[106] Gordon, D. Are There Any Limits to Natural Rights?

[107] Ibid.

favorably with its rivals in terms of plausibility, coherence, and consistency with facts about the nature of human beings."[108] Therefore, our purpose in evaluating the importance of self-ownership is not to arrive at a blueprint of the acceptable regulatory limits of property rights within a comprehensive theory of natural law. The aim is to demonstrate that there is a good case to be made for the existence of such limits—a less ambitious goal but one which nevertheless has important implications in evaluating the normative underpinning of wealth redistribution.

Those who call for wealth redistribution, taking private property from some to give it to others, cannot merely presume that their cause is just because there is an economic gap that they wish to fix. It has long been presumed that property rights call be justified. But history has amassed so much evidence to support the integrity and value of property rights that the converse seems more likely to be true: those who wish to encroach upon property rights should justify their claim. Instead of calling for private property rights to be justified, they have a duty to justify the moral basis of their expropriation demands in light of the importance and value of property rights. This becomes even more important in contexts of claims for reparations designed to redress historical injustices, as the rule of law requires that laws do not apply retrospectively, seeking to judge the lawfulness of past actions by reference to new laws that were not in force at the time of that action.

Since *voluntary* wealth transfers are uncontroversial and raise no moral concerns about property rights as owners are entitled to dispose of their property as they wish, the debate concerns *coercive* wealth transfers. In this context, coercive means legally mandated, such as through compulsory acquisition or payment of taxes.[109] It is sometimes argued that consent to such transfers is implied in membership in society. However, the justification accepted by some classical liberals such as Hayek, who support a role for the minimal state in relation to social welfare provisions such as education and health, does not include an implied agreement to

[108] Friedman, M.D. (2015). *Libertarian Philosophy in the Real World: The Politics of Natural Rights*. Bloomsbury Academic, p. 17.

[109] Gordon, D. (2019, November 15). Yes, Taxation Is Theft. *Mises Wire*. https://mises.org/wire/yes-taxation-theft; see also Casey, G. (2012). *Libertarian Anarchy: Against the State*. Continuum Books: "Through taxation, the state aggresses against the property of the individual": p. 3.

correct historic wrongs committed by one race against another. Wealth redistribution aimed at redressing racial injustice is inherently unjust in "adjudging guilt by the culpability of genealogy, a charge of guilt by connection to the past merely by the color of skin."[110] It forms no part of society's implied social contract.

Those who disagree that human beings have an essential nature, who see humanity merely as a social construct, would not agree with the philosophy of natural rights. But although it would be incorrect to suppose that natural rights are always, in practice, safeguarded or capable of being defended, the issue here is not what happens in practice but the essential inescapable nature of humanity and the normative ideal to which we should aspire.[111] It may therefore be concluded that from a natural-rights perspective, justice cannot be attained by wealth redistribution based on collective group duties owed by one race to another or owed by the state to specified racial groups. "For the ethical collectivist, the group itself is the moral atom. Individuals are agents of the group and are obliged to suppress their interests for the sake of the group."[112] It is in that sense that collectivism violates the principle of individual liberty which lies at the heart of natural law.

References

Alchian, A. A. (2007). Private Property. In D.R. Henderson (Ed.), *The Concise Encyclopedia of Economics*.

Aylmer, G. E. (Ed.). (1975). *The Levellers in the English Revolution*. Cornell University Press.

Baudin, L. (1962). *A Socialist Empire: The Incas of Peru*. Duke University Press.

Bauer, P. (2000). *From Subsistence to Exchange and Other Essays*. Princeton University Press.

110 Bell, R. (2020). The Unintended Consequences of Promising Black Americans Reparations. *Journal of Higher Education Theory and Practice*, 20(4), 11.

111 "To assert the right is not to deny that such violations occur; it is to condemn those violations": Mack, E. Natural Rights.

112 Posner, E. A. and Vermeule, A. (2003). Reparations for Slavery and Other Historical Injustices. *Columbia Law Review*, 103, 689, p. 707.

Bell, R. (2020). The Unintended Consequences of Promising Black Americans Reparations. (May 9, 2020). *Journal of Higher Education Theory and Practice, 20*(4), 11. Available at SSRN: https://ssrn.com/abstract=3597158

Block, W. (2019). *Property Rights: The Argument for Privatization.* Palgrave Macmillan.

Block, W., & Epstein, R. A. (2005). Debate on Eminent Domain. *NYU Journal of Law & Liberty, 1*(3), 1148.

Brenkert, G. G. (1998). Self-Ownership, Freedom, and Autonomy. *The Journal of Ethics, 2*(1), 27.

Cohen, G. A. (1995). *Self-Ownership, Freedom, and Equality.* Cambridge University Press.

Cooter, R. D. (2006). An Escape from Poverty: Developing Productive Organization. *Southwestern Journal of Law and Trade in the Americas, XII*(2), 186.

Deist, J. (2021, June 3). *A Libertarian Approach to Disputed Land Titles.* https://mises.org/wire/libertarian-approach-disputed-land-titles.

Delsol, J.-P., Lecaussin, N., & Martin, E. (Eds.). (2017). *Anti-Piketty: Capital for the 21st Century.* Cato Institute.

Devine, D. J. (2021). *The Enduring Tension: Capitalism and the Moral Order.* Encounter Books.

Duggan, L. (2019). *Mean Girl: Ayn Rand and the Culture of Greed*. University of California Press.

Easterly, W. (2006). *The White Man's Burden: Why the West's Efforts to Aid the Rest Have Done So Much Ill and So Little Good*. Oxford University Press.

Epstein, R. A. (1989). The Utilitarian Foundations of Natural Law. *Harvard Journal of Law and Public Policy, 12*, 711.

Epstein, R. A. (2018). Meeting the Fundamental Objections to Classical Liberalism. In M. T. Henderson (Ed.), *The Cambridge Handbook of Classical Liberal Thought*. Cambridge University Press.

Epstein, R. A. (2022, June 22). California's Reparations Overreach. *Defining Ideas*. https://www.hoover.org/research/californias-reparations-overreach

Finnis, J. (1980). *Natural Law and Natural Rights.* Oxford University Press.

Friedman, M. D. (2015). *Libertarian Philosophy in the Real World: The Politics of Natural Rights.* Bloomsbury Academic.

Gasper, G. E. M., & Gullbekk, S. H. (Eds.). (2015). *Money and the Church in Medieval Europe, 1000–1200: Practice*. Ashgate Publishing.

Gordon, D. (1995, October 1). A New Socialism? *Mises Review.*

Gordon, D. (1998, April 1). A Reluctant Marxist. *Mises Review.*

Gordon, D. (2012, August 9). Waldron's Rule of Law. *Mises Daily Articles*. https://mises.org/library/waldrons-rule-law

Gordon, D. (2017). *An Austro-libertarian View*. Volumes I, II and III. Ludwig von Mises Institute.

Gordon, D. (2019, November 15). Yes, Taxation Is Theft. *Mises Wire*. https://mises.org/wire/yes-taxation-theft

Gordon, D. (2021, February 19). Are There Any Limits to Natural Rights? *Friday Philosophy*. https://mises.org/library/are-there-any-limits-natural-rights

Harris, J. W. (1996). *Property and Justice*. Oxford University Press.

Kay, J. (2003). *The Truth about Markets—Why Some Nations Are Rich but Most Remain Poor*. Harper Collins.

Kim, J. (2019). Black Reparations for Twentieth Century Federal Housing Discrimination: The Construction of White Wealth and the Effects of Denied Black Homeownership (December 1, 2019). *Boston University Public Interest Law Journal*, (29), 135 (Winter 2019), Available at https://ssrn.com/abstract=3615775

Kukathas, C. (2019). Libertarianism Without Self-Ownership. *Social Philosophy and Policy, 36*(2), 71.

Kurrild-Klitgaard, P. (2000). Self-Ownership and Consent. *Journal of Libertarian Studies, 15*(1), 43.

Law, R. (1980). Wheeled Transport in Pre-Colonial West Africa. *Africa: Journal of the International African Institute, 50*(3), 249.

Locke, J. (1980). *Second Treatise of Government*. (C. B. Macpherson, Ed.). Hackett Publishing.

Maritain, J. (1961). *On The Use of Philosophy: Three Essays*. Princeton University Press.

Mises, L. v. (2005). *Liberalism: The Classical Tradition* (B.B. Greaves, Ed.). Liberty Fund. (Original work published 1927).

Mises, L. v. (2012). *Human Action: A Treatise on Economics*. Martino Publishing.

Molloy, D. (2022, June 29). Bruce's Beach returned to family nearly a century after seizure. *BBC*.

Muhammad, P. M. (2020). The Trans-Atlantic Slave Trade's African Elephant in the International Courtroom: African Nations Owe Blacks of the Diaspora Reparations (December 31, 2020). 27:1 UC Davis Journal of International Law & Policy 81 (2020), Available at SSRN: https://ssrn.com/abstract=3863452

Murphy, L. and Nagel, T. (2002). *The Myth of Ownership: Taxes and Justice*. Oxford University Press.

Newman, D. G., & Binnion, L. (2015). The Exclusion of Property Rights from the Charter: Correcting the Historical Record. *Alberta Law Review, 52*(3), 543.

Olsthoorn, J. (2019). Self-Ownership and Despotism: Locke on Property in the Person, Divine Dominium of Human Life, and Rights-Forfeiture. *Social Philosophy and Policy, 36*(2), 242–263. https://doi.org/10.1017/S0265052519000438

Posner, E. A., & Vermeule, A. (2003). Reparations for Slavery and Other Historical Injustices. *Columbia Law Review, 103*, 689.

Roemer, J. (1994). *A Future for Socialism*. Harvard University Press.

Rothbard, M. N. (2002). *The Ethics of Liberty*. New York University Press (original publication 1982).

Rothbard, M. N. (1995). *An Austrian Perspective on the History of Economic Thought*. Edward Elgar.

Samuel, J. (2022, April 30). Nothing Can Give the Victims of Slavery Justice – And Certainly Not Money. *The Telegraph*. https://www.telegraph.co.uk/news/2022/04/30/nothing-can-give-victims-slavery-justice-certainly-not-money/

Samuel, J. (2022, August 27). The Case of the Benin Bronzes, or How the Woke Monster is Eating Itself. *The Telegraph*. https://www.telegraph.co.uk/news/2022/08/27/case-benin-bronzes-how-woke-monster-eating/

Schmidt, J. (Ed.). (1996). *What is Enlightenment?* University of California Press.

Swerling, G. (2021, September 14). Britain Should Pay Reparations for Slavery, Says Cambridge Dean. *The Telegraph*. https://www.telegraph.co.uk/news/2021/09/14/britain-should-pay-reparations-slavery-says-cambridge-dean/

Thomas, D. A. (1996). Adverse Possession: Acquiring Title to Stolen Personal Property. *Probate & Property, 10*, 12.

Waldron, J. (1990). *The Law*. Routledge.

Waldron, J. (2002). *God, Locke and Equality: Christian Foundations of John Locke's Political Thought*. Cambridge University Press.

Waldron, J. (2002). Redressing Historic Injustice. *The University of Toronto Law Journal, 52*(1), 135.

Waldron, J. (2012). *The Rule of Law and the Measure of Property*. Cambridge University Press.

Wick, J. (2022, August 5). L.A. voters to decide whether hotels must rent vacant rooms to homeless people. *Los Angeles Times*. https://www.latimes.com/california/story/2022-08-05/initiative-would-require-l-a-hotels-to-provide-rooms-to-homeless-people

Widdowson, F. (2019). *Separate but Unequal: How Parallelist Ideology Conceals Indigenous Dependency*. University of Ottawa Press.

Zwolinski, M., & Ferguson, B. (Eds.). (2022). *The Routledge Companion to Libertarianism*. Routledge.

3

Legacies of Injustice and Racial Inequality

One argument often advanced in support of paying reparations is that former imperialist states ought to pay compensation to racial groups which suffered injustice associated with slavery and colonialism. The claim is that these states should implement wealth transfers to atone for their historical crimes. Although little is said in these debates about the fact that states rely on taxation as a source of funds, proposed reparations schemes nevertheless seek to redistribute wealth through tax-funded social welfare schemes. They propose by this means to transfer wealth from groups whose ancestors are said to have benefited from past injustices to groups whose ancestors are said to have suffered from exploitation. Further recompense is sometimes sought through measures such as land expropriation, which is depicted as a form of restitution for stolen land. Such proposals imply that a defence of property rights must give way to the demands of racial justice, or at any rate that a defence of property rights should not impede wealth redistribution designed to satisfy the demands of racial justice. Building on the importance of self-ownership highlighted in Chapter 2, this chapter aims to identify the normative standard by which we should evaluate the coherence of

D. Gordon and W. Njoya, *Redressing Historical Injustice*, Palgrave Studies in Classical Liberalism,
https://doi.org/10.1007/978-3-031-26584-6_3

these demands. The chapter evaluates racial justice arguments within the broader context of historical injustice and contemporary wealth redistribution initiatives.

Is wealth inequality unjust? Is it automatically an injustice for some people to have more wealth than others? Political debates about the obligations of contemporary society to redress historical injustice approach these questions from different perspectives. The meaning of justice is itself in dispute as there is no consensus on whether all must have equal material circumstances in order for the demands of justice to be satisfied and there is no common ground on this point between socialist and capitalist ideologies. Therefore the debate about redressing historical injustice is not simply about how to satisfy the demands of justice but also concerns what is meant by justice in the first place.

The scholarly debates on reparations proceed within a somewhat narrow frame of reference, as they presume that the contested ground concerns *how* to pay reparations for historical injustice and what types of claims should be included in paying reparations, rather than *whether* to pay such reparations. The definition of reparations is for that reason loosely defined to include any type of claim that acknowledges a duty to make recompense for historical injustice and the definition of reparations varies from one author to the next. Posner and Vermeule describe as follows the key features of reparations claims made in most cases:

> They typically refer to schemes that (1) provide payment (in cash or in kind) to a large group of claimants, (2) on the basis of wrongs that were substantively permissible under the prevailing law when committed, (3) in which current law bars a compulsory remedy for the past wrong (by virtue of sovereign immunity, statutes of limitations, or similar rules), and (4) in which the payment is justified on backward-looking grounds of corrective justice, rather than forward-looking grounds such as the deterrence of future wrongdoing.[1]

Posner and Vermeule are concerned with the analytical coherence of the various claims defined as reparations, including claims which fall within

---

[1] Posner, E. A. and Vermeule, A. (2003). Reparations for Slavery and Other Historical Injustices. *Columbia Law Review*, 103, pp 689, 691.

recognised legal categories and those which do not. They observe that in attempting to analyse reparations "The overall picture is that reparations schemes stand poised, uneasily, between ordinary remedies and large-scale transfer programs. They share the backward-looking, corrective justice focus of many ordinary remedies, but share with transfer programs a willingness to do mass or aggregate justice by dispensing with individualized moral justification for the transfer."[2] For purposes of this chapter, as our discussion focuses on the normative implications of reparations for the rule of law, the key issue with which we are concerned relates to a misconception about the justice of reparations claims, howsoever defined. Claims which fall within the parameters of the legal framework do not, on the face of it, raise concerns for the rule of law in that sense; or at any rate no more so than ordinary legal claims. The distinction we draw here is similar to that drawn by Nozick between rectification and redistribution: "returning stolen money or compensating for violations of rights are not redistributive reasons" and thus do not fall within the critique of wealth redistribution with which we are concerned.[3] But claims which seek "mass or aggregate justice" for racial groups "by dispensing with individualized moral justification" are redistributive in that they are concerned with the racial wealth gap which they see as the outcome of historical injustice. They are also founded in notions of collective guilt and responsibility which are incompatible with the protection of self-ownership and individual liberty. As such, these are the types of cases that raise grave normative concerns for the rule of law.

The gravity of these normative concerns is underestimated in the scholarly debates because these debates presume general consensus on the meaning of justice. The discourse blithely assumes that we all agree that reparations should be paid, and thus sees no need to question the philosophical justification of their claim. Many opponents of reparations are not opposed to the idea of reparations, but simply quibble about the form to be adopted by the implementation scheme such as who will pay and who will benefit. Having presumed that the moral basis of the proposals is self-evidently just, they proceed as if the debate were

[2] Ibid.

[3] Nozick, R. (1974). *Anarchy, State and Utopia.* Blackwell Publishing, p 27.

merely an analytical debate about the classification of legal remedies: should reparations be classified as breach of contract cases or restitution cases? How should borderline or difficult cases be classified? What type of evidence should be presented as proof of membership of the specified race: is genealogical evidence sufficient, or is DNA evidence also required? In California, for example, the proposal is for "Black Californians to trace their lineage by determining the birth year of a great or great-great grandparent in the South – and that would likely be sufficient evidence for eligibility."[4] Nobody appears to notice that in principle this proposal is little different from the racial laws of Apartheid or Jim Crow.

The dominant reparations discourse, therefore, fails to acknowledge that the premise itself, the justice of the reparations case, is in dispute. By describing reparations as a way to meet the demands of social justice or restorative justice, the presumption is that we all agree on the meaning of justice and simply disagree on *how* best to give effect to it in terms of practical implementation. For example Waldron writes "Arguments can be imagined, of course, in this context, for wiping the slate clean, or for treating the grievances of persons or peoples as mere historic sentiments, irrelevant to issues of justice."[5] But in framing the debate that way, referring to "issues of justice," Waldron presumes general agreement on what is meant by "justice," and it soon becomes clear that he presumes justice to mean *distributive* justice. If all were agreed that the concept of justice contains a distributive component then the debate would indeed concern the relevant factors to take into account in achieving distributive justice and the significance to be attached to historical grievances in pursuit of that goal. At the very least that way of framing the debate presumes that

[4] "Only those Black Californians who are able to trace their lineage back to enslaved ancestors will be eligible for the state's reparations. Other Black Californians — such as Black immigrants — will not be eligible… Don Tamaki, the only non-Black member of the Reparations Task Force, said that during the Japanese American Redress Movement – which sought reparations and an apology for Japanese internment during World War II – organizers faced similar questions about determining eligibility. 'It's rough justice,' Tamaki said. 'We had to exclude groups too within our community … practical and very difficult decisions were made.'" Kalish, L. (2022, March 30). California Task Force: Reparations for Direct Descendants of Enslaved People Only. *Cal Matters*. https://calmatters.org/california-divide/2022/03/california-reparations-task-force-eligibility/.

[5] Waldron, J. (2002). Redressing Historic Injustice. *The University of Toronto Law Journal*, 52(1), pp 135, 141.

we have a shared understanding of the types of claims that would constitute a "just" claim and are merely debating what factors are relevant in satisfying that claim.

The case for reparations is essentially an egalitarian case, based on the argument that the "economic gap" between different groups, communities or nations is caused by injustice and that wealth transfers designed to close that gap will thereby remedy the injustice. If the matter is to be debated only among egalitarians, then the only relevant questions would concern the factors to be taken into account and how reparations should be implemented. But if all members of society are to be included in this debate then two further issues arise: whether inequality is automatically an injustice, and what evidence is relied on to show that contemporary wealth inequality was caused by historical injustice. This chapter addresses those questions by evaluating what is meant by stating that wealth inequality between racial groups is "unjust." The chapter also questions the presumption that contemporary patterns of wealth distribution were caused by historical injustice. The argument is that poverty and inequality have multiple causes, and are not simply the outcome of racial discrimination or legacies of historical injustice.[6] Understanding the causes of inequality in turn has significant implications for both the pursuit of economic equality as well as the demands of justice.

The idea that we can reverse historical injustice by reallocating wealth is rooted in what Sowell describes as an intertemporal view of justice: the idea that past injustice can be retrospectively corrected by action taken in the present.[7] Unlike Sowell, Waldron regards the intertemporal view of justice as persuasive. He observes that many people view "events temporally prior to the establishment of the [prevailing property] distribution" as the cause of unfairness in the present distribution of wealth.[8] Waldron

[6] Williams, W. E. (2011). *Race and Economics: How Much Can Be Blamed on Discrimination?* Hoover Institution Press.

[7] Sowell, T. (1999). *The Quest for Cosmic Justice*. Touchstone.

[8] Waldron, J. (2002). Redressing Historic Injustice. *The University of Toronto Law Journal*, 52(1), pp 135, 142.

argues that since there are good reasons to be concerned about the historical events that gave rise to injustice, we ought to take appropriate steps in the present to redress the "ramifications" of that injustice.[9]

Waldron argues that "Of course, we cannot hope now to regulate [historical] events. But we do have control over the ramifications that those events are taken to have in our present-day system of property rights, and those ramifications can intelligibly be informed by the sense of justice established after the events in question took place."[10] The argument is that contemporary views of distributive justice ought to "inform" our understanding of the "ramifications" of historical events. He suggests that contemporary wealth redistribution should take historical injustice into account, and may be deemed unfair to the extent that it takes no account of historical injustice. That would mean, for example, that to achieve a fair distribution of wealth we might reallocate property from descendants of those who committed historical injustices, in favour of descendants of those who suffered from those injustices.

In that sense intertemporal perspectives imply that justice demands equal, or at least "fair," distribution of property whose distribution has been rendered unequal or unfair by past injustice. While many scholars debate the extent or form of redistribution, they generally take it as read that *some* form of redistribution is required to satisfy the demands of justice. By linking historical injustice to existing inequality and thence to claims for reparations, that discourse presumes that the concept of justice supplies the necessary analytical link between the claims made and the proposed solutions. This would mean that we require no further explanation for equalising wealth beyond describing inequality as "injustice."[11] The concept of justice is relied on to explain why taxpayers should fund the bill for such payments: simply put, doing so would amount to justice. By invoking the notion of justice in that simplistic way, it is presumed that no further reason or rationale need be supplied to substantiate the case. The social justice discourse has in that way shifted over time from

[9] Ibid.

[10] Waldron, Redressing Historic Injustice.

[11] For example Baradaran argues that reparations are 'necessary and theoretically justified' to satisfy the demands of justice by 'closing the racial wealth gap': Baradaran, M. (2020). Closing The Racial Wealth Gap. *New York University Law Review Online*, 95(1), p 57.

focusing on the causes of wealth inequality to debating "how [wealth] should now be shared," highlighting "historical and structural injustice" as a cause of inequality.[12]

As Flew observes, this presumption—that inequality is unjust and redistribution is required to satisfy the demands of justice—derives from Rawls's theory of distributive justice.[13] Yet the Rawlsian idea of an "overlapping consensus" with which all reasonable people would be expected to agree is rather narrowly constituted. It reflects a consensus of egalitarian perspectives, variations on a theme of socialism, and excludes from its compass the libertarian perspectives advanced in this book.[14] The deeper ideological schism between classical and progressive liberalism therefore concerns not the various factors to be included in a just system of property, but rather how we should understand the ideal of justice itself. Rather than being a more superficial dispute concerning which system does or does not uphold "justice," it is a fundamental ideological difference concerning the importance of self-ownership, property and liberty in a theory of justice, and sharp disagreement over the egalitarian insistence that justice must only be understood in a distributive sense.

The desire for justice, therefore, means different things to different people. All parties agree that justice must be done, but do not agree on what justice entails in specific contexts or on the normative requirements of justice. To derive a clear understanding of the interplay between racial inequality and justice it is, therefore, necessary to clarify the different perspectives on how justice ought to be understood. The aim in seeking clarity is not to come to an agreement, as those who value liberty will never agree with those who prioritise the pursuit of equality even when that pursuit requires the destruction of liberty. The aim is instead, to

---

[12] Forrester, K. (2019). Reparations, History and the Origins of Global Justice. In Bell, D. (Ed.), *Empire, Race and Global Justice*. Cambridge University Press.

[13] Flew, A. (1986). Enforced Equality—Or Justice? *Journal of Libertarian Studies*, 8(1), p 31; Rawls, J. (1999). *A Theory of Justice*. Belknap Press.

[14] For further discussion of this point see Njoya, W. (2021). *Economic Freedom and Social Justice: The Classical Ideal of Equality in Contexts of Racial Diversity*. Palgrave Macmillan; Njoya, W. (Ed.). (2023). Symposium on Economic Freedom and Social Justice: The Classical Ideal of Equality in Contexts of Racial Diversity. *Cosmos + Taxis*, 11(1).

achieve a clear understanding of the issues in dispute. No peaceful settlement, in which all parties agree to disagree, can be achieved if the matters in dispute are not clearly delineated.

The first point to clarify is that the dispute is of course not simply about whether justice is important, but rather how the demands of justice are to be understood. In evaluating that debate we must go beyond mere labels, to identify the essential points being advanced by the different perspectives as well as their implications. This involves looking behind the labelling words that are used to describe the various ideological positions. Approaching with caution the terminology used by various protagonists is necessary because people often mean entirely different things by the same words, or may use entirely different words to mean the same thing. As Sowell observed, "Adam Smith and John Rawls each said that justice was the prime virtue of a society, and yet they said it in such different senses that they meant nearly opposite things."[15] Thus the aim should not simply be to identify a variety of goals that may plausibly fall under the label of "justice" but also to identify what precisely is meant in describing various proposals as "just."

The debate about reparations to redress historical injustice therefore reflects the political and philosophical contestation surrounding the meaning and demands of justice. Despite the presumptions of many scholars, Rawls did not settle this question for all time. No honest debate can proceed on the basis that we are all agreed on the meaning of justice as equality or indeed on the importance of equality. Given that equality has now been redefined to mean substantive equality, a socialist principle which prioritises equality of outcome, it can no longer even be assumed that everyone agrees on the importance of equality defined in that way.[16]

Rawlsian theories of distributive justice are but one way to understand justice, not the only way. When people demand that wealth be redistributed between different racial groups in order to meet the demands of distributive justice, that gives rise to debate between egalitarians on the best way to design such a redistributive scheme. Distributive justice

---

[15] Sowell, *Cosmic Justice*, p 29.

[16] For a discussion of substantive equality see Barnard, C., and Hepple, B. (2000). Substantive Equality. *Cambridge Law Journal*, 59(3), p 562.

might for example justify wealth transfers from descendants of oppressors to descendants of victims, aiming to achieve a more fair distribution of wealth, although there may be differences of opinion on the most effective mechanisms to give effect to that goal. But for those who are not egalitarians, the concept of distributive justice in itself violates the idea of self-ownership and the concept of justice based on individual liberty.

Thus the debates as framed by egalitarians are merely internal debates about different shades of egalitarianism. These debates ignore the existence of other interpretations of justice. Wealth redistribution schemes may indeed achieve the goals of collectivist and egalitarian ideologies, but in doing so they create a new form of injustice which violates the tenets of justice in the classical liberal ideal, including the ideals of formal equality, self-ownership, and individual liberty. This in turn has serious implications for the rule of law as well as the legitimacy of democracy and the role of the state. Any state which exists to promote the partisan ideology of some of its citizens and not others ultimately relies more on coercion than on consent.

To help further an understanding of the ideological schism between classical and progressive views of justice the next part of the discussion explains the importance of formal equality and individual liberty to the classical ideal of justice. The aim is to highlight the point that simply excluding these perspectives from the reparations debate is likely to lead to more social and political polarisation, rather than to encourage a better understanding of the different perspectives which many people in society value.

3.1 The Classical Ideal of Justice: Formal Equality and Individualism

The classical ideal of justice is reflected in the principle of formal equality. Everyone has equal rights in the eyes of the law and nobody is permitted to infringe upon the rights of others. As Roman law expressed it, justice is to give every man his own. As Flew defined it, justice in the classical sense is not synonymous with equality of condition or equality of outcome.[17] The absence of equal conditions is not in itself unjust, as account must be taken of how the inequality is manifest and what has caused that inequality. Flew is therefore critical of arguments that presume justice and equality to be synonymous, so that they make no attempt to explain *why* inequality should automatically be treated as an injustice.[18] As Flew shows, classical liberalism does not define justice as substantive equality, nor does it promise the equal distribution of wealth and fortune.

Further, justice in the classical liberal tradition is based on individual responsibility and thus regards any attempt to enforce notions of collective guilt as unjust. As Lewis argues, individual responsibility is a basic ethical principle:

> no one can be responsible, in the properly ethical sense, for the conduct of another. Responsibility belongs essentially to the individual... For "a structure" cannot be the bearer of moral responsibility; neither can "society in general," for these are both abstractions which we must be careful not to hypostatize.[19]

The impetus behind the reparations claims is inherently collectivist, as it seeks to hold people collectively responsible for historical crimes.[20] In arguing that wealth discrepancies between racial groups can only be reversed by redistributing wealth between groups, the concern with wealth gaps overrides any desire to understand the causes of individual

---

[17] Flew, A. (2009). Justice: Real or Social? *Social Philosophy & Policy*, 151.

[18] "No doubt it appears to one and all utterly obvious that a just society must be an equal one; if not perhaps, if this is conceivable, 'a society which is equal in all respects.' For, given that equation, there would indeed be no need for further justification on either count": ibid., p 152.

[19] Lewis, H. D. (1948). Collective Responsibility. *Philosophy*, 23(84), pp 3, 13. See also Gordon, D. (February 21, 2020). Individual Responsibility and Guilt. *Mises Wire*. https://mises.org/wire/individual-responsibility-and-guilt.

[20] "Although ethical collectivism has enjoyed few philosophically sophisticated defenses, it does reflect powerful intuitions held by many people. The propensity to attribute moral qualities to nations and races is deeply ingrained and difficult to shake.": Posner, E. A. and Vermeule, A. (2003). Reparations for Slavery and Other Historical Injustices. *Columbia Law Review*, 103, pp 689, 707.

life outcomes. People become willing even to countenance new injustices in order to fix the "gap" between the fortunes of different groups, for instance overlooking the injustice of making innocent people pay for crimes they did not commit. As Friedman argues:

> even if our legislators could somehow devise an effective rectification strategy, this enterprise must respect the rights of citizens who were neither the perpetrators of such historical wrongs nor the beneficiaries of them. On Nozick's principles, to which I subscribe, it would be morally impermissible to burden blameless persons with the cost of remedying injustices committed by others. Because the misdeeds in question occurred at least many decades ago, most of the perpetrators and victims are dead. Thus, other than with respect to the return of identifiable property, rectification would have to be enforced against innocent people.[21]

The preoccupation with group disparities compares racial groups, often referred to as "communities," without regard to individual fortunes, so that any individual member of a community who deviates from the community "norm" by being successful is deemed to be irrelevant. Thus in critical race theories which designate racial groups as either oppressor or oppressed, black millionaires are deemed to be irrelevant in describing black people as oppressed, and white philanthropists are deemed to be irrelevant in describing white people as oppressors. Comparing groups of people by reference to whether the group is classified as oppressor or oppressed, measuring various gaps between the groups, and reallocating rights between the groups is a collectivist approach that eschews the concept of the individual or notions such as free will or choice that are associated with individual liberty.

The classical ideal of justice is based on individual liberty, predicated on the idea of normative individualism. Normative individualism expresses "the belief that each individual is an end in his or her self, not

[21] Friedman, M. D. (2015). *Libertarian Philosophy in the Real World: The Politics of Natural Rights*. Bloomsbury Academic, p 20.

to be sacrificed (or coerced) for the benefit of others."[22] Methodological individualism is the idea that "social phenomena are to be understood exclusively in terms of the beliefs, motives, and choices of individuals."[23] If each individual is an end in himself, not simply a representative of a racial or national group, then society is best understood by reference to the individuals within it not by reference to the fortunes of differentiated racial groups. In addition, political individualism "hold[s] that the sole legitimate function of the state is the protection of individual rights, or the promotion of individual welfare. Libertarians are thus opposed to the idea of 'group rights,' at least to the extent that such rights are not derivable from the rights of the individuals who constitute those groups."[24] Methodological individualism does not deny that society exists or that nations, communities or interpersonal relationships are important. Rather, it recognises that

> all actions are performed by individuals. A collective operates always through the intermediary of one or several individuals whose actions are related to the collective as the secondary source…a social collective has no existence and reality outside of the individual members' actions. The life of a collective is lived in the actions of the individuals constituting its body. There is no social collective conceivable which is not operative in the actions of some individuals.[25]

Racial justice claims make no attempt to establish (as distinct from merely asserting) the causes of the collective harm and responsibility which they advance as the basis of their claims, as they consider collective harm and responsibility to be inherent in membership of a racial group. Claims for racial justice are therefore based entirely on the membership of the race or tribe that suffered historical injustice. The following example involving a claim to fishing rights said to vest in the iwi tribe is given by Waldron: "since iwi had had the fishing rights wrongfully taken

---

[22] Zwolinski, M., and Ferguson, B. (Eds.). (2022). *The Routledge Companion to Libertarianism*. Routledge, p 4.

[23] Ibid.

[24] Ibid.

[25] Mises, *Human Action*, p 42.

away from them, it is to iwi that they should be returned."[26] In this situation fishing rights are determined not only by the membership of a native tribe, but membership of only one specific tribe, the iwi. The only basis on which such fishing rights can now be enjoyed is upon proof of tribal membership, and the only way to ensure that nobody wrongfully enjoys the rights without belonging to the tribe is to scrutinise the tribal antecedents or lineage of anyone who purports to exercise the rights. Tribal associations founded after the seizure of the property rights would therefore not qualify for restitution of the property wrongfully seized. In Waldron's example, "UMA had not suffered comparable injustice, for they did not exist at the time the expropriations took place, and so they were not entitled to any redress."[27]

This example shows how claims of collective ownership based on race raise difficult issues. Entitlement to the rights claimed can only be substantiated by tracing blood lines and genetic lineage. This unwholesome prospect, which in effect resurrects the old racial categories that were once used to oppress and exploit, but now promotes the same racial categories as a basis for allocating entitlement to reparations, has been much debated by the California reparations committee. The committee proposes to pay reparations only to genetic descendants of slaves and not to all black Californians who may in many cases be relatively recent immigrants to the state.[28] Not only are people divided by race, but they are to be further subdivided into different groups within that race to ensure that payment is not made to members of the race who do not qualify. When this type of racial classification was implemented by the Apartheid regime in South Africa, under Jim Crow, or by other race essentialists who have historically regarded race as a legitimate basis for

---

[26] Treaty of Waitangi Fisheries Commission, discussed in Waldron, Redressing Historic Justice, p 150.

[27] Ibid.

[28] Those eligible for proposed payments will need evidence of genetic lineage. "The task force voted in March to approve a motion that defines an eligible person as an "individual being an African American descendant of a chattel enslaved person or the descendant of a free Black person living in the US prior to the end of the nineteenth century."" Kalish, L. (2022, April 13). California's Reparations Task Force Explained. *Cal Matters*. https://calmatters.org/california-divide/2022/04/californias-reparations-task-force/.

assigning legal rights, it was denounced as evil. It is no less evil when it is proposed as a basis for the payment of reparations.

As Shaw has argued, a historical claim to title based on legal and archaeological evidence is quite different from a claim based purely on membership of a racial group said to have originally inhabited the land.[29] Justice ought to be based not on what one group, tribe or race owes to another, but what rights and liabilities individuals owe to each other in a just society. Thus the argument here is not that historical property claims ought not to be vindicated, but that vindication of property claims ought not to be based on racial identity.

It is sometimes argued that if proposals for racial justice conflict with classical perspectives of justice, perhaps that simply means that classical perspectives of justice have no relevance in contemporary debates and we need new theories of justice. This is not a new critique. Adam Smith addresses the argument that a concept of justice which does not express all the ideals that everyone in society might desire from the conduct of others is too bare and minimal. Smith defends a negative concept of justice which delineates the appropriate scope of compulsion and the use of state force to prevent people from infringing upon the rights of others. Justice does not confer a positive power that can be wielded to instil in others desirable personal virtues such as compassion or generosity. Justice is a concept that defends the scope of individual rights. Justice does not give the power to encroach upon the rights of others. As Smith describes this concept of negative justice:

> Mere justice is, upon most occasions, but a negative virtue, and only hinders us from hurting our neighbour. The man who barely abstains from violating either the person, or the estate, or the reputation of his neighbours, has surely little positive merit. He fulfills, however, all the rules of what is peculiarly called justice, and does everything which his equals can with propriety force him to do, or which they can punish him for not doing.[30]

---

[29] Shaw, W. H. (2003). They Stole Our Land: Debating the Expropriation of White Farms in Zimbabwe. *The Journal of Modern African Studies*, 41(1), p 75.

[30] Smith, A., Raphael, D. D., and Macfie, A. L. (1982). *The Theory of Moral Sentiments*. Liberty Classics; see Flew, Justice: Real or Social? p 152.

The reason why the concept of justice does not encompass all the social or moral expectations of good conduct we might desire from others is that failure to meet social expectations of admirable conduct does not in itself constitute an injustice. Justice backed by the force of law expresses a minimal basis on which we are entitled to invoke the use of force to defend our rights against infringement by others. Justice is not a concept that appropriately expresses aspirations for all the noble and worthy conduct we might expect from our fellow citizens. It is self-evident that we do not all agree on what constitutes worthy conduct, so if we regarded the use of coercion as justified to enforce worthy conduct we would end up in endless conflict, each group trying to enforce their ideals on others.[31] Thus we encourage people not to be selfish, to give to charity and help the less fortunate, but if some people are selfish that is not, in itself, an injustice for which legal sanction is appropriate and we do not wage war on people for being (in our perception) selfish. First, we cannot all agree on what amounts to selfish conduct. Second, even if we were able all to agree that a particular group of people is selfish, that would not constitute grounds to wage war upon them. Were it otherwise, frail humanity itself would have to be outlawed. Those who fail to meet the expectations of their neighbours would face legal sanctions. In the end tyranny, not liberty, would prevail.

One of the main problems in contemporary discourse is precisely a failure to distinguish between social ideals and aspirations, dreams we would wish to see come true in an ideal world, and the concept of justice. For example, one may wish to achieve certain goals in life, but a failure to achieve those goals does not necessarily mean that an injustice has occurred for which legal recompense ought to be available. Further, neither the socialist ideal nor the capitalist ideal should be forced on those who do not share that ideal. It is not the case that one or other must be enforced upon dissenters so that we should simply fight to see which ideology prevails—that approach would end in constant upheaval and conflict. History has shown through many centuries of experience

---

[31] On the importance of distinguishing between private and public law in this context see Njoya, W. (2021). A Critique of Equality Legislation. *Journal of Libertarian Studies*, 25(1), p 272.

that the only approach to moral and ideological disagreement which is compatible with peace is the edict "live and let live."

3.2 Stolen Property and Counterfactual Analysis

In evaluating how reparations may help to redress historical wrongs, Waldron conceptualises the challenge as legally and morally analogous to returning stolen property to its rightful owner.[32] But when centuries have passed since an alleged theft it is no straightforward matter to ascertain whether a theft occurred in the first place, and if so to identify the original or rightful owner to whose descendants the property should be returned. In cases of theft there is no presumption that an accused person is guilty unless he can prove his innocence, nor that if anyone is accused of having stolen property he must prove that it was lawfully acquired. The presumption of natural justice is the converse: "Possession is nine-tenths of the law and the burden of proof is always on those who seek to overturn present property titles."[33] In the context of historical injustice, an allegation that the presumptive owner derived their title from stolen property could only be substantiated by a historical inquiry into the original ownership of the disputed land. As Rothbard points out: "We can only find the answer through investigating the concrete data of the particular case, i.e., through 'historical' inquiry."[34]

Such a historical inquiry would be necessary not only to ascertain the facts of the original acquisition but also to identify the rightful descendants of the original owner. In many cases even if the original owner is known it is no straightforward matter to identify the rightful descendants. The break from the past constituted by colonialism and conquest with all the attendant social and cultural upheaval of such events, followed by subsequent migration of many different groups of people, makes it difficult to see how title can be traced back through

[32] Waldron, Redressing Historic Injustice.

[33] Block, W. (2019). *Property Rights: The Argument for Privatization.* Palgrave Macmillan, p 31.

[34] Rothbard, M. N. (2002). *The Ethics of Liberty.* New York University Press, p 51.

time to identify the original "owner" much less trace that owner's line of descendants. Family lines, locations, occupations, and land use patterns of family groups, have not remained the same since the time of the expropriation to the present day. Communities have long since broken up, intermarried, moved away, or may have been demographically transformed by incoming groups.[35] A similar idea is reflected in Nozick's argument that in evaluating the justice of property holdings a principle of rectification "uses historical information about previous situations and injustices done in them…and information about the actual course of events that flowed from these injustices, until the present."[36] It is not simply about ascertaining what happened in a historical event, but also what has happened in the course of time that has transpired since that event.

Therefore several difficulties arise in tracing property entitlements through generations. Not only are rightful owners and heirs difficult to trace, but the property itself, even if proved to have been stolen, may have been so transformed in the meantime that it cannot justly be treated as the same resource that was originally stolen. Such cases regularly arise in relation to personal property, for example, when a thief steals corn and transforms it into whiskey. In such a case, can the original owner of the corn claim ownership of the whiskey? Such questions are even more intractable in relation to land, for example where land is reclaimed from a river and a city is subsequently constructed on the reclaimed land: do the owners of ancient fishing rights in the rerouted river now have title to the city?[37] The landscape itself may have changed: part of the seabed may have been reclaimed and converted to farmland, and what was once open grassland may now be a city of skyscrapers. Waldron argues that in such cases, "Even if we were sure that we had the right entity – the right right-bearer – we would need additional assurance that the right

---

35 Waldron, Redressing Historic Injustice.

36 Nozick, *Anarchy, State and Utopia*, p 152.

37 For an example in relation to land on which a university now stands, see Korn, M. (2022, July 13). University of Washington Professor Sues School Over Alleged Free-Speech Violation. *Wall Street Journal*. https://www.wsj.com/articles/university-of-washington-professor-sues-school-over-alleged-free-speech-violation-11657733575?page=1: "In other words, Mr. Reges says, citing philosopher John Locke's theory that those who improve upon land own it, the Coast Salish people historically owned nearly none of the campus land."

in question had survived…So now we have to ask whether the rights remain stable during the prodigious lifetime of the group. On the face of it, it seems implausible that [the rights] would remain stable."[38] Waldron argues that in cases where land use has changed unrecognisably over time it cannot be assumed that the original rights to use the land have survived in the same form.[39]

Therefore it would not be obvious that a settlement made in the nineteenth century should be interpreted as a claim to benefit from evolving land use in perpetuity, several generations after the original parties to the agreement, who could not have foreseen how circumstances would change centuries into the future. Paradoxically, it is often said that colonial treaties are "living trees" but the reinterpretation of such treaties to keep up with changing times tends only to be in the direction of the continued expansion of treaty rights to include new forms of land use, rather than to question whether such rights have survived the evolving land use including the costs attendant upon the expansion of the welfare state and of the general population size.[40] Waldron therefore observes that the initial injustice of conquest may therefore be "superseded by circumstances."[41]

Waldron further emphasises that fairness does not amount simply to restoring the descendants of historical injustice victims to the position they would have occupied if the injustice had not occurred. Some legal scholars regard that as the goal of compensation, for example in cases of breach of contract, namely to restore the claimant to the position he would have occupied but for the breach. Waldron acknowledges the difficulties entailed in achieving that in relation to historical crimes. Asserting

38 Waldron, J. (2002). Redressing Historic Injustice, p 151.

39 "the land and other resources of the country [New Zealand] are now used on a basis that is staggeringly different from the basis on which they were used at the time the violations took place. This, I think, has to make a difference to how we think about rights – even violated rights – that are alleged to have survived from that earlier era into the present." Ibid.

40 "Quite apart from anything else, the changes that have taken place over the past 200 years mean that the costs of respecting primeval entitlements are much greater now than they were in 1800. Two hundred years ago, a small aboriginal group could have exclusive domination of 'a large and fruitful Territory' without much prejudice to the needs and interests of very many other human beings. Today, such exclusive rights would mean many people going hungry who might otherwise be fed." Ibid., p 156.

41 Ibid., p 152.

that "the task of reparation is to transform the present so that it matches as closely as possible the way things would be now if the injustice had not occurred" demands an almost impossible calculation.[42] He points out that "The difficulties in this task are those of all counterfactual speculation. How can we know what would have happened if some event that in fact did occur had not taken place?"[43]

Nozick envisages a counterfactual analysis being conducted in rectifying property holdings: "The principle of rectification presumably will make use of its best estimate of subjunctive information about what would have occurred (or a probability distribution over what might have occurred, using the expected value) if the injustice had not taken place."[44] But as Posner and Vermeulen point out, the counterfactual analysis required by historical injustice cases raises questions even more intractable than those which arise in, for example, tort or contract cases, as they require consideration of how entire lifetimes across generations would have unfolded; for example: "How does one value the loss of an education that was denied because of political activities? Should it matter if the education would not have increased one's income?"[45]

Counterfactual historical analysis is especially difficult where we no longer have all the details necessary to evaluate the truth of what took place centuries ago and how matters have unfolded since then. We can date the time and sequence of particular conquests or settlements, but while conquest is always wrong it is not asserted that all historical conquests ought to be compensated for—this would not be possible as the history of humanity has for millennia been the history of conquest. The idea behind most reparations arguments is to select only those cases of historical conquest that have given rise to present racial inequalities. But even if we select only cases of contemporary racial injustice it is still necessary to evaluate which particular settlements of foreign lands where those races were involved was *wrongful*. The wrongfulness does not arise automatically from the presence of the specified races

42 Ibid., p 144.

43 Ibid.

44 Nozick, *Anarchy, State and Utopia*, p 152.

45 Posner and Vermeule, Reparations for Slavery, p 700.

but from the conduct itself. In the case of nineteenth-century exploration, settling on unowned property and mixing one's labour with it gives rise to a just and moral claim to ownership in the Lockean sense. For the same reason a claim by any native tribe to prior ownership of settled land cannot meaningfully extend over entire continents including uninhabited land.[46]

In addition to the difficulties of evidence and counterfactual speculation, Waldron points out that free will and choice intervene in human interactions and experiences over time so that we cannot be certain that if those historical events had not occurred, the economic outcomes of their descendants today would be different.

> Would they have held on to the land and passed it on to their children and grandchildren? Or would they have sold it – but this time for a fair price – in response to the first honest offer they were given? And, if they had, then what would the purchaser have done with it? Sold it again? Passed it on to his children? Lost it in a poker game?[47]

Waldron's argument is not simply that we cannot predict the choices people might hypothetically have made, but that no choice was *in fact* made. Thus although Waldron favours acknowledging and redressing historic injustice in contemporary formulations of distributive justice, he doubts the feasibility of that particular sort of counterfactual analysis.[48] It fails to take due account of changes that have occurred over time which make it impossible simply to restore people to the position we think they would have occupied had history unfolded differently: "we must come to terms with each other here and now, irrespective of how we all got here."[49] We might perhaps speculate about hypothetical choices that were not in fact made, but we cannot attach moral authority to

---

[46] "Crusoe, landing upon a large island, may grandiosely trumpet to the winds his "ownership" of the entire island. But, in natural fact, he owns only the part that he settles and transforms into use." Rothbard, *Ethics of Liberty*, p 64.

[47] Ibid., p 144.

[48] "the approach that aims, as it were, to wind the tape back to the injustice and try to make the world as though the injustice had never happened…the counterfactuals that that involves are impossible to figure out (if not incoherent)." Ibid., pp 158, 159.

[49] Ibid.

our hypothesis and use that to inform a theory of justice. We simply do not know how things would be now if the historical injustice had not occurred, and it is just as easy to suppose that things now might have been much worse if history had taken a different path from the path it in fact took.

It might equally well be, for example, that for all we know Africa would be economically much worse off today if large parts of it had never been colonised. It is interesting to hypothesise and speculate, but we cannot call our musings a theory of justice and rely on it to justify coercive redistribution of wealth as a way to satisfy the putative demands of justice. This means that any attempt to derive a theory of justice based on the counterfactual interpretation of historical events would amount to restructuring the present "so that it matches as closely as possible the way we would *hope* or *wish* things to have turned out"[50] rather than to produce just outcomes.

These difficulties are typically overlooked where claims are made about "stolen land" or land that is said to have been expropriated or seized. No details are typically given, as the general understanding in contemporary political debates seems to be that the mere fact of exploration, settlement and colonisation is sufficient to establish that land was wrongfully seized. Yet it has long been acknowledged that people have a right to explore, and to settle in other lands. It is not the mere settlement, but the fact of violent conquest, that is wrongful:

> Each person, says Kant, and each group has the right to approach other peoples in the world with a view to "offering to engage in commerce." Though the privilege is terribly abused, still "such abuse cannot annul the right of citizens of the world to try to establish community with all [others] and, to this end, to visit all regions of the earth.[51]

Kant does not endorse the use of force to settle on land that is already inhabited. But what is meant by "inhabited" land? What historical and archaeological evidence would suffice to establish who was the first

[50] Ibid., p 144.

[51] Waldron, Redressing Historical Injustice, p 135.

possessor of the land, and should it be based on what would have been understood by the parties at the time as a claim to possession or ownership, or by reference to what we now think possession or ownership of land should entail?

Shaw argues that historical claims to title should be based on the same principles of property acquisition that apply in general cases: "According to entitlement theorists like Nozick and Locke, one justly acquires a previously unowned resource only by mixing one's labour with it. Thus, if some whites settled on unused land and started working it, then they would have established a property right to it."[52] Like Kant, Shaw does not condone criminal acts, such as resorting to violence to evict people from their lands, but argues that a case of violent expulsion is distinct from a case of settlement. Each case turns on its own historical facts: "This is a question for historians and archeologists to settle on a case-by-case, and farm-by-farm, basis."[53]

It has not been suggested in the reparations debates that an attempt should be made to make reparation for all historical injustice, to encompass all land that has ever been historically expropriated by anyone. But that being the case, how it would be decided which stolen land to return and which stolen land may be kept within a theory of justice? Waldron's example of the theft of his car sheds little light on the matter. In principle all stolen goods ought to be returned to their owners. But title to personal property such as cars vests in a named owner (whether a human or legal owner) while in cases of disputed land, there was often no clear title in the first place and the claim to ownership is based on tribal history that is buried in the mists of time. Leaving aside arguments about compensation, to say that the theft of a car persists until the car is returned is in material respects not the same thing as saying the theft of land from one group persists until the land is returned to the group. Either the original owners with title to the land can be traced or they cannot. As argued in Chapter 2, if title can be traced restitution is a straightforward legal claim. The absence of a straightforward legal claim in the types of cases referred to as "stolen land" is in itself indicative of the fact that no title

52 Shaw, *They Stole Our Land*, p 75.

53 Ibid.

can be established (if title could have been established, the claim would have been brought).

As Kant says in the passage quoted by Waldron, people have a right to explore and to settle, but not to steal. Thus the legal problem is not simply whether theft ought to be remedied even after considerable time has passed since the theft occurred—the problem here is that it is not clear whether, where, if, or how the alleged theft occurred. To say that the mere presence of settlers proves that some theft must have occurred begs the very question which falls to be answered, namely whether settling new lands automatically amounts to theft or expropriation. Here it is important to resist the tendency which has been termed presentism, which involves evaluating past interactions and communications based on what they would mean if they were expressed today.[54] This approach to understanding history may tell us much about our own understanding of the world, but tells us nothing about how matters were understood at the time by those who lived through those events. The prevailing idea that historical exploration and settlement on foreign lands is wrongful in itself, so that land settled on by European settlers should now be regarded as stolen land, is an interpretation based on presentism. It evaluates the wrongfulness of past events by reference to contemporary expectations. Presentism cannot assist in deciding whether the historical land acquisition was just or unjust. We can acknowledge that conduct regarded in the past as perfectly acceptable might no longer be so today, without going further to demand reparations for past conduct which was not regarded as wrongful at the time.

Therefore in ascertaining legal liability for historical events, the relevant standard ought to relate to the circumstances that prevailed at the time those events occurred. In all cases the applicable principle would be that the burden is on the claimant to prove the claim to rightful ownership: "the burden of proof lies on someone who disputes a land title to make good his claim. If he cannot do so, the present possessor owns his land legitimately. Absent a clear proof by the objector that land has been

[54] Miles, J., and Gibson, L. (2022). Rethinking presentism in history education. *Theory & Research in Social Education*, 50(4), p 509; Black, J. (2008). Contesting the Past. *History*, 93(2), p 224; McCarthy, A. (2022). Historians, Activists and Britain's Slave Trade Abolition. *Scottish Affairs*, 31(3), p 325.

forcibly wrested from him or his ancestors, the current possessor's claim holds good."[55] Based on that principle, the just outcome of each case would vary from one type of historical event to another, as settling on uninhabited land or selling land to a colonial power calls for a different analysis than a violent conquest and forcible expulsion of people from their homes. In reality, the facts on the ground in different historical contexts varied widely.[56]

In many cases where historical events are described as wrongful, that means no more than that we wish now that those events had not occurred, but that is no just basis on which to dispossess the current owners of the property. If dispossession were given effect based on a mere assertion by a claimant to ancestral entitlement, with no requirement for evidence or proof, that would not amount to justice in any recognisable sense of the term justice. The idea of ancestral guilt, that innocent people living today must atone for the crimes of their ancestors by paying reparations, perpetrates an injustice of its own. It risks lending credence to the threat described by Sowell as a cycle of revenge and counter-revenge, where in a bid to reverse historical injustices by punishing the descendants of those who perpetrated the original injustice, unjust methods are relied upon to redress the original injustice.

3.3 Legacies of Injustice

Those concerned about legacies of historical exploitation do not necessarily claim that the case is analogous to that of returning stolen property to its rightful owner. They have a different argument based on legacies of exploitation—the idea is that new injustices have arisen over time, and that these new injustices were triggered by the original injustices. Their argument is that slavery and colonialism have persistent effects, which

[55] Gordon, D. (2009, September 25). Private Property's Philosopher. *The Mises Review*, 5(1). https://mises.org/library/private-propertys-philosopher.

[56] "Tribes were systematically dispossessed of their lands by purchase, confiscation or legal artifices": Waldron, Redressing Historic Injustice, p 149. Clearly acquisition by these three different methods would give rise to varying outcomes: a purchase is not the same thing as a confiscation. Similarly much depends on whether the confiscation or legal artifice entailed the use of force.

can now be seen in new and evolving forms of racial discrimination. Discrimination is thus described as a historical legacy the existence of which is illustrated by endemic economic inequality. The argument then is that contemporary economic inequality would not exist without the original historical unfairness and its persistent legacy of discrimination.[57]

The claim framed in this way is not one for the restoration of stolen property, nor does it seek compensation for the original injustice of exploitation or conquest. Instead, the aim is to resolve the injustice of currently prevailing economic unfairness said to be caused by racial discrimination which daily produces fresh victims. If economic inequality between racial groups is caused by discriminatory legacies emanating from oppressive and exploitative historical events, that would suggest that redistributive schemes would be the best response to the residual legacy of those events.[58] In this way, the racial justice arguments increasingly shift attention away from the original injustice and more onto the idea that contemporary wealth redistribution through race-based payments would help to resolve enduring patterns of racial inequality. Although this perspective is consistent with Waldron's idea about the "ramifications" of historical injustice, it differs in its emphasis on emerging outcomes of the original injustice rather than seeking to redress the original injustice itself.

Proponents of the "legacies" argument derive their contemporary understanding of racial injustice and the racial wealth gap from their understanding of historical events and thus express their experience of contemporary life in light of how they consider it to be affected by historical events. This in turn leads them to argue that the economic gap that persists between racial groups is an outcome of historical events, and that the demands of distributive justice are to be satisfied, today, by wealth transfers to disadvantaged groups. This is what is meant by those who say that they have been waiting for their reparations for 400 years—not that they are aggrieved by the original injustice, but that the original injustice has replicated itself anew throughout that time, and its legacy

---

[57] See Williams, W. E. (2011). *Race and Economics: How Much Can Be Blamed on Discrimination?* Hoover Institution Press.

[58] See Perry, A. (2020). *Know Your Price: Valuing Black Lives and Property in America's Black Cities*. Brookings Institution Press.

operates in the same way today. In sum, that perspective is concerned not with whether we can or ought to engage in an intertemporal analysis of justice but claims that by transferring wealth to descendants of those who suffered historical disadvantage we can satisfy the contemporary legacies of that disadvantage.

It can be seen that the "legacies" argument is generally constructed upon a set of causal relations the validity of which is taken by critical race theories to be self-evident.[59] The first presumption relates to a connection between historical injustice and contemporary discrimination. This discrimination is said to be "systemic" in nature, so that systemic racism is said to be manifest not in individual conduct or individual life experiences but in the very systems on which society, in general, is constructed such as the legal system or the criminal justice system. The society itself, as a whole, is said to be systemically racist. Merely by being present in society, one can be said to experience that injustice. A further presumption relates to a causal connection between racial discrimination and patterns of wealth distribution, with a further presumption that "ending discrimination" today would result in equal outcomes for all racial groups. Unequal outcomes are said in this theoretical perspective to be a legacy of the exploitative relationship between historical "oppressors" and the historically "oppressed."

The emphasis on historical injustice as the cause of an enduring legacy of racial discrimination and economic inequality explains why the reparations debates devote much attention to detailing examples of past unfairness. It is not that they simply wish to rehash the past, but that they believe rehashing the past is the best way to understand and explain economic outcomes today. In that sense redressing the original injustice, by itself, would not satisfy the claim. For example, ancient fishing rights might be restored to dispossessed native tribes, but as long as there persists an economic gap the historical injustice will continue to count as unredressed.

Based on the interdependent series of presumptions on which the legacies argument relies, merely showcasing historical grievances suffices to prove the case for paying reparations. For example, the California

[59] See for example Kendi, I. X. (2019). *How to Be an Antiracist*. Penguin Books.

reparations report states: "For hundreds of years, the American government at the federal, state, and local levels has systematically prevented African American communities from building, maintaining, and passing on wealth."[60] The defined harm lies in the allegation of having been prevented from making economic progress. The perpetrator is identified broadly as all levels of government. The victims are broadly defined as African American communities. Numerous historical examples are then cited to substantiate the claim of "systemic" or general harm to the community, as the claim is based generally on membership of that community. It is not concerned with the personal outcomes of any individual person who can prove that the government has impeded his own progress, in the sense that he would be experiencing different life outcomes today if the government had not so impeded his ancestors. Instead, the claim is based on harm constituted purely by the claimant's membership of the African American community as a disadvantaged community. In framing these claims as community claims it is not alleged that no other community has historically suffered harm or disadvantage based on unjust government action. Indeed it is not necessary for any such allegation about other communities to be made in order to advance the argument that an enduring legacy of exploitation persists in relation to the African American community, since reparations claims are in this context framed in a way that is specific to the racial group whose grievances are showcased. On that basis they would argue that whether other communities have suffered comparable harm or not is irrelevant to evaluating their own claims.

Some might argue that any wealth transfers implemented by the state as racially targeted social welfare are part of the welfare state to which everyone implicitly consents as a member of society. This may appear to be simply a case of social welfare that targets beneficiaries who are said to be particularly vulnerable due to the legacies of oppression from which they suffer. For example, the proposals in California to pay reparations to descendants of slaves do not propose that descendants of slaveholders should be identified and singled out as being liable to pay reparations:

[60] California Task Force to Study and Develop Reparation Proposals for African Americans: *Interim Report* (June 2022), p 474. Available at https://oag.ca.gov/system/files/media/ab3121-reparations-interim-report-2022.pdf.

rather, reparations are paid from general taxes. Everyone pays into the public purse from which reparations are drawn. Two arguments may be advanced in response. First, paying compensation for historical crimes through taxes amounts to attempting to make all members of society pay for historical crimes in which they played no part: "if there is any case for reparations, these should come from guilty parties, not from the entire citizenry through the tax system. To make all citizens pay for the crimes of a few would be to extend—not diminish— the effects of robbery."[61]

Further, the insistence that the economic gap sought to be corrected by reparations is in some way caused by historical crimes perpetrated by one race upon another puts racial history at the heart of contemporary debates about economic inequality. The case cannot be treated simply as a social welfare case such as, for example, disability support payments. Reparations might superficially be said to be merely a way to allocate social welfare funds in a manner deemed to be just since the payment is based simply on the existence of an economic gap which it is desired to eradicate. Indeed some "climate reparations" and "covid pandemic reparations" proposals, such as that in Rhode Island, are open to everyone who requires support rather than being allocated on the basis of race.[62] It is often said that after all, we pay taxes to fund many things we may personally disagree with, and it makes no real difference to any individual taxpayer if public funds are used for racially based social welfare schemes.

Taxation seems to be no undue imposition on any individual, and is therefore relatively tolerable to many people as the price for living in society even in cases where social welfare allocation is unjust. For example in the UK where schools and hospitals are funded by taxes, many complaints are made about fairness in the distribution of tax funds to different localities but in general, the complainants do not assert that these things ought not to be publicly funded through taxes. The

---

[61] Block, *Property Rights*, p 29.

[62] "Because the $10 million is money the city received under the federal American Rescue Plan Act, the program does not limit eligibility to Black residents. The eligibility criteria include Black and Indigenous residents and people facing poverty:" Chavez, N. and Gamble, J. (2022, December 3). Rhode Island's Capital City Will Spend $10 Million in Reparations, and It Could Benefit White Residents. *CNN*. https://edition.cnn.com/2022/12/03/us/providence-rhode-island-reparations-reaj/index.html.

complaints relate simply to the implementation of the scheme. Similarly, many people quibble about the particular form in which reparations would be distributed but do not question the payment of reparations in principle. Yet the justification for payment of social welfare on racial lines is weak. Unlike schools and hospitals which in theory are available to everyone, reparations are based on racial entitlement. Moreover, payment of reparations is intrinsically connected to ideas of collective racial guilt or retribution for historical crimes, and the entire case for payment of reparations is constructed upon narratives of racial injustice substantiated by a long list of racial grievances and harms for which atonement is demanded.

Wealth transfers based on collective racial guilt and responsibility cannot, therefore, be deemed acceptable as social welfare simply because they are satisfied from the common purse. Given that payment of taxes is not optional, and there is little direct democratic control of the precise uses to which taxes are put, it seems to many people pointless to debate the moral foundations of tax expenditure. However, it matters for the integrity of the legal system and in upholding respect for the rule of law. It is an important value that the law should be widely regarded as just and fair, not as a weapon to punish some racial groups at the behest of other groups in an attempt to reopen old wounds and resolve historical grievances. Moreover, it casts into doubt the foundational legitimacy of a state which devotes taxation and social welfare schemes towards the prioritisation of one race to the exclusion of other races.

3.4 Why the Causes of Inequality Matter

Without understanding the factors that drive economic failure or economic success, public policy responses risk exacerbating, rather than resolving, concerns about racial inequality. To understand why wealth transfers will not resolve the problem of inequality, it is important to look beyond race and racial grievances and make the effort to understand the causes of inequality in a more comprehensive sense. The extent to which economic inequality is rooted in historical events is disputed. The causal connection between unequal outcomes and historic exploitation, or indeed present discrimination, cannot be presumed to be the only explanation for economic outcomes. Economic outcomes are influenced by multiple variables, so the causal connection between historical injustice and economic inequality must be established, not simply asserted.

The view that discrimination is the cause of life outcomes presumes that were it not for discrimination, economic outcomes of all racial groups would be equal in all material respects. This idea has been influential in development economics. As Bauer observes:

> The idea of Western responsibility for Third World poverty has also been promoted by the belief in a universal basic equality of people's economic capacities and motivations. This belief is closely related to egalitarian ideology and policy which have experienced a great upsurge in recent decades. If people's attributes and motivations are the same everywhere and yet some societies are richer than others, this suggests that the former have exploited the rest.[63]

The presumption that people will experience equal life outcomes in the absence of exploitation or injustice ignores the reality that people have different skills, talents and other attributes relevant to explaining economic outcomes. As Mises observes: "In any social system the main issue is how to promote peaceful co-operation among people markedly different from one another not only in bodily characteristics but also in mental capacity, willpower and moral strength."[64] All these differences would logically be expected to influence economic experiences and outcomes. In addition, there are cultural, geographical and other variations that explain why different racial groups may experience different economic outcomes over time.

The importance of understanding the causes of economic progress derives from the very need to solve economic problems. Historical grievances in themselves do not constitute an explanation for economic

---

[63] Bauer, P. (2000). *From Subsistence to Exchange and Other Essays*. Princeton University Press, pp 60, 61.

[64] Mises, L. v. (1962). Foreword. In Baudin, L. (1962). *A Socialist Empire: The Incas of Peru*. Duke University Press, p v.

outcomes, nor does itemising historical crimes amount by itself to an explanation for economic inequality. Instead, we need a theoretical interpretation that identifies and clarifies the implications of those historical facts, helping us to gain a deeper understanding of historical events. It is one thing to highlight historical facts, and quite another to evaluate their implications. The reparations movement errs in simply presenting historical facts as if they supply their own argument for wealth distribution. The facts are what they are, and what we learn from those facts is a matter of interpretation. Learning from history involves an element of logical analysis: "In order to learn something from history, we need a theoretical background. We can understand the records of the past only if we approach them equipped with a body of doctrinal knowledge acquired from other sources than the study of history."[65]

It is not sufficient to observe that a social phenomenon such as racial wealth disparity exists. It is necessary to understand what causes it and why it persists. If the causes of the disparity and the reasons for its persistence remain unknown, then policy responses are simply wild stabs in the dark. Causal analysis is important in the reparations debate because the causes of things matter. This is why science investigates the causes of things: it "aims at tracing back every phenomenon to its cause."[66] The rational course of action is that which is likely, as far as we can tell, to produce the outcome we desire. We must endeavour to understand the causal factors that contribute to the desired outcome, and not simply assume that redistributing wealth will suffice. Superficial and subjective perceptions can be deceptive, and merely to assume that wealth transfers will resolve the problem of inequality with no attempt to understand what causes inequality in the first place will lead to failed outcomes or, even worse, potentially create new injustices.

[65] Ibid., p vii.

[66] Mises, *Human Action*, p 17.

3.5 Moral Emotion and the Causes of Inequality

Hayek described the concept of social justice as "the chief outlet for moral emotion, the distinguishing attribute of the good man, and the recognized sign of the possession of a moral conscience."[67] The influence of moral emotion goes a long way in explaining why the causes of inequality are glossed over in the reparations debate. Historical injustices are deemed to be so significant, so morally abhorrent and horrifying it may be said, that the need to atone for them in a quasi-religious sense seems so compelling as to render their causes and effects irrelevant in considering how appropriately to atone for them. The reparations argument is framed with direct reference to the horror of historical events. For example the California report devotes a notable amount of space to descriptions and even photographs of horror.[68] The moral claim for slavery reparations is based, like the moral claim for slavery abolition, in large part on the ability to shock people by detailing the horrors of slavery. But while the abolition movement aimed to persuade people to back ending the slave trade, the reparations movement seeks compensation centuries after the event to transfer wealth from people who were not present at the time to those who never suffered its injustice. The idea of historical legacies is designed principally to create the impression that present-day governments are complicit in the horrors of the past, and that present-day populations suffer from those horrors in the same way as their ancestors.

---

[67] Hayek, F. A. (1973). *Law, Legislation and Liberty: A New Statement of the Liberal Principles of Justice and Political Economy*. Routledge, p 66.

[68] California Task Force to Study and Develop Reparation Proposals for African Americans: *Interim Report* June 2022 states: "This report contains discussions of racial discrimination, sexual assault, torture, lynching and other forms of extreme violence. The report contains unedited historical quotations and photographs of white supremacist hatred, torture, lynching, autopsy, and other forms of graphic violence." The table of contents includes "Enslavement, Racial Terror, Political Disenfranchisement, Housing Segregation, Separate and Unequal Education, Racism in Environment and Infrastructure, Pathologizing the Black Family, Control Over Creative Cultural and Intellectual Life, Stolen Labor and Hindered Opportunity, An Unjust Legal System, Mental and Physical Harm and Neglect" among other similar topics. Available at https://oag.ca.gov/system/files/media/ab3121-reparations-interim-report-2022.pdf.

To argue that culpability need not be established where a historical crime is overwhelming in its abhorrence, that the occurrence of that historical crime in itself demands that someone, anybody, must now atone for it, and that emotional attachment to historical events is the same as being present at the time of those events, is incompatible with justice. Justice predicated on the rule of law demands that even the worst crime, murder most foul, does not justify a policy that anybody, or everybody, must make recompense for that crime without fair trial and without evidence of culpability. The rule of law upholds a presumption of innocence and the principle that accusers must prove their case with verifiable evidence. Objective evidence, something more than subjective feelings, is an imperative. Truth stands on shaky ground indeed if "lived experience" based on feelings about the past suffices as evidence of moral or legal culpability. As Mises points out, it also ignores the complexity of experience:

> any experience in the field of social events is experience of complex phenomena, i.e., of the joint effects of a multiplicity of chains of causation. It is specifically historical experience as distinct from the experience of laboratory experiments, in which we are in a position to observe the effects of the change in one factor only, while all other factors that could possibly influence the outcome remain unaltered. Historical experience can therefore neither verify nor falsify any theorem in the sense in which verification or falsification of a hypothesis can be attained in the experimental procedures of the natural sciences.[69]

We must also emphasise the analytical distinction between violence as a feature of historical events, and claims to compensation specifically for the racial violence associated with slavery or colonialism. While the moral case in support of reparations draws heavily on the history of violence, historical events such as slavery and conquest would be morally unjustifiable even if they did not involve violence. It is true that violence is endemic in the nature of exploitation, as it could be argued that nobody (or few people) would submit to slavery or colonialism in the absence

[69] Mises, L. v. (1962). Foreword. In Baudin, L. (Ed.). *A Socialist Empire: The Incas of Peru.* Duke University Press, p vii.

of violence. But human subjugation is abhorrent even in the absence of violence or evidence of harmful legacies. The central role played by graphic accounts of violence in the reparations debates risks framing the moral debate as *purely* about eradicating violence, which in turn implies that expropriation is acceptable as long as no violence is involved. Slavery, being inherently a violation of the principle of self-ownership, is inherently wrong. The Roman law of slavery understood slavery to be an emanation of war or conquest, and it is thus by its very nature coercive and can never be regarded as voluntary or benevolent.[70] On that basis, no form of slavery is acceptable whether or not violence and brutality are involved in specific cases and even in cases where the slaveholder is proved to have behaved with benevolence and kindness towards his slaves. Morally and ethically, slavery is simply wrong. It is not necessary to itemise the attendant violence or showcase pictures of horror in order to understand that it is wrong; the violence and horror exacerbate an institution that is wrong in itself.

A similar observation may be made about the exploitative nature of colonialism. The case for reparations is often based on arguing that colonial forces committed brutal acts of violence. The case for reparations is then thought to be conclusively proved simply by providing a comprehensive list of violent events or giving a platform to survivors to explain what they endured.[71] This in turn creates an incentive to focus exclusively on the violence of colonialism, if only by omitting to mention any benefits that might also have resulted from it in an attempt to create the impression that colonialism entailed nothing but violence on the presumption that this makes the case for reparations more compelling.[72] If the claim to be compensated for historical events is weak, that claim cannot be made stronger simply by pointing to contemporaneous acts of violence. Brutality that occurred centuries ago cannot, in itself, offer a good foundation for contemporary wealth transfers from people who

---

[70] Buckland, W. W. (1908). *The Roman Law of Slavery: The Condition of the Slave in Private Law from Augustus to Justinian.* Cambridge University Press.

[71] See for example Elkins, C. (2022). *Legacy of Violence: A History of the British Empire*. Penguin. For a review of *Legacy of Violence* see Black, J. (2022, May 12). Professor Good, Empire Bad. *Quadrant Online.* https://quadrant.org.au/magazine/2022/05/professor-good-empire-bad/.

[72] Ogot, B. A. (2005). Britain's Gulag. *The Journal of African History*, 46(3), p 493.

were not there at the time of the brutal events and had no hand in them. When the argument based on legacies of history shifts to highlighting contemporary economic disparities, the claim for compensation at once becomes even weaker, because the economic legacy of historical events is not simply one of exploitation—it is also one of benefit and economic progress. As Bauer highlights: "Since the middle of the nineteenth century, commercial contacts established by the West have improved material conditions out of all recognition over much of the Third World" which is surely a relevant fact in evaluating the economic legacy of colonialism.[73]

The conclusion is inescapable that wealth transfer arguments are not based simply on a moral interpretation of justice as they imply when they frame the claim as one for social justice. These arguments also represent an ideological political programme animated by socialist ideology. Reparations are seen as the appropriate remedy for economic inequality because they are intended to equalise the material conditions of victimised peoples and nations by transferring wealth from rich to poor, within a socialist worldview that regards the equalisation of wealth as a worthy goal. Whether such wealth transfer schemes work in resolving social problems (or in this case, given that wealth transfers have been running for several decades, understanding why the favoured remedy never seems to work) must depend in the first place on understanding the causes of the problem. Yet the relevant causal factors are barely mentioned in the policy debates about reparations and equity. Instead, the debate is dominated by concerns about how racial groups should be defined for purposes of receiving race-based payments, which suggests that the proponents of such schemes have little interest in whether their proposals will in fact improve anyone's material conditions.

The claims about racial injustice as the main determinant of economic outcomes in that way reveal themselves to be based less on reason and logic than on rhetoric and myth. Reasoned debate cannot be entirely effective in responding to claims of that nature. Political disputes about racial injustice need not, and indeed seldom do, rely on reason and rationality and to a large extent it does not matter to the claimants

[73] Bauer, *From Subsistence to Exchange*, p 58.

whether their demands are reasonable or logical given the political significance and weight of their case. Perceptions of inequality, especially racial inequality, periodically result in public protests or even riots and thereby imbue activist social justice movements with the necessary political significance required to influence policy outcomes. Indeed, one of the arguments often advanced to support socialist wealth redistribution schemes is that it will ensure social peace. Piketty for example argues that "too high inequality generates a risk of revolution, and chaos could follow."[74] This assumes that envy and resentment are greater motivators than aspiration and self-reliance, which is not empirically true but serves an important rhetorical purpose in the advance of socialist ideology. Reparations claims also derive theoretical comfort from critical race theories which consider reason and rationality to be in any case "problematic" in that they are associated with an Enlightenment tradition in which white men, deemed to be representative of both patriarchy and imperialism, notably feature.

Owing in large part to the emotional sensitivity associated with the legacies of slavery and colonialism, there seems to be a widespread view that the causes of inequality are rendered irrelevant by the urgency of satisfying strong feelings of historic unfairness. The racial justice debates in that sense reject the objective search for truth. Instead, they embrace ideologies of inclusiveness which regard all subjective "truths" based on lived experience as putatively valid.[75] Furedi argues that the classical liberal tradition, which regarded the advancement of knowledge as a meaningful ideal, has fallen under pressure from "the cumulative impact of Western society's disenchantment with the legacy of the Enlightenment" which rejects the relevance of truth in favour of ideas with broader popular appeal.[76] But as Furedi highlights, the relevant issue for public policy is not whether emotions and personal experience are important but whether they ought to displace the role played by logic and reason in advancing the quest for knowledge and justice.

---

[74] Delsol, J.-P. (2017). The Great Process of Equalization of Conditions. In Delsol, J.-P., Lecaussin, N. and Martin, E. (Eds.). *Anti-Piketty: Capital for the 21st Century*. Cato Institute, p 11.

[75] Furedi, F. (2004). *Where Have All the Intellectuals Gone?* Continuum Books, p 4.

[76] Ibid., p 13.

Progressive policies which are justified as an attempt to improve upon our concepts of justice and fairness overlook the fact that after millennia of human progress we have valuable resources to draw upon in addressing questions of racial justice. History shows that attempts to achieve justice which deny the importance of individual liberty and self-ownership eventually result in tyranny. The threat to liberty and prosperity is often overlooked in the haste to resolve social problems presented by racial inequality and the plight of the vulnerable. Classical liberal ideals are therefore under pressure from the great political weight behind the claim that property rights must now give way to restorative justice in recompense for past wrongs. In the haste to address the legacies of slavery and colonialism the redistribution debates fail to take due account of the role of self-ownership and property rights in promoting prosperity. In doing so the prevailing policy framework precludes a clear understanding of the nature of productive activity and forecloses more promising avenues for addressing the challenges of inequality through free markets.

3.6 A Consistent Approach to Comparative Analysis

One of the most intractable issues in the reparations debates concerns comparative analysis of the historical experiences of different racial groups. Williams has shown that there is no evidence to support the view that historical suffering causes some groups to suffer economic disadvantage in the long run while other groups are able to overcome their disadvantage over time.[77] It is well known that many different groups suffered historically. Of the American experience Williams observes that "In addition to black Americans, the Irish, Italians, Jews, Puerto Ricans, Poles, Chinese, Japanese, Swedish, and most other ethnic groups have shared the experience of being discriminated against by one means or another."[78]

77 Williams, *Race & Economics*.

78 Ibid.

An objection often heard in response to Williams's comparative studies is that lessons for one racial group cannot be extrapolated from the experience of another group. The claim is made, for example, that trans-Atlantic slavery is not like other experiences of slavery, that forced labour suffered by slaves was not like forced labour suffered by serfs or indentured servants, or that colonialism in Africa was not like that experienced in other realms of the British Empire such as, say, India. Similarly, it is argued that there are material differences between trans-Atlantic slavery and slavery in the Roman Empire when measured for example by reference to survival rates. If the claim for special treatment of specific racial groups is distinguished on grounds of the specific unique nature of the historical event where the oppression of that racial group arose, such as trans-Atlantic slavery, then the question arises as to what makes that specific event unique. In the case of trans-Atlantic slavery it is not alleged to be the only form of slavery perpetrated in history, and those who attempt to distinguish this specific form of slavery based on its brutality also cannot show that this is the only case of brutality perpetrated in history. The historical experience of slavery was global, with "a long history and a broad geographical scope. [It] encompasses the ancient and modern world, Atlantic and Islamic trades, and it is scarcely surprising that slavery does not have a single meaning, nor a uniform context."[79] In discussing the historical experience of slavery little attention is paid, for example, to the slave ships of the Soviet gulags.[80] This suggests that it is not the historical fact of slavery, in itself, which animates the moral ideology of the debates with which we are concerned, but the historical fact of *selected* forms of slavery coupled with the economic fortunes of the specific groups proposed as potential beneficiaries of wealth redistribution. The focus on trans-Atlantic slavery attracts the most attention precisely because it is closely linked to racial economic inequality in the West, not because it raises different moral concerns than other types of slavery.

---

[79] Black, J. (2011). *A Brief History of Slavery*. Robinson Press, p xii.

[80] Bollinger, M. (2003). *Stalin's Slave Ships: Kolyma, the Gulag Fleet, and the Role of the West*. Praeger.

Comparative analysis becomes more complex still when we distinguish between legal or formal definitions and the practical experiences of different types of forced labour experienced by slaves, serfs, servants, and even employees who claim to be working in slavery conditions. The legal distinctions between these categories do not neatly map onto the extent to which these different groups of labourers were, in practice, "free." Williams highlights, for example, the experience of "the self-hired and quasi-free" slaves in the American South who were legally and formally slaves but in practice as free as other disadvantaged people who depended on their labour for a livelihood in the same social and economic context.[81]

All experiences in life are of course different in many respects, and no comparison of historical experiences can be entirely exact, so the point here is not that the experiences of all groups are exactly the same. The point is that in establishing the causal connection between historical experience and socioeconomic outcomes over time consistency of argument and analysis is important. For example, in one context it was said by defenders of reparations for black people in the US that the economic success of Japanese immigrants is irrelevant in evaluating the validity of their own group's claims that their economic outcomes are a product of racial discrimination, but in a different context the same proponents will argue that since reparations were paid to the Japanese for wrongful incarceration during the second world war, they too are entitled to reparations for their own grievances. This means that comparisons between different racial groups are relied upon only when they assist the case for reparations, but where they do not advance that case comparisons are deemed to be irrelevant and inappropriate.

An unwholesome attempt is sometimes made to ascertain whose grievances were "worse" than others, even though there is no objective measure by which we can ascertain whose historical grievances ought to be considered more grievous than others for purposes of public policy and wealth transfers. Given that racial discrimination is the common experience of all human beings the comparative question is why some forms of racial discrimination are "worse" than others, and how we would

[81] Ibid., p 21.

determine which type of racial discrimination is worse (or "worst"). It would imply not only a stepped scale of comparative harm, where a qualitative evaluation is made about which group suffered the "worst" historical injustice but also a stepped scale of reparations where those who suffered "worse" get higher levels of compensation than those who suffered "less."

A further observation about comparative analysis in this discourse is that arguments in favour of reparations are not based on historical injustice in general, but are specifically concerned with the historic injustice suffered by a particular race, usually black people or others considered to be ethnic minorities in the West. The stunning silence surrounding the expropriation of white-owned farms in Zimbabwe and South Africa shows the double standards that apply in the selection of which cases of injustice merit attention. Those who advance claims on behalf of only their own racial group may well point out that it is open to other racial groups to advance their own racial claims for reparations, should they wish. All racial groups could potentially make claims to reparations, as all racial groups have suffered historical injustice at some point in their history. Recent examples include Asians expelled from East Africa and white families driven out of Zimbabwe and South Africa. We could all descend into a global melee in which each race claims reparations against the others. But it is clear that no economy could thrive based on a system in which public funds are allocated as "reparations" for historical injustice to *all* racial groups living in that society. That would simply amount to a system of paying out public funds based not on public welfare provision but on account of the recipients' race. Ultimately, the question must be whether there is any coherent theoretical foundation for allocating public funds based on race. As it cannot credibly be argued that race-based reparations should be paid to *all* people, the question then is why specific races are deserving of reparations while others are not.

A similar difficulty arises in relation to the concept of justice in a more amorphous sense, and how that concept is harnessed to mount racial claims. In claiming that racial justice relates to some races and not others the question is why all groups who have suffered historical injustices are not also entitled to justice, and what type of justice would be achieved if all groups of humanity were to make claims for reparations against each other. It would resemble some kind of race war rather than a quest for justice. After all, the proponents of this amorphous type of justice do not claim that there are races that have never suffered historical injustice. Their claim instead is based on racial exceptionalism, namely that there is some unspecified exceptional quality of one type of racial grievance that entitles it alone to be recompensed from the public purse, while other historical injustices need not be redressed.

It can be seen therefore that the arguments in favour of reparations are based on a selective approach to comparative analysis. If reparations are not claimed on behalf of all people who have ever suffered historical injustice but only in relation to specific groups, an explanation is required for why any particular group should be treated as a special case. No such explanation has been supplied, other than a vague unsubstantiated attempt to suggest that some types of exploitation are worse than others. Although the reparations debate is heavily linked to the idea of racial justice, historical injustice is not of course confined to races or other social groups. There are many other factors that make people vulnerable and have caused them to suffer historical injustice, such as social class or religion. Nor is there evidence that in relation to economic outcomes such historical disadvantage can only be overcome through wealth transfers. Williams therefore argues that "The experience of several ethnic minority groups in the United States and elsewhere seriously calls into question arguments that disadvantaged minorities must acquire political power and need measures to 'end racism' in order for socioeconomic growth to occur."[82]

The issue then becomes one of consistency in comparative analysis. The argument for racial exceptionalism relies on double standards, for example by arguing that whether conduct is exploitative or not depends entirely on the respective races of the parties involved.[83] In some cases,

---

[82] Ibid., p 15.

[83] "This being typical: "Carter G. Woodson, the pioneering African American historian. In his 1924 book *Free Negro Owners of Slaves in the United States*...Woodson did acknowledge that there were black slaveholders who bought slaves for the same reason that whites did–to gain economic advantage from their forced labor–but he believed that such exploitation of blacks by blacks was relatively rare." Lightner, D. L. and Ragan, A. M. (2005). Were African American Slaveholders Benevolent or Exploitative? A Quantitative Approach. *The Journal of Southern History*, 71(3), p 535.

these double standards are justified by reference to neo-Marxist "critical race theories" which hold that relationships of power require the application of double standards in order to account for power differences between groups. Critical theorists maintain that a member of an oppressor race is not to be judged by the same standard as members of oppressed races. In practice this means, for example, that only white people can be "racist" and that only black slaveowners can be "benevolent" while any benevolence exhibited by a white slaver is irrelevant because white slavers belong to the "oppressor" race.[84] This race essentialist approach, which evaluates conduct by reference to the race of the perpetrator, is incompatible with the principle of formal equality.

3.7 The Lessons of History

Understanding why many different groups have thrived *despite* discrimination and historical oppression is important, not least because there would be much of value to be learned by understanding those reasons. Williams explains:

> Obvious examples are the Chinese, Indians and Jews – all despised aliens in racially hostile climates…the same is true of Armenians, Greeks, and Jews in the successor states of the Ottoman Empire, and Igbos in Nigeria. The fact that such alien minorities sometimes make significant economic gains questions at least two assumptions made in the literature on race. Benevolence on behalf of the larger society is neither a necessary nor sufficient condition for an ethnic minority to achieve economic predominance; and economic progress can occur in the absence of what is traditionally considered political power.[85]

The important question in comparing the historical experiences of different groups is not whether there are different types of exploitation, but rather, to what extent the differences in experiences of historical

[84] Lightner, D. L., and Ragan, A. M. (2005). Were African American Slaveholders Benevolent or Exploitative? A Quantitative Approach. *The Journal of Southern History*, 71(3), p 535.

[85] Williams, *Race & Economics*, pp 13, 14 (references omitted).

injustice are significant in explaining contemporary economic outcomes. Economic inequality cannot be explained, or explained primarily, by historical events such as slavery or colonialism. As Williams shows, many societies that have suffered similar (and worse) histories have nevertheless thrived. "Racial and ethnic preference, grouping, and conflict have been a permanent global feature of man's history…Contrary to what is often thought, no racial or ethnic group has a monopoly on racial oppression and discrimination."[86]

A similar observation may be made in relation to colonial history, as the experience of colonialism varied widely and valuable lessons about economic progress may be derived from comparing them. As Bell observes: "identifying imperialism and its legacies, though, is not always a straightforward matter. This is because empire and imperialism come in different forms, and moreover, there is considerable dispute about how best to define them. There are also a range of thorny empirical problems concerning causality, of how to identify the relationship between past and present."[87] The fact that some former colonies thrived while others fell into even deeper poverty shows that colonialism is not itself the cause of poor economic outcomes. Bauer points out that there is no evidential basis for linking colonial history to poverty, as "The poorest and most backward countries have until recently had no external economic contacts and have often never been Western colonies. It is therefore obvious that their backwardness cannot be explained by colonial domination or international social stratifications."[88]

Finally, the implications for equality and justice must be considered. The natural-rights philosophy holds all people to be equal in virtue of their humanity, and equal before the law. To promote justice it is necessary first to defend the principle of equality before the law. This means that rights and liabilities ought not to be prescribed based on racial groups. For example, as noted earlier the main reason why slavery is morally and ethically wrong is not because it creates economic inequality between racial groups, but because it reduces human beings to the legal

[86] Ibid., pp 11–12.

[87] Bell, D. (Ed). (2019). *Empire Race and Global Justice.* Cambridge University Press, p 5.

[88] Bauer, P. (2000). *From Subsistence to Exchange*, p 54.

status of chattels. Thus slavery remains wrong irrespective of the races of the slaver and the enslaved, and also irrespective of whether it involves physical brutality and violence which are always wrong *in themselves* regardless of the races involved and regardless of the respective racial outcomes. The slogan of the abolitionists, "Am I not a man and a brother" reflected this belief in our common humanity. It was rooted in religious beliefs, primarily deriving from Anglicans and Quakers, that all men are created equal, and it was not in any sense an "antiracism" doctrine about economic or power relations between races or eradicating economic gaps between racial groups. As it was put by the American Anti-Slavery Convention, abolition was based on the equality and liberty of all individuals:

> The right to enjoy liberty is inalienable... all these laws which are now in force, admitting the right of slavery, are, therefore, before God, utterly null and void...and therefore they ought instantly to be abrogated.[89]

By focusing on racial identity and the wealth gap between different racial groups, the racial exceptionalism approach discounts the value of liberty and equality. It also discounts successful ethnic minority individuals as exceptions to the group norm that do not matter in evaluating the experience of their racial group. Thus for example the fact that some slaves prospered in the American economy is deemed to be irrelevant in evaluating the legacy of slavery. Williams points out that "during the colonial period, some slaves bought their freedom and acquired property" and indeed acquired their own slaves.[90] But entrepreneurial slaves are deemed to be irrelevant in evaluating the legacy of slavery, even though "so common was the practice of self-hire [by slaves] that historians have described the people so employed as "Quasi-Free Negroes" or "Slaves

[89] William Lloyd Garrison, "Declaration of Sentiments of the American Anti-Slavery Convention" discussed in Rothbard, *Ethics of Liberty*, p 24.

[90] "During colonial days, slaves learned skills and found that they could earn a measure of independence by servicing ships as rope makers, coopers, and shipwrights. Some entered more skilled trades...some slaves bought their freedom and acquired property." As Williams highlights, this included owning their own land and their own slaves: Williams, *Race & Economics*, pp 15, 16.

Without Masters."[91] So widespread and successful were the economic activities of both free and unfree black people in the American South that Jim Crow legislation became necessary to restrict them and also to restrict the choices of anybody who chose to interact with black people. This legislation punished slave owners who "allowed a slave to go at large as a freeman."[92] The legislation was not primarily designed to punish slaves (as no *new* legislation would be needed to achieve that) but to punish masters who allowed freedom to their slaves in return for a fee. Levying fines on such masters would, in principle, also make it no longer financially attractive for them to permit self-hire by slaves. That entire historical record is dismissed as irrelevant by a focus on "equal outcomes" for racial groups as a whole. While slavery is wrong in itself regardless of its economic effects, the existence of slaves who forged their own economic path casts doubt on the argument that the legacy of slavery has greater economic implications today than the legacy of other historical injustices suffered by different groups throughout history.

Ultimately egalitarian philosophy demands equal outcomes based on group identity. In their preoccupation with comparing group outcomes, egalitarians focus exclusively on inequalities between groups as a whole, and ignore any cases of success and prosperity no matter how widespread or significant. The egalitarian worldview is also highly selective in choosing which historical injustices to redress and which to ignore. Unless we propose simply to abandon the idea of property rights altogether, it surely cannot be argued that we should reopen all the wars in history, relitigate events like the enclosure system which prevent people from having access to their ancestral lands, and demand reparation for every historical injustice that has ever occurred since the beginning of time. Indeed nobody makes the claim that all historical events should be reversed. For example, the claim has not been advanced that Corsair pirates, or their descendants, should pay for kidnapping English people from the villages of Devon and Cornwall and selling them as

[91] Ibid., p 20.

[92] Ibid.

slaves, or for many other historical experiences of slavery.[93] Most importantly, in failing to consider the implications for classical liberal views of justice, distributive justice falls into the danger of responding to historical injustice by creating new injustices.

References

Baradaran, M. (2020). Closing The Racial Wealth Gap. *New York University Law Review Online, 95*(1), 57.

Barnard, C., & Hepple, B. (2000). Substantive Equality. *Cambridge Law Journal, 59*(3), 562.

Baudin, L. (1962). *A Socialist Empire: The Incas of Peru*. Duke University Press.

Bauer, P. (2000). *From Subsistence to Exchange and Other Essays*. Princeton University Press.

Bell, D. (Ed.). (2019). *Empire*. Cambridge University Press.

Black, J. (2022, May 12). Professor Good, Empire Bad. *Quadrant Online*. https://quadrant.org.au/magazine/2022/05/professor-good-empire-bad/

Black, J. (2008). Contesting the Past. *History, 93*(2), 224.

Black, J. (2011). *A Brief History of Slavery*. Robinson Press.

Block, W. (2019). *Property Rights: The Argument for Privatization*. Palgrave Macmillan.

Bollinger, M. (2003). *Stalin's Slave Ships: Kolyma, the Gulag Fleet, and the Role of the West*. Praeger.

Buckland, W. W. (1908). *The Roman Law of Slavery: The Condition of the Slave in Private Law from Augustus to Justinian*. Cambridge University Press.

California Task Force to Study and Develop Reparation Proposals for African Americans. (June 2022). *Interim Report*. https://oag.ca.gov/system/files/media/ab3121-reparations-interim-report-2022.pdf

Chavez, N., & Gamble, J. (2022, December 3). Rhode Island's Capital City Will Spend $10 Million in Reparations, and It Could Benefit White Residents. *CNN*. https://edition.cnn.com/2022/12/03/us/providence-rhode-island-reparations-reaj/index.html

---

[93] Black, J. (2011). *A Brief History of Slavery*. Robinson Press.

Delsol, J.-P. (2017). The Great Process of Equalization of Conditions. In J.-P. Delsol, N. Lecaussin, & E. Martin (Eds.), *Anti-Piketty: Capital for the 21st Century*. Cato Institute.
Elkins, C. (2022). *Legacy of Violence: A History of the British Empire*. Penguin Books.
Flew, A. (1986). Enforced Equality—Or Justice? *Journal of Libertarian Studies, 8*(1), 31.
Flew, A. (2009). *Justice: Real or Social?* Social Philosophy & Policy, 151.
Friedman, M. D. (2015). *Libertarian Philosophy in the Real World: The Politics of Natural Rights*. Bloomsbury Academic.
Furedi, F. (2004). *Where Have All the Intellectuals Gone?* Continuum Books.
Gordon, D. (2009, September 25). Private Property's Philosopher. *The Mises Review, 5*(1). https://mises.org/library/private-propertys-philosopher
Gordon, D. (2020, February 21). Individual Responsibility and Guilt. *Mises Wire*. https://mises.org/wire/individual-responsibility-and-guilt
Hayek, F. A. (1973). *Law, Legislation and Liberty: A New Statement of the Liberal Principles of Justice and Political Economy*. Routledge.
Kalish, L. (2022a, March 30). California Task Force: Reparations for Direct Descendants of Enslaved People Only. *Cal Matters*. https://calmatters.org/california-divide/2022/03/california-reparations-task-force-eligibility/
Kalish, L. (2022b, April 13). California's Reparations Task Force Explained. *Cal Matters*. https://calmatters.org/california-divide/2022/04/californias-reparations-task-force/
Kendi, I. X. (2019). *How to Be an Antiracist*. Penguin Books.
Korn, M. (2022, July 13). University of Washington Professor Sues School Over Alleged Free-Speech Violation. *Wall Street Journal*. https://www.wsj.com/articles/university-of-washington-professor-sues-school-over-alleged-free-speech-violation-11657733575?page=1
Lewis, H. D. (1948). Collective Responsibility. *Philosophy, 23*(84), 3.
Lightner, D. L., & Ragan, A. M. (2005). Were African American Slave-holders Benevolent or Exploitative? A Quantitative Approach. *The Journal of Southern History, 71*(3), 535.
McCarthy, A. (2022). Historians, Activists and Britain's Slave Trade Abolition. *Scottish Affairs, 31*(3), 325.
Miles, J., & Gibson, L. (2022). Rethinking Presentism in History Education. *Theory & Research in Social Education, 50*(4), 509.
Mises, L. v. (1962). Foreword. In Baudin, L. (1962). *A Socialist Empire: The Incas of Peru*. Duke University Press.

Mises, L. v. (2012). *Human Action: A Treatise on Economics*. Martino Publishing.

Njoya, W. (2021a). *Economic Freedom and Social Justice: The Classical Ideal of Equality in Contexts of Racial Diversity*. Palgrave Macmillan.

Njoya, W. (2021b). A Critique of Equality Legislation. *Journal of Libertarian Studies, 25*(1), 272.

Njoya, W. (Ed.). (2023). Symposium on Economic Freedom and Social Justice: The Classical Ideal of Equality in Contexts of Racial Diversity. *Cosmos + Taxis: Studies in Emergent Order and Organization, 11(1).*

Nozick, R. (1974). *Anarchy, State and Utopia*. Blackwell Publishing.

Ogot, B. A. (2005). Britain's Gulag. *The Journal of African History, 46*(3), 493.

Perry, A. (2020). *Know Your Price: Valuing Black Lives and Property in America's Black Cities*. Brookings Institution Press.

Posner, E. A., & Vermeule, A. (2003). Reparations for Slavery and Other Historical Injustices. *Columbia Law Review, 103*, 689.

Rawls, J. (1999). *A Theory of Justice*. Belknap Press.

Rothbard, M. N. (2002). *The Ethics of Liberty*. New York University Press (original publication 1982)

Shaw, W. H. (2003). They Stole Our Land: Debating the Expropriation of White Farms in Zimbabwe. *The Journal of Modern African Studies, 41*(1), 75.

Smith, A., Raphael, D. D., & Macfie, A. L. (1982). *The Theory of Moral Sentiments*. Liberty Classics.

Sowell, T. (1999). *The Quest for Cosmic Justice*. Touchstone.

Waldron, J. (2002). Redressing Historic Injustice. *The University of Toronto Law Journal, 52*(1), 135.

Williams, W. E. (2011). *Race and Economics: How Much Can Be Blamed on Discrimination?* Hoover Institution Press.

Zwolinski, M., & Ferguson, B. (Eds.). (2022). *The Routledge Companion to Libertarianism*. Routledge.

4

Property Rights and the Rule of Law

The terminology of proprietary entitlement is often employed in seeking redress for historical injustice. Any demand for the return of stolen property or repayment of debts owed appears to be self-evidently justified because it appeals to the popular understanding of entitlement: the social justice claimant seems to demand no more than what rightfully belongs to him. The purpose of the legal system and courts of law is precisely to settle such disputes about entitlement. For the rule of law to prevail the meaning of legal entitlements must be clear, generally applicable, certain and predictable, as well as capable of being defined and understood by all parties to the dispute. Understanding the implications of self-ownership and property rights in jurisdictions where popular opinion favours wealth redistribution therefore requires a deeper and more critical inquiry into the meaning of the rule of law. What is meant by the rule of law in the context of redressing historical injustice?

This book has argued so far that self-ownership is an essential component of individual liberty. This chapter analyses in more detail why self-ownership and individual liberty are essential to the rule of law. The analysis treats the principle of self-ownership as "a guidepost for

D. Gordon and W. Njoya, *Redressing Historical Injustice*, Palgrave Studies in Classical Liberalism,
https://doi.org/10.1007/978-3-031-26584-6_4

shaping and reshaping whatever positive law may be in existence" to evaluate whether rules of positive law conform to the precepts of reason.[1] As explained in chapter one, our argument is not that the natural law offers the only theoretical lens through which the rule of law may be understood, but rather that it offers a theoretical lens which accords to self-ownership and property rights the importance which these concepts merit in constructing a philosophical defence of individual liberty. This normative standard is helpful in evaluating not only situations where it is sought to abolish property rights altogether, but also cases where control over private property is so heavily circumscribed by state control that it bears little resemblance to private property. As Mises observes, private property is under constant threat not only from those who seek to abolish it altogether but also from those who view it as an impediment to the pursuit of social welfare goals and wish therefore to restrict it:

> property rights as they are circumscribed by laws and protected by courts and the police, are the outgrowth of an age-long evolution. The history of these ages is the record of struggles aiming at the abolition of private property. Again and again despots and popular movements have tried to restrict the rights of private property or to abolish it altogether.[2]

The rule of law goes beyond a requirement that state conduct must be legal or that the state must follow due process in regulating private property. After all, compulsory acquisition of property is lawful in jurisdictions where legislation permits the state to seize property without the owner's consent or even, as in the case of South Africa, without compensation. Article 17 of the Universal Declaration of Human Rights and similar human rights instruments which purport to protect property rights do not resolve the prior question under consideration here, namely how we define property rights in the first place and how we ascertain the content and scope of such rights. Designating the content of legal concepts is ultimately a rule of law question, in the sense that legal categories must make sense and accord to the precepts of reason. A "right," if

[1] Rothbard, M. N. (2002). *The Ethics of Liberty*. New York University Press (original publication 1982), p 17.

[2] Mises, L. v. (2012). *Human Action: A Treatise on Economics*. Martino Publishing, p 650.

that right is to be meaningful and coherent within the rule of law, must be something more than a mere wish, desire or demand.

In defining rights it is important to distinguish between property rights as an emanation of self-ownership in the natural law normative sense, and property rights understood as a technical matter of legal definitions in the formal sense of positive law. If understood purely as a matter of positive law it would seem that property rights can take any form that a jurisdiction desires, so that any jurisdiction could choose to define as "property rights" any rights including communal licence to use the property with title vesting in the state. For example, Vancouver in Canada declares that title to the city's lands vests in the native peoples who historically inhabited the lands, but there is an expectation that the city is entitled to continue in possession of the land subject to paying specified sums of money to those groups.[3] The question is: does this scheme reflect property rights? The city has after all, democratically elected to define and understand land ownership in this way. In ascertaining the nature of property rights in different societies and cultures the question then is, as Kukathas frames it:

> Are any conventions of property permissible so long as they are accepted by the community that abides by them? This issue is not an easy one to settle because insisting on a certain core understanding of property supplies a warrant for intervening in the practices and lives of people who might not accept that understanding—something of which the European colonizers of new worlds were certainly guilty—but denying that there is any core leaves one unable to distinguish between genuine or valid or legitimate property claims from spurious, invalid, or illegitimate ones.[4]

[3] "Rights and title holders in the City of Vancouver are the Musqueam, Squamish, and Tsleil-Waututh within the meaning of UNDRIP [United Nations Declaration of the Rights of Indigenous Peoples] …The City of Vancouver has the responsibility to provide rights-based programming and services to the diverse Indigenous populations": City of Vancouver's UNDRIP Strategy: Report of the UNDRIP Task Force to the City of Vancouver Mayor & Council (2022, October 25) https://council.vancouver.ca/20221025/documents/p1.pdf.

[4] Kukathas, C. (2019). Libertarianism Without Self-Ownership. *Social Philosophy and Policy*, 36(2), 71, p 86.

For purposes of analytical clarity there must be a way to distinguish legitimate from spurious claims, otherwise any democratically elected civic body could simply vote in favour of giving away the land in the expectation that this would be considered a valid disposition of property. The idea in the context of Canada is twofold: first that this is simply an evolving way of implementing rights defined in nineteenth-century treaties, and second that it implements "reconciliation" by recognising indigenous land rights as recommended by the United Nations Declaration on the Rights of Indigenous Peoples. The question remains, is this still recognisably private property?

All jurisdictions purport to protect the right to property, but that right is in all cases stated to be subject to the state's right to control or regulate land use. It is in accordance with this proviso that land expropriation often occurs. No state blatantly announces an intention to steal, but rather claims to be proceeding within the scope of exceptions set out in accordance with the law. In his discussion of the protection of property rights under the European Convention on Human Rights Lord Bingham gives the example of expropriation without compensation of white farmers in Zimbabwe, an example which illustrates the deeper questions that arise concerning the meaning of the rule of law where action taken by the state accords with the procedure set out for compulsory acquisition and therefore cannot be said to be "unlawful" in a formal sense.[5]

Although this book is not concerned with the regulation of land use or eminent domain (referred to in English law as compulsory acquisition), the debate on the scope of the eminent domain principle may shed light on the underlying conceptualisation of property rights and the scope of state power to encroach upon private property. In that context Eagle argues that the increasing scope of state power to regulate land use "results from deference to legislators, faith in government expertise, and doubts about the solidity of property rights."[6] There is a growing perception that property rights are whatever the majority desires them to be, or

[5] Bingham, T. (2010). *The Rule of Law*. Allen Lane, p 82.

[6] Eagle, S. J. Assembling Land for Urban Redevelopment: The Case for Owner Participation. In Benson, B. L. (Ed.). (2010). *Property Rights: Eminent Domain and Regulatory Takings Re-Examined*. Palgrave Macmillan, p 8.

whatever the legislature declares them to be, and that the only constraint on regulatory takings is that the legislature should consider the taking to serve a "public purpose." For example the South African legislature justified a statute enabling expropriation without compensation in pursuit of racial "land justice" on grounds that this was not incompatible with the basic legal framework of liberal democracies which all have land use regulation authorising compulsory acquisition.

The rationale given to defend the power to act in the public interest is that voters can correct legislative overreach through democratic channels. In theory that is how a functioning democracy would work. But a system of private property in which the owner's property rights can be extinguished if that serves a public purpose is no longer a system of private property except in the most technical sense. It amounts to no more than a licence to use and occupy land at the discretion of the legislature. It leaves the property rights of the minority at the mercy of majority whims. The fact that in practice there may be democratic controls on legislative power would not safeguard the basic principles of private property from the threat of extinction by the state—it would mean only that property rights are extinguishable if the public interest demands it. In the context of eminent domain this implies that "as long as cities, states, and other government agencies follow the letter of the law and formal procedures, property can be condemned and transferred to the public sector or other private parties."[7]

Subjecting private property to state encroachment in that sense is incompatible with the individual liberty that lies at the heart of the rule of law. Locke emphasises the defence of individual liberty as the essential purpose of law: "The end of the law is, not to abolish or restrain, but to preserve and enlarge freedom. For in all the states of created beings capable of laws, where there is no law there is no freedom. For liberty is to be free from restraint and violence from others; which cannot be where there is no law: and is not, as we are told, a liberty for every man

[7] Staley, S. R. The Proper Uses of Eminent Domain for Urban Redevelopment: Is Eminent Domain Necessary? In Benson, B. L. (Ed.). (2010). *Property Rights: Eminent Domain and Regulatory Takings Re-examined*. Palgrave Macmillan, p 27.

to do what he lists."[8] The appeal to democratic controls on state power therefore does not suffice to defend self-ownership and liberty.

The need to restate fundamental ideals of liberty in response to evolving political debates is therefore imperative. As Hayek wrote, in reference to the ideal of freedom:

> If old truths are to retain their hold on men's minds, they must be restated in the language and concepts of successive generations. What at one time are their most effective expressions gradually become so worn with use that they cease to carry a definite meaning.[9]

This applies not only to the concept of individual liberty but also to the rule of law itself, an ideal whose meaning and significance has been undermined by the highly partisan nature of modern legislative programmes. The dominance of party politics leads to strongly partisan legislation, which reflects ideological positions that are unacceptable to the opposing side of the political divide. The view has thus come to prevail that while law must be *obeyed*, it need not be respected; indeed it is not expected to be respected by the political opposition but merely enforced upon them. The rule of law has thus come increasingly to be associated with obeying the legislative edicts issued by one's political opponents despite the fact that one may disagree with them.[10]

But the rule of law in its traditional meaning evokes something more than simple obedience. Waldron suggests that law "ought to command the obedience and respect of everyone"[11] and that, to ensure that all parties feel able to respect it, law should not be "so politically extreme as to strain the respect that members of the community – including their political opponents—have for law as such."[12] If the rule of law is simply about obedience to law in the face of threats from the state then the rule of law would no longer signify following legal principles rather than the

[8] Locke, J. (1980). *Second Treatise of Government* (C. B. Macpherson, Ed.). Hackett Publishing.

[9] Hayek, F. A. (1960). *The Constitution of Liberty*. University of Chicago Press, p. 1.

[10] Waldron, J. (2012). *The Rule of Law and the Measure of Property*. Cambridge University Press.

[11] Ibid, p 12.

[12] Ibid., p 14.

caprice of men but would mean the opposite—following the caprice of men that bears the empty labels and slogans of legal terminology.

4.1 Natural Law as a Normative Ideal

The meaning of the rule of law has been much debated by jurists over the centuries. Leoni describes the rule of law as a "juridical ideal" whose meaning varies not only over time but also from one jurisdiction to the next.[13] Dicey's concept of the rule of law reflects the idea that the law, rather than the will of the ruler, is supreme, meaning that "no man is punishable or can lawfully be made to suffer in body or goods except for a distinct breach of law established in the ordinary legal manner before the ordinary courts of the land."[14] This implies that the meaning of legal rights ought to be clear and well understood in advance, rather than being arbitrarily reformulated to accord with whimsical political ideologies.

The natural-rights libertarian ideal establishes a normative standard by reference to which the rules of property law can be evaluated: "the natural law provides an objective set of ethical norms by which to gauge human actions at any time or place."[15] While there are many different interpretations of natural law, this chapter is concerned with that which grounds individual liberty in the principle of self-ownership rather than other values which might be used to defend individual liberty, such as the principle of equality. In this interpretation of natural-rights philosophy the principle of the rule of law requires that formal law ought not to violate self-ownership and property rights.

Natural law and natural-rights are distinct from positive law and from what Mises refers to as "man-made law." Natural law principles, derived from reason, are universal laws whose "violation penalizes itself" and does not rely entirely on state sanctions for their enforcement.[16] The

[13] Leoni, B. 1961. *Freedom and the Law*. D. Van Nostrand Company, pp 58, 59.

[14] Bingham, *The Rule of Law*, p 3.

[15] Rothbard, *Ethics of Liberty*, p 17.

[16] Mises, *Human Action*, pp 755, 756.

consequences of failing to safeguard property rights are not simply determined by legislation, but by the natural laws of cause and effect. As will be examined in more detail in chapter five, that is the sense in which economic progress and individual liberty are inextricably dependent on property rights. It means that failure to safeguard property rights, while it may technically accord with the requirements of specific legislation, will nevertheless undermine liberty and justice.

In upholding the natural law as a normative guidepost in this way, we do not of course mean that only natural lawyers uphold the rule of law. For example, although Hayek rejects the natural law as a normative ideal, he considers individual liberty and formal equality to be essential to the rule of law. Hayek defines individual liberty not by reference to self-ownership, as we do in this book, but as "The state in which a man is not subject to coercion by the arbitrary will of another".[17] Hayek's regards individual liberty as central to the normative foundations of the rule of law, so that a legal system which failed to uphold individual liberty would fail to uphold the rule of law:

> [The rule of law] is a doctrine concerning what the law ought to be, concerning the general attributes that particular laws should possess. This is important because today the conception of the rule of law is sometimes confused with the requirement of mere legality in all government action. The rule of law, of course, presupposes complete legality, but this is not enough: if a law gave the government unlimited power to act as it pleased, all its actions would be legal, but it would certainly not be under the rule of law. The rule of law, therefore, is also more than constitutionalism: it requires that all laws conform to certain principles.[18]

Similarly, although both Waldron and Dicey regard the rule of law as a political ideal, and indeed "one of the great values of our political system" as Waldron expresses it, neither of them would consider a defence of self-ownership or private property to be essential to the rule of law.[19] For

[17] Hayek, *The Constitution of Liberty*, p 11.

[18] Ibid., p 205.

[19] See Waldron, *The Rule of Law*, p 6, for a discussion of Dicey's view: "Nor did Dicey make any connection with property except obliquely in a reference to "goods" … "No man is

example Waldron argues that "a society which fails to protect property rights against legislative restriction" is not thereby "failing to support the Rule of Law" although he considers the connection between the rule of law and property rights to be at least "worth entertaining" given that this idea is, as he says, "familiar in the vernacular use that is made of the Rule-of-Law ideal".[20] He also observes that while Hayek is concerned by the threat posed by "social justice" to the rule of law, Hayek's argument "seems to implicate private property, at least indirectly"—meaning that property rights are of concern in Hayek's analysis of the rule of law only by indirect implication from the importance Hayek attaches to individual liberty.[21] Safeguarding the concept of individual liberty indirectly confers upon property rights an essential role in any legal system that claims to uphold the rule of law. Further, as Waldron also observes, although Epstein does not consider the defence of private property to be an intrinsic element of the rule of the law in an analytical sense, he considers the rule of law to be "impoverished" if it lacks a robust defence of private property.[22]

These interpretations of the rule of law illustrate that different classical liberal theories uphold the rule of law despite differences in the concerns they choose to prioritise and the specific priority they may accord to property rights. The different perspectives are nevertheless valuable, in different ways, in understanding the meaning and significance of the rule of law. As Gordon highlights:

> Classical liberals like Friedrich Hayek and Richard Epstein have often claimed that the rule of law imposes strong constraints on the state's regulation of private property. If they are right, this would be a very effective argument against such regulation, as the rule of law is an

punishable or can be lawfully made to suffer in body or goods except for a distinct breach of law", p 16.

[20] Waldron, *The Rule of Law*, p 17.

[21] Ibid., p 18.

[22] Ibid., p 19. See Epstein, R. A. (2011). *Design for Liberty: Private Property, Public Administration, and the Rule of Law*. Harvard University Press.

> ideal commanding wide respect, by no means confined to those of classical-liberal or libertarian inclinations.[23]

At the same time, it can be seen that in this context, the divergence between natural law libertarianism and utilitarian libertarianism or classical liberalism has considerable normative implications. This is precisely because the rule of law relies on normative ideals rather than being concerned with the selection of legal rules with which all classical liberals might agree despite their philosophical differences: all classical liberals may agree that property rights are important, but vary greatly in the degree of importance they attach to such rights in upholding the rule of law.

In conceptualising self-ownership as the primary foundational value for the rule of law, and in treating any violation of self-ownership as unjust even where it is said to be in "the public interest", we derive an approach to the rule of law which treats any encroachments upon property rights as unjust. Self-ownership and property rights are thus absolutely essential for the rule of law, so that the rule of law is not compatible with extinguishing or eroding property rights. Any encroachment upon property rights, and any permutation of socialist law and policy, could after all be justified on grounds that it is necessary to advance social welfare or the public interest. In arguing that formal definitions of property rights must accord with essential tenets of justice, and that reconceptualising property rights in a manner which violates the principles of justice cannot properly be understood as an ethical foundation for the rule of law, we therefore highlight the centrality of property rights to the moral legitimacy of law as enforced by the state.

---

[23] Gordon, D. (August 9, 2012). Waldron's Rule of Law. *Mises Daily Articles*. https://mises.org/library/waldrons-rule-law.

4.2 Self-Ownership, Democracy and the Rule of Law

Previous chapters have argued that property rights are central to evaluating the debates surrounding historical injustice. Property rights provide a conceptual framework for defining entitlements, thus clearly delineated and robustly defended property rights are essential for resolving conflicting claims to ownership and for the peaceful settlement of disputes. To the extent that correcting historical and economic injustice is implemented through wealth transfers, that approach to redressing injustice erodes institutions of private property and is ultimately inimical to both economic well-being and to the rule of law. In that context Dorn argues that where confiscatory taxes amount to "legal plunder," that "would undermine the rule of law, which is meant to safeguard persons and property, and turn the concept of justice on its head. Instead of meaning the prevention of injustice (i.e. the protection of individual rights to liberty and property), justice has come to mean distributive justice—namely, the use of force to dictate some politically favoured distribution of income and wealth" which violates the very principles of justice that it purports to defend.[24]

Why do we argue that self-ownership ought to be central to the rule of law? After all there are many other liberal values that might feasibly suffice to define the essential content of the rule of law, so it is necessary to justify the importance that this book accords to self-ownership. For this purpose it is not necessary to revisit the general theory of the rule of law formulated by the "many canonical figures in the Rule-of-Law literature who seem to have no interest in making any explicit connection between property and the Rule of Law."[25] Nor indeed is it necessary to formulate a general theory of the rule of law for all purposes. Instead, our aim is to address the specific question concerning the importance of property rights in the historical injustice debates. The key issue concerns

---

[24] Dorn, J. Piketty's Plan for Equality Would Reduce Personal Freedom and Undermine Growth. In Delsol, J.-P., Lecaussin, N., and Martin, E. (Eds.). (2017). *Anti-Piketty: Capital for the 21st Century*. Cato Institute, p 235.

[25] Waldron, *The Rule of Law*, pp 16, 17.

the implications for the rule of law if the content of property rights is capable of being redefined to enable more socially-desirable wealth redistribution that benefits some races at the expense of others.

If property rights can be redefined to encompass anything at all that people desire to have, and if a "socially just" distribution of property should be decided based on racial and ethnic heritage, that raises serious questions about the degree of respect which we would expect to be accorded to the rule of law. Part of the difficulty is that in recent decades individual liberty has come to be regarded as an optional extra in liberal democracies and has thus fallen outside what might now be regarded as the essential content of the rule of law. Democracy has come to occupy centre stage in the popular understanding of the rule of law. The impression is thereby given that as long as the democratic will of the majority is expressed in legislation that suffices to accord with the rule of law. Regardless of how it is defined or whether it has democratic support, the rule of law cannot be stretched so far as to legalise theft. As Block asks: "[this] argument is a variation on legal positivism, the claim that the law is always just, since it can trace its beginnings back to a majority vote. Why is a forced transfer of money rendered any less of a theft because more than half the voters supported it?"[26]

Hayek adverted to these difficulties when he cautioned that the phrase "the rule of law" has lost much of its meaning as it has become divorced from the idea of liberty and formal equality. As Hayek explains, "Liberalism [in the classical tradition] is a doctrine about what the law ought to be, democracy a doctrine about the manner of determining what will be the law."[27] Hayek is correct to observe that democracy does not guarantee that the law is compatible with classical liberal values of liberty and equality, as democracy reflects only a majority view of what law ought to be. As Hayek puts it, classical liberalism "accepts majority rule as a

[26] Block, W. (2019). *Property Rights: The Argument for Privatization.* Palgrave Macmillan, p 23.

[27] Hayek, *The Constitution of Liberty*, p 103.

method of deciding, but not as an authority for what the decision ought to be."[28]

Hayek rightly emphasises that the rule of law is not simply an edict about obedience to law, but rather reflects a normative standard to which positive law should aspire. Indeed most proponents of the rule of law recognise that it reflects a political ideal. In Waldron's view it reflects "one star in a constellation of ideals that dominate our political morality; others include democracy, human rights and economic freedom."[29] Hayek also highlights this sense in which the rule of law reflects a political ideal:

> The rule of law is therefore not a rule of the law, but a rule concerning what the law ought to be, a meta-legal doctrine or a political ideal. It will be effective only in so far as the legislator feels bound by it. In a democracy this means that it will not prevail unless it forms part of the moral tradition of the community, a common ideal shared and unquestioningly accepted by the majority.[30]

This appeal to moral tradition does not mean that the ideal of the rule of law is too esoteric to be expressed in man-made law. Hayek explains that this is essentially what was attempted by the US constitution, in defending individual liberty by limiting government power: "The conception of a higher law governing current legislation is a very old one. In the eighteenth century it was usually conceived as the law of God, or that of Nature, or that of Reason. But the idea of making this higher law explicit and enforcible by putting it on paper, though not entirely new, was for the first time put into practice by the Revolutionary colonists."[31]

Hayek, like Smith, defends liberty as a negative concept that means nothing more than the absence of coercion. Yet Hayek is too hasty in

---

[28] Ibid., p 104.

[29] Waldron, *The Rule of Law*, p 12.

[30] Hayek, *Constitution of Liberty*, p 206.

[31] Ibid., p 179.

presuming that individual liberty defined in that way can stand alone without the foundations of natural law that he relegates to the eighteenth century. It is not enough to state that law ought to reflect a political or normative ideal, or that it ought to uphold individual liberty, because it still remains necessary to explain *why* individual liberty is essential to the rule of law. Otherwise the underlying question remains unanswered: why must the law uphold individual liberty in the face of attacks from proponents of social justice? Something more than a utilitarian answer is required to meet, and to robustly oppose, the collectivist moral arguments.

It is true, as Hayek observed, that those who proclaim the virtues of social justice often have little idea what they propose or why: "The people who habitually employ the phrase [social justice] simply do not know themselves what they mean by it and just use it as an assertion that a claim is justified without giving a reason for it."[32] Yet the ideological power of the mantle of social justice, and the extent to which it now threatens to override individual liberty, is such that a moral and ethical response to claims concerning historical injustice is nevertheless required. The case for defending liberty as a core component of the rule of law itself requires a normative justification in light of debates about redressing historical injustice. It is not sufficient to depict liberty as "one star in a constellation" alongside democracy and human rights, as these ideas have also been harnessed to undermine the principle of individual liberty.

Similarly, it is sometimes thought that it is unnecessary to seek a further normative foundation for liberty as that may be found in the ideal of formal equality. It is true that the classical ideal of equality lies at the heart of the rule of law.[33] All are equal in virtue of their humanity. The ideal of formal equality is therefore an essential component of justice. In the *Constitution of Liberty* Hayek argues that "The great aim of the struggle for liberty has been equality before the law."[34] In Hayek's view

---

[32] Ibid.

[33] "the laws of the land should apply equally to all, save to the extent that objective differences justify differentiation": Bingham, T. (2007). The Rule of Law. *Cambridge Law Journal*, 66(1), 67, p 73.

[34] Hayek, *The Constitution of Liberty*, p 85.

"It is of the essence of the demand for equality before the law that people should be treated alike in spite of the fact that they are different."[35] He defends formal equality against the argument that material equality requires different rules for different people, emphasising that "Equality before the law and material equality are therefore not only different but are in conflict with each other; and we can achieve either the one or the other, but not both at the same time."[36]

But even on this point a further defence of liberty is required as the principle of equality is increasingly attacked on distributive justice grounds. While formal equality is essential for the rule of law, it is still important to reiterate the reasons *why* it is essential. The concept of formal equality is rooted in that body of natural law that is based on reason, which explains that equality is not essential for its own sake. It is essential because it is a component of liberty and is essential to the protection of self-ownership which undergirds individual liberty.[37] Equality in the natural-rights tradition means that any right one claims for himself, he claims also for others. Property rights are therefore intrinsically linked to the classical ideal of equality in that property rights are human rights that apply equally to all.

But the idea that property rights are human rights has over time come to be construed as equality of outcome or equal wealth distribution, for example in the claim that different demographic groups should have equal wealth. This has given rise to special "protected characteristics" and quotas for particular racial groups, which confer special privileges upon them to which other groups are not entitled, which are then treated as a basis for equalisation of income and other resources. Rights based on membership of a racial group, to the exclusion of other groups, are not compatible with the principle of formal equality. The concept of liberty, including economic liberty, is one that treats everyone as equally entitled to rights protected by law. This in turn raises the question: what are rights? For example, is there a "right" to live the same lifestyle as others in the same society? The answer must be no, as inequality between different

[35] Ibid., p 86.

[36] Ibid.

[37] Rothbard, *The Ethics of Liberty*.

groups in society is the reality of human existence. Sometimes material inequality gives rise to social discontent and upheaval or even violence, but it does not follow that embracing egalitarian ideals and values is the best theoretical or philosophical lens through which to approach such problems. That would amount not to the rule of law but to the rule by democratic opinion or even mob rule: if property rights are defined as whatever is necessary to keep the mob from the gates that would mean that political or demographic might makes right.

If the concept of material or substantive equality is held as the gold standard, then wealth redistribution becomes in itself the paramount policy goal. Rather than being a strategy likely to yield equality, given that perfect equality is unachievable and even approximate equality is an elusive goal with so many variables, wealth redistribution is then pursued for its own sake. If wealth redistribution itself becomes the goal then strategies designed to redistribute wealth, such as racial quotas and targets, are implemented without regard to the wider social and economic implications. Sight is lost of any further goal other than to identify repositories of wealth and redistribute them to the designated groups.

The impossibility of equalising the human experience or human outcomes is not regarded as a problem by egalitarians who see human nature as a challenge to be overcome. But human nature is a fact of life, not a problem to be fixed. This is not to say that social problems are insignificant. It is not necessary to regard inequality as wrong in itself, in order to understand the nature of inequality and how best to respond to it by alleviating poverty and raising material conditions. The point here is that solutions to social problems are more likely to be fair, just and effective if they take account of human nature, than if they attempt to override, ignore or subvert human nature. While the egalitarian sees reality as a suggestion that calls to be reshaped or reframed, reality is not optional.[38] Reality is what it is, and we are more likely to succeed in our endeavours if we begin from that premise than if we regard reality as one out of a number of different social constructs.

[38] Sowell, T. (1993). *Is Reality Optional? And Other Essays*. Hoover Institution Press.

4.3 Unjust Acquisition of Title

The debate about redressing historical injustice encompasses a number of disparate claims, some of which rely on the "stolen property" and "legacies of oppression" arguments considered in chapter three. Other types of claims seek property transfers purely as a remedy or compensation for a variety of historical wrongs. Such claims may involve restitution of wrongfully acquired property or compensation for wrongful deprivation of property, or they may be based on claims that are not proprietary (for example breach of a contract or promise) but seek a proprietary remedy as the best way to compensate for the loss claimed. These types of claims may give rise to intricate doctrinal legal puzzles, but they are not the type of claim of direct concern for this book. The question to be addressed here is not simply how law resolves property disputes, but how the principle of the rule of law ought to be understood where racial justice claims demand the reconceptualization of property rights.

Most demands for reparations are not cases of "true reparations" in the legal sense, involving restitution or compensation for infringement of proprietary entitlements. The fact that politically driven reparations claims are not litigated through the ordinary legal process, but instead seek resolution through direct tax transfers from the public purse to specific races, reveals that the language of property law used to frame the claim is no more than rhetorical. The unjust enrichment argument is that wealthy individuals, corporations or nations were unjustly enriched by slavery and colonialism which gives rise to a duty in equity to disgorge their profits.[39] In that sense, as Sherwin highlights, "the notion of unjust enrichment is a comparative idea that draws on resentment and the desire for retaliation, rather than the desire to be made whole."[40] That is not, it soon becomes clear, a principle of unjust enrichment as developed in the law of restitution, but rather a more amorphous claim said to reflect "racial injustice." Although the language of "unjust enrichment" or "breach of contract" is sometimes deployed, the remedy sought is not

[39] Rhodes, C. (2021). *Woke Capitalism: How Corporate Morality Is Sabotaging Democracy*. Bristol University Press.

[40] Sherwin, E. (2004). Reparations and Unjust Enrichment. *Boston University Law Review*, 84(5), 1443.

in fact a legal remedy but one which appeals for vindication to people's feelings of collective guilt and retribution based on racial histories.

An example can be seen in California, where much effort has been devoted to tracing corporate history such as the history of insurance companies which once insured slaveholders. California's Assembly Bill 3121 establishes a Task Force to Study and Develop Reparation Proposals for African Americans, building upon existing law relating to "the economic benefits of slavery that accrued to owners and the businesses, including insurance companies and their subsidiaries" for example SB 2199 "Slavery Era Insurance Policies" which amends the California Insurance Code (CIC).[41] The aim is to trace the legacy of harm from slavery and provide for compensation. Such claims are superficially framed using the common law language of obligations (property, contract and tort) or within evolving principles of unjust enrichment in the law of restitution:

> Many reparations schemes are based on a claim that one group of people wrongfully harmed another group of people and therefore owe compensation to the extent of the harm. Others are based on a claim that one group of people was unjustly enriched by another group of people and therefore must make restitution of the benefit obtained.[42]

When the case is framed in that way the legal principles relevant to evaluating claims for reparations ought not to call for special consideration beyond the ordinary debates about the conceptual nature of legal claims. In such cases recourse may be had to establish principles of compensation for harm and restitution for unjust enrichment. The issues may be particularly complex, but complexity is inherent in many legal principles so that would not in itself raise any concerns about the rule of law. Similarly, cases involving stolen property in which disputed claims to title lie between the heirs of the original thief and the heirs of a subsequent

41 https://oag.ca.gov/ab3121.

42 Posner, E. A. and Vermeule, A. (2003). Reparations for Slavery and Other Historical Injustices. *Columbia Law Review*, pp 103, 689, 698.

innocent purchaser of the stolen property are frequently litigated and do not call for a special set of rules to take racial history or racial group inequalities into account. Such cases may instead be resolved by ordinary legal principles. For example Block explains how cases involving stolen property claims may be resolved. He observes that "a classical liberal perspective certainly could justify reparations in the case of slavery" in cases where the claim is simply one for the return of stolen property.[43] In that case it would be less a claim for "reparations" and more a claim for the return of stolen property decided in the same way as any other case relating to the return of stolen property:

> If A is the rightful owner, B steals property from A, sells it to C, and then disappears, there is only one correct answer to the question of who should keep it, according to libertarianism: A. C is out of luck, unless he can somehow locate B.[44]

Leaving aside statutory rules that may apply to such cases, this relatively straightforward example reflects the established common law position, subject to equitable principles that may arise in specific cases based on the parties' respective knowledge and conduct, and subject also to practical considerations such as the available evidence, the existing state of the property, and who happens now to be in possession of it. Some of these claims would fall squarely within the law of restitution, such as the example given by Posner and Vermeule: "If a communist government wrongfully harms a property owner, and in the process obtains his land, and the government gives the land to an official or supporter, then the beneficiary is unjustly enriched, and has a duty to return the benefit to the original owner."[45] In these situations there is almost a complete unity between the common law and libertarian principles concerning the return of stolen property. Block notes, in that context, that "if [reparations] payments are to be morally enacted, several conditions must be met" such as imposing liability specifically on the person who stole the property or who is now in possession of the stolen property, rather

---

[43] Block, *Property Rights*, p 140.

[44] Ibid.

[45] Posner and Vermeule. Reparations for Slavery and Other Historical Injustices, p 700.

than being enforced against the general population through taxation. It would also be important to ensure sufficient proximity of claimants to the events for which compensation is sought for instance through evidence of direct victimhood.[46]

These are all principles that would apply under the common law, where nobody is liable for the actions of another or for outcomes which are not proximally caused by their actions. Claims for reparations which satisfy those prerequisites would therefore fall within the purview of the ordinary law. Nothing is added to the analysis by the racial element, or even by describing the case as one involving "reparations". Any practical difficulties associated with the evidentiary burden, such as the difficulty in tracing titles in respect of property of which former slaves claim to have been expropriated or, once the titles have been confirmed, tracing the true heirs, would present merely practical rather than moral or ethical difficulties. This is not to say that practical difficulties are insignificant, but that practical difficulties may arise in any type of legal case and not just cases involving stolen property. In so far as Block distinguishes between general or popular claims for reparations such as all whites owing reparations to all blacks, and refers to "true reparations" concerning the straightforward return of stolen property where the title is traceable to the original owner and subsequent dispositions of title are undisputed, Block's libertarian analysis of "true reparations" may therefore be said to follow well-established legal principles.

The same unity between the common law and natural law is seen in cases where ownership and land use have evolved over time. In most legal systems titles are quieted over time precisely because the original land use has changed. The resource is no longer used for the same purpose as successive owners have over generations found a new way to organise economic activity. As Waldron argues: "this is the case with some of the groups that are now claiming the benefit of historic reparations: that whereas [the original group] was a group oriented to its members' subsistence and treasured its property rights accordingly, [the contemporary group] is a group oriented mainly to its historic grievances and treasures its (violated) property rights as a source of lingering claims against

[46] Ibid., p 29.

others, well aware that its members have now for several generations been organizing their subsistence on a different basis altogether."[47]

The common law recognises the importance of quieting titles rather than endlessly relitigating claims to have been the "first" owner of property which has passed through many hands through the centuries with its original use lost in the mists of time. The law of adverse possession or the limitation of actions is founded in this principle. This principle is essential to the avoidance of endless uncertainty and war, and at common law it will quiet titles even when the original acquisition was wrongful:

> A cherished tenet of American law is that a thief acquires no title to stolen property; nor may a thief pass title, even to a good faith purchaser. Behind that simple doctrine, however, lies the possibility that both thieves and good faith purchasers can acquire new and paramount titles to stolen goods through operation of the adverse possession rules.[48]

Waldron refers to this as a "common sense" approach: "if a new settlement – originally wrong and unlawful under principles of cosmopolitan right – becomes established over several generations, then the descendants of the original settlers are likely to have nowhere to return to."[49] It is certainly a pragmatic approach, and as discussed in chapter two it is also compatible with natural law principles of justice in cases where the original acquisition is just or, which amounts to the same thing from a rule of law perspective, cannot be shown to be unjust.

4.4 Redefining Property Rights

The claims with which this book is concerned fall into three broad categories: historical entitlements to property whose ownership or control is

[47] Waldron, Redressing Historic Justice, p 158.

[48] Thomas, D. A. (1996). Adverse Possession: Acquiring Title to Stolen Personal Property. *Probate & Property*, 10(12), p 12.

[49] Waldron, Redressing Historic Injustice, p 137.

said to have changed (sometimes referred to as "stolen property" claims), entitlements arising as a form of compensation for historic injustice, and new forms of entitlement said to be created by modern notions of racial equity. The previous part of this discussion has shown that common law rules of ownership and title based on theft are well established, and in cases where claimants have these types of legal claims to property, their cases could be brought in the usual way. They may face evidentiary burdens, if the claim is disputed, but the first two types of claims do not involve a challenge to property rights per se, or to the rule of law.

But the historical grievance and racial inequality claims which dominate the social justice debates primarily involve claims which fall outside that legal framework. Most claims do not satisfy the prerequisites of the established legal principles concerning the settlement of property disputes. Rather, the claim for reparations often involves people who were never in possession or control of the land in the first place, for example in vast swathes of Africa or North America. In other cases they may have laboured on land that was in the possession or control of another as in the case of slavery, and thus do not have a claim to ownership of the land based on Lockean principles. There is also the practical difficulty, especially after the passage of time, of proving the claim. Evidence is of course always required to prove legal entitlement and reparations claims are no different in that respect. As Block explains, it is not sufficient for newcomers to declare that property should be transferred to them as reparations for historical crimes without proof of ownership, nor does membership of a specific race or tribe in itself prove a claim to title:

> Most important, in all such cases, we must cleave mightily to the basic legal axiom: "Possession is nine-tenths of the law." That is, the presumption must always be that the present owner is the rightful owner. It is the burden of the one who would upset property titles to prove beyond a reasonable doubt that reparation is justified.[50]

[50] Ibid., p 30.

In such cases the public discourse is therefore geared towards law reform to create new legal entitlements and new rights which would enable reparations claims to bypass these legal strictures. The question then arises as to the philosophical or ethical foundations of such new claims to property. The roots of property rights lie in legal antiquity, and the issue here concerns the implications for the rule of law of deviating from that path. As Block highlights, from a libertarian perspective "there is only one type of entitlement the citizen may properly receive from the state: security of his person and property".[51] This is an important principle to bear in mind in the debate on redefining property rights.

Where a legal claim within established parameters of property law is not feasible the claimants seek new democratically driven legislative "rights" to vindicate their sense of injustice. For example, in the "land justice" claims in Zimbabwe, the argument was not that the claimants had been dispossessed of their farms, but that the white farmers who homesteaded the land ought in fairness to share it with those who need it. The claim thus set up was deemed to be self-evident based on membership of a racial group that did not own comparable amounts of farmland. This, then is the claim that calls to be substantiated in a coherent sense. As Shaw argues, what is in dispute here is not whether some people lack as much wealth as others, but whether they are lawfully entitled to the wealth of others:

> Rather, what is being disputed here is the following inferential chain: people are poor; therefore, they need land; therefore, they have a claim to other people's farms.[52]

Contemporary claims for racial and social justice in that sense reflect what Block refers to as "disappointed hopes" which fall outside the purview of property rights and indeed outside the established disciplinary rules of law.[53] The claims advanced by proponents of reparations for slavery and colonialism are to that extent not akin to claims for the

---

[51] Ibid., p 19.

[52] Shaw, W. H. (2003). They Stole Our Land: Debating the Expropriation of White Farms in Zimbabwe. *The Journal of Modern African Studies*, 41(1), 75.

[53] Block, *Property Rights*.

return of stolen property or claims in the tort of conversion.[54] The claims are based purely on lineage and descent from slaves, and they are not required to establish proof of dispossession in order to qualify for reparations. The claim is based on the suffering caused by slavery, which is said to have caused a legacy of trauma. This is not, in any meaningful sense, a proprietary claim except in the sense that it seeks a transfer of property as the remedy for the claimed injustice. Nor is this claim similar to the limited and direct claims arising immediately after a war, for example, reparations paid to Japanese-Americans after the second world war. In many cases involving racial injustice during slavery or colonialism, there was no identifiable property lost in the first place (at least not in the sense now claimed as a remedy) in existence at the time the alleged claim arose—for example in the case of pre-colonial Africa the property in its current economically valuable form was itself a product of colonialism.[55]

Such claims are not generally framed within the common law of property but appeal instead to notions of reconciliation or compassion. For example, Miller argues that reparations claims ought to be advanced less in the adversarial style of defined legal claims and more in what he terms a "conversational model" which offers "a more inclusive discussion of the future of race".[56] Similarly Butt argues that there is a "connection between past and present actions on a moral level – leading to the necessity of reparation payments between states in a post-colonial world".[57] Such moral claims are not based on any recognisable legal claim, but on a more general moral vision of universal justice. This reflects an ethos described by Sowell as a form of intertemporal justice, the idea being that current interventions can cure past injustices in a cosmic sense, absolving current populations from the wrongs of their forebears.[58]

---

[54] See for example Loth, M. (2020). How does Tort Law deal with Historical Injustice? On Slavery Reparations, Post-Colonial Redress, and the Legitimations of Tort Law. *Journal of European Tort Law*, 11(3).

[55] Howard-Hassman, R. (2011). *Reparations to Africa*. University of Pennsylvania Press.

[56] Miller, E. (2004). Reconceiving Reparations: Multiple Strategies in the Reparations Debate. 24 B.C. Third World L.J. 45.

[57] Butt, D. (2014). 'Reparations and the End of Empire'. https://blog.politics.ox.ac.uk/reparations-happen-end-empire/; see also Butt, D. (2012). Repairing Historical Wrongs and the End of Empire. *Social & Legal Studies*, 21(2).

[58] Sowell, *Cosmic Justice*.

One argument sometimes put forward is that these claims could be defended in a manner consistent with the priority of property rights as long as we redefine the meaning and concept of property itself. But property rights cannot be delinked from the idea of self-ownership. Property ownership in this context refers not to that particular bundle of rights which may be formally designated as "ownership" in a legal system but "full control of the services that can be derived from a good".[59] Full ownership means "the ability to use one's property, to control it, to earn income from it, to exclude others from it, to dispose of it, etc."[60] The rule of law encompasses full ownership in that sense.[61] Property rights are privately held if these rights are in the control of private owners, so that it is not sufficient if these rights are privately held but subject to state control. In cases where the state dictates what private owners may do with their property that is more accurately understood as a form of public ownership.

> However, nowadays there are tendencies to abolish the institution of private property by a change in the laws determining the scope of the actions which the proprietor is entitled to undertake with regard to the things which are his property. While retaining the term private property, these reforms aim at the substitution of public ownership for private ownership.[62]

If property rights are seen as free-floating rights whose content expresses nothing more than aspirations of social justice that are malleable at the behest of a democratic majority, then any type of social desire is capable of being defined as a "property right" which ought to be included in the definition of basic rights and whose integrity may be defended by the

---

59 Mises, *Human Action*, p 678.

60 Sternberg, E. (2015). Defining Capitalism. *Economic Affairs*, 35(3), 380, p 386.

61 "Comprehensive private property presupposes the existence of private property, and thus the rule of law. Rule of law here only requires the operation of some institution(s) capable of enforcing the absence of coercion and the performance of contracts. Neither private property nor the rule of law requires the existence of an institution that claims a monopoly on the legitimate use of physical force in a geographical area–government as it is often understood": Sternberg, Defining Capitalism, p. 386.

62 Mises, *Human Action*, p 679.

use of force. The result of that would be conceptual confusion, where it becomes no longer clear what is encompassed by property rights and such rights become vulnerable to yield to any claim described as "justice." Clear legal rules and precise definitions of legal entitlements are necessary if we are to avoid fighting endless disputes about whatever one might perceive as "justice," which is bound always to differ from what others perceive to be just, and if "that's mine" is not to become nothing more than an expression of wishful thinking rather than a claim to ownership. Precision and clarity in defining legal principles is itself an essential principle of the rule of law, which prescribes governance according to laws and not according to the arbitrary or capricious will of men.

4.5 Legislative Reform

In ascertaining the requirements of the rule of law it is important to avoid semantic debates. We could in theory attach any label to any concept which we prefer to think of as a "right" but the concern here is with rights of property understood in a natural law sense, rather than a semantic or legalistic sense.[63] We can agree with Waldron's point about the importance of ensuring that the concepts of "*mine* and *thine* (or even *ours* and *theirs*) can be determined as a matter of positive law"[64] but it is also necessary for positive law in turn to reflect some underlying meaning if the exercise is to be more than a random attachment of labels to ideas with little regard to what the concepts mean. Defining property rights in a purely legalistic sense serves little purpose if that definition breaks with the general understanding on what property is. There must be clarity on the meaning of words and definitions, if communication is to be meaningful.

If the real goal is to overhaul what has heretofore been meant by "property" then we are engaged not in the delineation of property rights but in revolution, in which case it matters little what labels we attach to the new concepts created to uphold the new legal order. But the old labels ought

63 Rothbard, *Ethics of Liberty*.

64 Waldron, Redressing Historic Injustice, p 140.

not to be retained deliberately to create the impression that nothing has changed. As Lord Selborne LC said in discussing the evolution of the doctrines of equity and trusts:

> It is equally important to maintain the doctrine of trusts which is established in this court, and not to strain it by unreasonable construction beyond its due and proper limits. There would be no better mode of undermining the sound doctrines of equity than to make unreasonable and inequitable applications of them.[65]

The point is that legal doctrines serve their purpose only if they have a meaningful definition and are not randomly construed in ways which have no reasonable connection to their established meaning. Indeed this is one reason why the social justice debates have also entailed debates about the meaning of words, and whether words even have any meaning or just mean, as Humpty Dumpty says to Alice in Wonderland, whatever the speaker chooses to mean.[66] For example in property law the common law *numerus clausus* principle traditionally reflected the idea that property rights ought to be clearly defined and understood, and new rights appurtenant to property ownership should not generally be created by the courts: "The common law approached this problem in connection with land utilization primarily by discouraging novel interests in land, stating that "incidents of a novel kind" cannot "be devised and attached to property at the fancy or caprice of any owner".[67] The problem with creating new rights to protect emerging interests such as social welfare or the public interest, is that it strays into the realm of political disputation in which words often carry the opposite meaning from one person to the next. If property rights simply mean "land justice" then there are no property rights but simply political disputes on what is meant by justice. While political and philosophical debates about the meaning of justice

65 *Barnes v Addy* (1874) 9 Ch App 244, 251.

66 "When *I* use a word," Humpty Dumpty said, in rather a scornful tone, "it means just what I choose it to mean—neither more nor less." "The question is," said Alice, "whether you *can* make words mean so many different things." "The question is," said Humpty Dumpty, "which is to be master—that's all." Carroll, L. (1934). *Through the Looking-Glass*. Dodge Publishing, p 205.

67 Eagle, Assembling Land for Urban Redevelopment, p 11.

are important, enforcement of legal claims must adhere to precise rules that are identifiable in advance and generally applicable to all without regard to race.

Although the reparations debate is usually framed in moral and political terms, legislation then follows by translating these moral and political claims into legally enforceable claims. South Africa's new law authorising expropriation without compensation is one of the most recent examples of this trend in which it is sought to institutionalise, by law, evolving social and political views on the appropriate scope of property rights. As noted during the parliamentary debate in South Africa, legislation providing for compulsory acquisition is by no means unusual. What makes the South African example particularly striking is that it links expropriation to racial justice. Although the South African legislation refers to "diversity" and "inclusiveness" generally rather than specifically in relation to race (it includes for example sexual or gender diversity) the discourse in the law reform debates has focused on racial claims framed as reversing the effects of apartheid. The Expropriation Bill empowers the government to seize land without paying compensation, in the "public interest". It provides that "Local, provincial and national authorities will use this legislation to expropriate land in the public interest for varied reasons that seek to amongst others, promote inclusivity and access to natural resources."[68] Although previous attempts to amend the constitution to permit expropriation without compensation failed, this new law permits compensation to be valued at "nil".[69] The power to expropriate property is not limited to land: "property is not limited to land" thus any property including movable property and immovable property may be expropriated."[70]

Those who favour these types of social justice amendments to property rights, designed to enable expropriation without *technically* breaking the

[68] The Expropriation Bill [B23-2020] https://www.parliament.gov.za/project-event-details/1670.

[69] Clause 12 of Bill B23-2020 "provides for situations wherein it may be just and equitable and in the public interest to pay nil compensation for land earmarked for expropriation" in certain circumstances for example where it is purchased as an investment rather than immediate practical use. https://www.parliament.gov.za/storage/app/media/Bills/2020/B23_2020_Expropriation_Bill/B23_2020_Expropriation_Bill.pdf.

[70] The Expropriation Bill [B23-2020] https://www.parliament.gov.za/project-event-details/1670.

law, are therefore primarily concerned with politically driven legislative law reform secured through political activism. Proposals to amend the constitution in order to permit expropriation in the public interest are political expressions of a social ideal, rather than being concerned with the conceptual and analytical structure of private law.[71] In Zimbabwe, the ruling party instigated "a massive, extra-legal programme of land redistribution, initially spearheaded by the party's informal para-military wing (the so-called war veterans) who began occupying white-owned farms around the country, dividing up the land, and selling or giving it to peasants and party supporters."[72] Similarly, the case for reparations is based on elaborating upon a set of historical grievances, depicting that set of grievances as a "legacy" for which the government is responsible, and for which compensation is demanded to be funded by government in the usual way through taxes as part of its social welfare programme. Steps are then taken to amend the law so that the scheme does not fall in breach of constitutional protection for property rights.

Such claims, although framed as legal claims, are in fact merely political arguments. This does not mean they are not worthy of consideration in the context of political debate, but it does mean that they should be subjected to open and robust debate in the same way as any other political proposals. By framing the historical injustice debate as one concerning legal claims, the impression is created that the case involves delineating or reconfiguring property rights to enable more effective enforcement of the underlying legal entitlements. Imbuing these demands with the character of legal rights implies that such

---

[71] For example a private members' bill in the Republic of Ireland: "This Bill seeks to delimit the protections given to private property in favour of the common good, which does allow, even under our Constitution, the Government to override private property rights." Thirty-ninth Amendment of the Constitution (Right to Housing) Bill 2020 available at https://www.oireachtas.ie/en/debates/debate/dail/2021-06-03/46/; similarly in South Africa: "The main objective of this Bill is to ensure that expropriation laws are in line with the Constitution of South Africa. The Bill will clearly outline how expropriation can be done and on what basis." Expropriation Bill, B23-2020 available at https://www.parliament.gov.za/project-event-details/1670 and B18-2021: "To amend the Constitution of the Republic of South Africa, 1996, so as to provide that where land and any improvements thereon are expropriated for the purposes of land reform, the amount of compensation payable may be nil" available at https://www.parliament.gov.za/project-event-details/285.

[72] Shaw, They Stole Our Land, p 76.

rights lie beyond the ordinary realm of political debate and that the matter requires technical expertise in complex legal principles which only trained lawyers are qualified to explicate. In Canada, for example, lawyers have been instrumental in framing the historical injustice debate as one involving legal entitlements: "lawyers have been one of the most significant actors in interacting with indigenous people, and various forms of transfers have been proposed as the solution to indigenous problems."[73] The reason for framing such claims as legal entitlements is to create the impression of impartiality, and of compatibility with the rule of law, rather than admit it to be based purely on the political ideology of socialist egalitarianism. Any demand that is based overtly on political ideology would immediately encounter opposition from those who adhere to a different political ideology, but framing the case as one of legality and justice gives it the appearance of one which all reasonable people should support. Yet paradoxically the vindication of these claims is then pursued *outside* the legal framework, expressed in the idea that the legal framework does not adequately recognise the claim being made or is complicit in the very exploitation for which redress is sought.[74] In South Africa, for example, constitutional reform has been debated on the question of expropriation without compensation, the idea being that the existing framework of compulsory acquisition which requires compensation is inadequate to reverse historical injustice.

A further implication of the discussion in this chapter is that for the rule of law to have a coherent meaning, legal constructs should have a clearly defined and ethical content. We distinguish natural law theories of property from legislative provisions to highlight the fact that the rule of law does not simply mean that whatever is enacted by legislation automatically acquires a clear and ethical legal content. While legislation inherently has a compelling claim to be categorised as law in any debate about the rule of law, especially in jurisdictions such as the UK

[73] Widdowson, F. (2019). *Separate but Unequal: How Parallelist Ideology Conceals Indigenous Dependency*. University of Ottawa Press, p 10.

[74] See for example discussions linking reparations to properties now owned by the National Trust: Cream teas at dawn: Hinsliff, G. (2021, October 16). Inside the War for the National Trust. *The Guardian*. https://www.theguardian.com/uk-news/2021/oct/16/cream-teas-at-dawn-inside-the-war-for-the-national-trust.

governed by the constitutional principle of parliamentary sovereignty, it should not be the case that legislation can impose any idea on citizens no matter how unjust, and then simply be defended on grounds that it is lawful. There ought to be a normative standard by which we can evaluate whether what the law decrees is indeed just. This implies that we cannot take any claim whatsoever, expressing the wishes and desires of particular groups of people, and define that as "property." An ethical evaluation must be made.

The final implication is that the claims advanced under the banner of redistributive justice fail to resolve the issues with which those claims are concerned. If the rule of law is to have any coherent meaning, it is not enough to assert that property which one desires has been stolen, since any general "all property is theft" argument merely takes us back to the root of all title without resolving contested issues concerning the current ownership of disputed property.

References

Benson, B. L. (Ed). (2010). *Property rights: Eminent domain and regulatory takings re-examined*. Palgrave Macmillan.

Bingham, T. (2007). The rule of law. *Cambridge Law Journal, 66*(1), 67.

Bingham, T. (2010). *The rule of law*. Allen Lane.

Block, W. (2019). *Property rights: The argument for privatization.* Palgrave Macmillan.

Butt, D. (2012). Repairing historical wrongs and the end of empire. *Social & Legal Studies, 21*(2).

Carroll, L. (1934). *Through the looking-glass.* Dodge Publishing.

City of Vancouver. (2022, October 25). *UNDRIP strategy: Report of the UNDRIP task force to the City of Vancouver Mayor & Council*. https://council.vancouver.ca/20221025/documents/p1.pdf

Delsol, J.-P., Lecaussin, N., & Martin, E. (Eds). (2017). *Anti-Piketty: Capital for the 21st century.* Cato Institute.

Epstein, R. A. (2011). *Design for liberty: Private property, public administration, and the rule of law*. Harvard University Press.

Gordon, D. (2012, August 9). Waldron's rule of law. *Mises Daily Articles.* https://mises.org/library/waldrons-rule-law

Hayek, F. A. (1960). *The constitution of liberty.* University of Chicago Press.

Hinsliff, G. (2021, October 16). Inside the war for the national trust. *The Guardian.* https://www.theguardian.com/uk-news/2021/oct/16/cream-teas-at-dawn-inside-the-war-for-the-national-trust

Howard-Hassman, R. (2011). *Reparations to Africa.* University of Pennsylvania Press.

Kukathas, C. (2019). Libertarianism without self-ownership. *Social Philosophy and Policy, 36*(2), 71.

Leoni, B. (1961). *Freedom and the law.* D. Van Nostrand Company.

Locke, J. (1980). *Second treatise of government* (C. B. Macpherson, Ed.). Hackett Publishing.

Loth, M. (2020). How does Tort Law deal with historical injustice? On slavery reparations, post-colonial redress, and the legitimations of Tort Law. *Journal of European Tort Law, 11*(3).

Miller, E. (2004). Reconceiving reparations: Multiple strategies in the reparations debate. 24 B.C. *Third World L.J.* 45.

Mises, L. v. (2012). *Human action: A treatise on economics.* Martino Publishing.

Mises, L. v. (1962). *Socialism: An economic and sociological analysis.* Yale University Press (first published 1951).

Posner, E. A., & Vermeule, A. (2003). Reparations for slavery and other historical injustices. *Columbia Law Review, 103,* 689.

Rhodes, C. (2021). *Woke capitalism: How corporate morality is sabotaging democracy.* Bristol University Press.

Rothbard, M. N. (1982). *2002.* New York University Press (original publication.

Shaw, W. H. (2003). They stole our land: Debating the expropriation of white farms in Zimbabwe. *The Journal of Modern African Studies, 41*(1), 75.

Sherwin, E. (2004). Reparations and unjust enrichment. *Boston University Law Review, 84*(5), 1443.

Sowell, T. (1993). *Is reality optional? And other essays.* Hoover Institution Press.

Sowell, T. (1999). *The quest for cosmic justice.* Touchstone.

Sternberg, E. (2015). Defining capitalism. *Economic Affairs, 35*(3), 380.

Thomas, D. A. (1996). Adverse possession: Acquiring title to stolen personal property. 10 *Probate & Property* 12.

Waldron, J. (2002). Redressing historic injustice. *The University of Toronto Law Journal, 52*(1), 135.

Waldron, J. (2012). *The rule of law and the measure of property*. Cambridge University Press.
Widdowson, F. (2019). *Separate but unequal: How parallelist ideology conceals indigenous dependency*. University of Ottawa Press.

5

Capitalism, Markets and Economic Equality

It is often assumed that there is a causal relationship between poverty and inequality, in the sense that poverty is said to be caused by inequality. If that were true it would imply that the reason some people are poor is because others are rich. This tends often to be regarded as a self-evident truth. The presumption is that wealth is created by exploiting the poor: "the belief that economic differences are anomalous and unjust and that they reflect exploitation."[1] But in reality wealth is not created through exploitation, nor is economic advancement driven by wealth redistribution. Economic progress is achieved through productivity and exchange. This means that unless it is proposed to construct an equal society by the simple expedient of levelling everyone down, it must be acknowledged that economic progress is essential to improving the material conditions of those who are left behind economically. Economic growth is ultimately the only effective route out of poverty. This chapter argues that

[1] Bauer, P. (2000). *From Subsistence to Exchange and Other Essays.* Princeton University Press, p 56.

D. Gordon and W. Njoya, *Redressing Historical Injustice*, Palgrave Studies in Classical Liberalism,
https://doi.org/10.1007/978-3-031-26584-6_5

by presuming inequality to be primarily the outcome of racial discrimination, the historical injustice debates pay too little heed to what is known about the causes of economic success. A better understanding of the causes of economic inequality is therefore essential in deliberating on how to redress historical injustice. By undermining private property in an attempt to resolve inequality through wealth transfers, we overlook the importance of property rights in incentivising economic progress and prosperity.

The case in favour of economic growth might seem to its proponents to be self-evident—few would declare themselves to be against the pursuit of growth and prosperity, though they might disagree on the priorities and limits of that pursuit. Yet the pursuit of wealth equalisation in practice causes economic growth and prosperity to be disregarded in public discourse. Egalitarians argue that public policy should focus on solving economic problems and ensuring more equal distribution of wealth, rather than being directly concerned with the causes of economic growth or progress. The causes of economic growth attract little interest in the inequality debates, owing to the preference for wealth transfers as a quick fix to address income disparities. The assumption that prosperity is best achieved through wealth transfers from richer to poorer groups or countries tends to be uncritically accepted.[2] If the reason for the wealth gap is attributed to historical legacies, that places the cause of the gap beyond our ability to resolve it as we cannot turn back time or reverse historical events. It seems then that the only alternative is to implement wealth transfers. This in turn diverts attention from the causal factors that influence economic outcomes.

Poverty is a default condition guaranteed to pertain simply by doing nothing to create or maintain wealth—the absence of productive activity will suffice to ensure that poverty prevails. As Sowell asks, "what reason was there ever to expect incomes to be even or approximately equal, given that whole groups, nations, races have evolved for thousands of years in radically different geographical environments and acquired very different cultures and so on. For example, why would you expect the people of

[2] Hay, D. (1984). Equality, the Third World and Economic Delusion. *Transformation*, 1(2).

sub-Saharan Africa to have the same income as people in Europe?"[3] The premise that a problem has arisen which causes countries to experience wealth inequality and that by fixing this problem (through wealth redistribution) we can restore equality, is therefore misguided. Our preoccupation with redistribution treats the causal factors of economic growth as irrelevant, yet we cannot pursue goals without understanding the factors likely to lead to success in achieving those goals. As Sowell argues, it is not poverty that requires to be explained, but progress and growth. It is the causes of wealth that ought therefore to concern us, so it is more accurate to frame this inquiry as an imperative to identify the causes of prosperity. To understand better how to achieve economic equality we ought therefore to be concerned not with income and wealth distribution but with factors such as human capital (for example education and skills) access to capital, health, life expectancy, and social mobility.

This also has implications for global inequality and the idea that wealth ought to be transferred from rich to poor countries. Those who consider wealth transfers necessary to alleviate poverty would presume that foreign aid, including its recent iterations in ideas such as reparations for climate change, is the best way to resolve global property. Easterly finds this argument unconvincing: "Over 1950–2001, countries with below-average aid had the same growth as countries with above-average foreign aid. Poor countries without aid had no trouble having positive growth".[4] Banerjee and Duflo also question the causal links between foreign aid and economic growth, citing Rwanda as one example of a country that defies all presumptions concerning whether aid does or does not work in lifting countries out of poverty.[5] Rwanda prospered under the gift of aid and subsequently continued to thrive without aid. This example points to the need to examine other causal factors that

---

[3] Henry, J. (2014, December 30). Thomas Sowell on the Root Causes of Income Inequality. *World*. https://wng.org/sift/thomas-sowell-on-the-root-causes-of-income-inequality-1617252316, discussing Sowell, T. (2014). *Basic Economics: A Common Sense Guide to the Economy*. Basic Books.

[4] Easterly, W. (2006). *The White Man's Burden: Why the West's Efforts to Aid the Rest Have Done So Much Ill and So Little Good*. Oxford University Press, p 35.

[5] Banerjee, A. and Duflo, E. (2011). *Poor Economics: The Surprising Truth about Life on Less Than $1 a Day*. Penguin Books.

may also have contributed to the relative prosperity of Rwanda in a time when other African countries remained mired in poverty, both with and without aid.

Development economists have observed that wealth transfers may be politically attractive but they do not materially improve the conditions of poor countries. Wealth transfers such as financial reparations, social welfare schemes, and new forms of "financial equity" seem to be much favoured by policymakers as a means of addressing economic inequality. Redistribution policies are politically attractive because they justify both fundraising through taxes as well as distribution to favoured political causes. Bauer observes that wealth redistribution as the appropriate solution to poverty constitutes an "article of faith" justifying ideas and policies which "are especially useful to politicians who have promised a prosperity which they cannot deliver. But such schemes are also useful to other influential local groups who expect to benefit from policies inspired by these ideas, especially from the expropriation of foreign enterprises or discrimination against minorities."[6]

Similarly Easterly observes that one explanation for why the foreign aid myth continues to beguile politicians is attributable to "the political appeal of utopian plans to rich-country politicians."[7] He observes that the foreign aid legend has been followed since the 1950s and continues to be implemented despite the lack of any evidence that it makes any difference to economic outcomes: "the poorest countries can grow and develop on their own" and there is no evidence that their success was caused by foreign aid or indeed by Western interventions.[8] For example, "the typical African country received more than 15 percent of its income from foreign donors in the 1990s…Aid accelerated as growth fell" suggesting that "the surge of aid was not successful in reversing or halting the slide in growth of income per capita toward zero."[9] Carving out an amount to pay in foreign aid is relatively straightforward and plays well to many voters as a mark of compassion. Attributing poverty to a lack of foreign

---

[6] Bauer, *From Subsistence to Exchange*, p 61.

[7] Easterly, W. *The White Man's Burden*, p 33.

[8] Ibid. p 35.

[9] Ibid. pp 39, 40.

aid also permits politicians to detract attention away from corruption in third world countries as a causal factor in explaining poor outcomes. Yet the reality is that economic growth is the only route to economic progress, and that in turn depends on free markets.

Economic history shows that wealth spreads between nations primarily through trade and commerce, not through state redistribution of wealth. As Bauer observes, "the spread of material progress from more to less advanced regions is a commonplace of history," a trend which can be observed across different regions of Europe and even between different regions within the borders of nation state.[10] Bauer shows that regions with the highest levels of "external contacts" through trade and cultural exchange have the highest levels of economic development, while those most isolated have the lowest levels.[11] No country or region has ever improved its material conditions purely through wealth redistribution.

Further, economic history shows that exploitation cannot be taken as the explanation for variations in wealth between groups and nations. Western countries are the most advanced in the modern age due to trade, not exploitation. The prevailing view is that "the West has in some way been the cause of poverty in the Third World".[12] But as Bauer points out, "The West was materially far ahead of the present Third World countries when it established extensive and diverse economic contacts with them in the nineteenth and twentieth centuries."[13] Moreover, many countries which are today very poor were never colonised and many rich countries never had colonies, so it cannot be presumed that colonialism is the cause of either poverty or wealth.[14] The widely asserted claim that the West became rich due to colonialism is therefore not historically accurate. There is no evidence to substantiate the claim that the wealth of modern capitalist nations can in any meaningful way be understood as a

---

[10] Bauer, *From Subsistence to Exchange*, p 58.

[11] Ibid. p 67.

[12] Hay, D. (1984). Equality, the Third World and Economic Delusion. *Transformation*, 1(2), p 27.

[13] Bauer, *From Subsistence to Exchange*, p 58.

[14] Bauer gives the examples of poor countries that were never colonised: Afghanistan, Tibet, Nepal and Liberia (Ethiopia was only colonised for 6 years); and rich countries that had no colonies: Switzerland and the Scandinavian countries, and other Western countries that became rich long before they acquired colonies: Ibid. p 62.

product of slavery, colonialism or other historical forms of exploitation. As Roy highlights, the British Empire was not simply a system of coercive control in its intention or design. It was also a system of free trade and commerce. Based on the economic history of India, Roy highlights some of the economic benefits of colonialism:

> Colonialism strengthened globalization also by setting up institutions and infrastructure necessary for a market economy to smoothly function, including uniform weights and measures, contract law, unified currency, the railways, the telegraph, a redefinition of private property as ownership right, and a commitment to protect it via a new set of courts of law. There is no doubt that the trading opportunities, the institutional changes, and the transportation and communications infrastructure encouraged peasant production for the market, in place of production for consumption or local exchange, and encouraged business growth.[15]

Roy observes therefore that "Although the idea that British rule made the Indians poor lives on in internet blogs, popular history, and nationalistic discourses, evidence-based history has long found it inadequate and untestable…Colonialism and globalization created opportunities for some people, were oppressive to some other people, and never either uniformly good or uniformly bad for all people."[16]

5.1 The Morality of Capitalism

The view that wealth is created through exploitation, and that wealth redistribution by the state is the best way to alleviate poverty, is rooted in egalitarian critiques of the morality of capitalism. The zero-sum assumption that the rich gain at the expense of the poor and that the only plausible explanation for why some people are poor is that others are rich is expressed in the egalitarian principle that wealth creation has no moral value unless it is equally shared. This in turn explains the view that where wealth is created it ought to be handed over to the state

[15] Roy, T. (2020). *The Economic History of India 1857–2010*. Oxford University Press, p 5.
[16] Ibid. pp 14, 15.

in order to equalise material conditions. This view explains much of the popular animus against capitalism, given that capitalism relies on markets rather than the interventionist state. A typical example is seen in Piketty's critique of capitalism, which presumes unequal wealth distribution to be inherently unjust: "Piketty takes the evilness of inequality as a given, ignoring the broader question of whether the same conditions that lead to growing wealth at the top of the pyramid also improve material well-being for those at the bottom."[17]

There seems to be an implicit presumption in socialist discourse that if some have more than others they must have achieved their position by some sort of trickery. Thus there is a widespread misconception that an unacceptable moral failing lies at the heart of capitalism, a failing which permits inequality to flourish and racial injustice to go without redress. Yet the assumption that wealth inequality is caused by unfairness ignores the complex factors that contribute to productivity. As Block puts it: "Mere poverty does not imply victimization by robbers since people can become rich without stealing and poor without being pilfered. It is only vulgar Marxism to contend that the rich are rich because the poor are poor."[18] This is not, of course, an argument that nobody ever acquires wealth through fraud and corruption, or that innocent people do not lose their wealth due to theft. The point is that theft and corruption are not the primary explanatory factors in understanding economic progress. As Bauer explains, the view that poverty is caused by exploitation has also influenced the discourse of development economics, where it is often assumed that some countries are poor because other countries are rich: "These assertions express the misconception that the incomes of the well-to-do have been taken from others…that the prosperity of some group means that others have been exploited."[19]

Sowell was therefore right to caution that this presumption, the expectation that all things being equal everyone should be equally rich, causes the existence of poverty to be viewed as a deviation from an expected norm and its causes to be overlooked. In an example highlighted by

[17] Tanner, M. Piketty Gets it Wrong. In Delsol, J.-P, Lecaussin, N. and Martin, E. (Eds.). (2017). *Anti-Piketty: Capital for the 21st Century*. Cato Institute, p 57.

[18] Block, W. (2019). *Property Rights: The Argument for Privatization.* Palgrave Macmillan, p 29.

[19] Bauer, *From Subsistence to Exchange,* p 61.

Bauer, Townsend argues that "the poverty of deprived nations is comprehensible only if we attribute it substantially to the existence of a system of international social stratification".[20] This assumes that without some sort of exploitative social stratification causing nations to have different levels of progress, all nations would be equally wealthy. Poor nations are presumed to have been "deprived" by someone of their wealth, and an explanation of the form or mechanism of that deprivation is then sought. The explanation is often said to be found in the "hierarchy of societies with vastly different resources in which the wealth of some is linked historically and contemporaneously to the poverty of others".[21] As Bauer argues, this interpretation of the relative wealth of nations is implausible. Bauer asks, "who deprived these groups, and of what?"[22]

The perception that the capitalist model of economic growth is socially harmful arises from the tendency of free markets to yield unequal, or at least uneven, results. Capitalism is in that sense incompatible with egalitarian notions of substantive equality. This is because the economic system of capitalism does not seek to promote justice or any other moral good, but seeks only to institutionalise economic freedom, productivity and free exchange. As Sternberg explains:

> Capitalism does not promise ideal distributions, or the greatest good for the greatest number, or any notion of justice or fairness. Although the spontaneous order that emerges from the workings of capitalism is likely to satisfy the preferences it reflects better than any imposed order could (Hayek 1945, p. 525), that order will only be better than others in respect of its responsiveness, and its exclusion of coercion: it is not one whose specific content will necessarily be desired, or considered desirable, by any, far less all.[23]

Economic freedom, although it does not aim to yield equal outcomes, tends in the long term to advance equality; not in the simplistic sense that growth trickles down, but in the sense that the most prosperous

---

[20] Ibid. p 54 (discussing Townsend, P. [1970]. *The Concept of Poverty.* Heinemann, pp 41–42).

[21] Ibid.

[22] Bauer, *From Subsistence to Exchange*, p 62.

[23] Sternberg, E. (2015). Defining Capitalism. *Economic Affairs*, 35(3), 380, p 388.

societies tend also to be the most free and equal. Conversely, the attempt to engineer equal outcomes through legislative interventions inevitably undermines the economic freedom that drives growth. As Hayek cautioned, it is not possible for governments to pursue both economic growth and equal outcomes concurrently, as the pursuit of equal outcomes requires measures that ultimately impede economic growth.[24] There are therefore sharp fault lines in contemporary discourse between those who prioritise wealth redistribution and those who prefer to pursue economic productivity and growth.

One of the challenges in understanding the morality of capitalism is that the term "capitalism" is often loosely associated with inequality but no clear definition is offered of what capitalism means. Sternberg defines capitalism as "an economic system characterised by comprehensive private property, free-market pricing, and the absence of coercion".[25] Importantly, profit maximisation is not part of the essential definition of capitalism. Sternberg explains that profits may be made within a socialist system, and not all capitalist projects entail the maximisation of profit:

> however common business, profit-seeking, and profit-making may be under capitalism, profits are not exclusive to capitalism, nor pursued by everyone in capitalist economic systems. Profits can be sought under mercantilism and socialism. And unless consumers are investors, they are typically not engaged in profit-seeking, even if achieving their preferences includes pursuing best value for money.[26]

This definition of capitalism is therefore distinct from "crony capitalism". Crony capitalism is a system based not on free markets but on special favours and subsidies for favoured firms, usually large banks and other economically powerful institutions or interest groups. Most features of crony capitalism emanate not from free markets or even from

[24] Hayek, F.A. 1960. *The Constitution of Liberty*. University of Chicago Press, p 86.

[25] Ibid. p 385: adding "'System' here merely indicates that the phenomenon involved is complex, and has interacting and interdependent elements. It does not indicate or imply that the phenomenon is the product of deliberate design."' Sternberg defines coercion as "Coercion is the non-consensual initiation of physical force, fraud, or the threat thereof by a person or persons against other persons or their property" Ibid. p 386.

[26] Ibid. p 387.

corporations or entrepreneurs, but from "politicians playing the good fairy, or from intellectuals trying to perfect society, or from bureaucrats thinking they can solve every problem given sufficient power."[27] As Casey observes, "much of what is described as capitalism is actually a contemporary form of mercantilism in which certain economic actors, usually powerful and wealthy ones, seek and obtain privileges from the state in return for their support. Capitalism (mercantilism) of this sort is simply an extension of the state's activities and so, from a libertarian perspective, is indefensible."[28]

The morality of capitalism, where capitalism is understood as defined by Sternberg, must therefore be sought not directly in the tenets of capitalism but in its capacity to promote individual liberty and human flourishing. A moral or ethical evaluation of capitalism is derived from a normative evaluation based on objective ethical standards by which we can evaluate social and economic systems. It is no more reasonable to seek a moral standard within the processes of free market exchange than it would be to seek a moral standard in hills or forests or other natural features. Instead, the tenets of capitalism ought to be evaluated according to an independent moral standard, namely the ethics of liberty. The concern to alleviate poverty arises from, and remains committed to, a concern for liberty as an essential element of human flourishing. Free market capitalism is moral not for its own sake but to the extent that it plays an essential role in achieving the goals of economic freedom and individual liberty. This idea is reflected in Sen's observation:

> To be generically against markets would be almost as odd as being generically against conversations between people ... The freedom to exchange words, or goods, or gifts does not need defensive justification in terms of their favorable but distant effects ... The contribution of the market mechanism to economic growth is, of course, important, but this comes

[27] Devine, D. J. (2021). *The Enduring Tension: Capitalism and the Moral Order*. Encounter Books, p 203.

[28] Casey, G. (2012). *Libertarian Anarchy: Against the State*. Continuum Books, p 5.

> only after the direct significance of the freedom to interchange—words, goods, gifts—has been acknowledged.[29]

Easterly also highlights the importance of economic freedom for development: "Economic freedom is one of mankind's most underrated inventions, much less publicized than its cousin political freedom. Economic freedom just means unrestricted rights to produce, buy, and sell."[30] Economic freedom is the only *sustainable* path to prosperity, and free market capitalism has been responsible for driving economic progress in prosperous market societies. It is only through economic freedom that society maximises its ability to resolve the social problems occasioned by inequality. With greater prosperity and opportunity social problems relating to inequality become less pressing and may be more effectively resolved. With that in mind, it becomes clear that the measure of inequality and the historical pathways of different nations are less important than the potential for any group or nation to succeed in attaining economic growth and prosperity. Economic growth in this context does not refer simply to technological supremacy, financialisation or stock markets, but refers more broadly to human progress and prosperity. Progress means, as Pinker phrased it, "improving the human condition."[31]

In improving the human condition it is important to distinguish between poverty and inequality. The distinction between scarcity and inequality may be illustrated by the example given by Locke: "No Body could think himself injur'd by the drinking of another Man, though he took a good Draught, who had a whole River of the same Water left him to quench his thirst."[32] In this example there is no moral value in comparing the amount of water drunk by everyone to ensure that

---

[29] Sen, A. (1999). *Development as Freedom.* Alfred Knopf, p 61. For discussion see Gordon, D. (2000). Development as Freedom by Amartya Sen. *The Quarterly Journal of Austrian Economics* 3(1) 89.

[30] Easterly, *The White Man's Burden,* p 63.

[31] Pinker, S. (2018). *Enlightenment Now: The Case for Reason, Science, Humanism and Progress.* Random House, p 39.

[32] Locke, J. (1980). *Second Treatise of Government.* (C. B. Macpherson, Ed.). Hackett Publishing; discussed in Waldron, J. (2002). Redressing Historic Injustice. *The University of Toronto Law Journal,* 52(1), 135, p 153.

everyone has equal quantities of water, nor does the opportunity to quench one's thirst entail any necessary comparative component. A more meaningful analysis would focus on the moral duties that arise in conditions of "desperate scarcity": one's fellow human being is parched, rather than one's fellow human being has a glass less full than that of another.

Where to draw the line in defining absolute poverty is debated, but the point here is that poverty does not simply refer to inequality and comparisons of relative wealth. For example resorting to theft to satisfy the need for food may seem morally compelling if the example is taken of a greedy selfish person needlessly hoarding food while caring nothing for those who are starving. In that light Hay regards Bauer's critique of Western interventionism, to the extent that Bauer's argument may be thought to imply that nobody need be concerned about helping others, as "scarcely a tenable position for those who are called to love their neighbour as themselves."[33] But the case is immediately cast in an entirely different moral light if it is recalled that those who seek to undermine property rights are demanding neither a basic supply of "food" nor representing starving people. They are simply involved in a comparative exercise in which the fact that one person has champagne and caviar while another has beans and potatoes is deemed to be morally unacceptable. They are simply measuring income gaps. In that context we would argue, in line with the natural law ethics of liberty, that "forcible interference with property rights cannot be justified by the need of others for food".[34] We may exhort others to share whatever they can in good conscience with those who are less fortunate, but without resorting to the use of force. The use of force is justified only to defend one's own rights against unjust aggression, and as discussed in Chapter 4 "rights" do not simply refer to any wish or demand people might make.

Of course, a socialist or egalitarian would evaluate inequality according to a quite different moral standard than that of liberty. The egalitarian might say that according to the tenets of socialism a

[33] Hay, D. Equality, the Third World and Economic Delusion. See discussion in Chapter One of the analytical distinction between economic analysis and personal morality.

[34] Gordon, D. *Development as Freedom.*

system which fails to equalise outcomes is an immoral system. Ideological perspectives vary and it is neither necessary, nor possible without resorting to the use of force, for all humanity to agree on a system of morality: one system violates the tenets of another system and so there cannot be consensus by adherents of all moral systems. Unless socialists and capitalists are simply to annihilate each other, the goal must be for open exchange, clarity of exposition, and mutual understanding, rather than enforcement of conformity. The inequality debate is not simply a moral debate as to whether all people ought to enjoy equal amounts of wealth, on which opinions may differ, but whether the use of state force to redistribute wealth in such cases is a justifiable use of force. The rule of law requires that legal principles be of general application, and simple rules cannot be formulated by listing different examples of when abrogating property rights would or would not be morally justified. People with different moral values would in any case never be able to reach an agreement on the content of such a list, without some attempting to coerce others into accepting their choice. An ethical defence of property rights is in that sense intrinsically linked to a concern for liberty.

Egalitarian perspectives therefore err in treating poverty and inequality as largely synonymous for purposes of moral evaluation, taking these concepts to be perhaps distinct in a technical dictionary sense but in practice treating them as synonymous for all intents and purposes. The result of treating inequality and poverty as synonymous is that equalisation of wealth, by solving inequality, is presumed to serve also as the appropriate solution to poverty. If economic inequality is presumed to be the *cause* of poverty, or in other words if it is presumed that inequality and poverty are two words describing the same essential social problem, it would seem to follow that in order to alleviate poverty we should focus on eradicating inequality. Moreover, if it is believed that some are poor *because* others are rich, the solution to poverty is then thought to lie in ensuring that some do not become richer than others. Wealth redistribution may well lessen inequality, as pointed out by those who defend Stalinist Russia on grounds that wealth was more equally distributed, but that does not address the goal of poverty alleviation. Poverty alleviation and wealth equalisation differ entirely as goals. The moral duty to be concerned for the welfare of one's fellow human beings relates not to gaps or multiples of wealth but to the alleviation of deprivation and want. Capitalism may not have a unique record in addressing inequality, but it has an unbeaten record in alleviating poverty and improving the human condition.

There is an important interrelationship between free markets, economic progress and poverty alleviation. Free market exchange is about "lifting people out of poverty and increasing prosperity around the world," not "unbridled consumerism" or "crony capitalism" but "[allowing] individuals to make choices in markets operating under a limited government that established basic rules of justice".[35] While systems other than free market capitalism, such as agrarian economies, may generate wealth, they do not generate sufficient wealth to benefit more than a small number of elite people. Lucas observes: "As we know from many historical examples, traditional agricultural society can support an impressive civilization. What it cannot do is generate improvement in the living standards of masses of people."[36] In that sense free markets are more effective in advancing equality than centralised wealth redistribution. Therefore individual liberty is ultimately the foundation of any moral defence of capitalism. As Devine expresses it, "the morality of individual freedom is the fundamental moral defense of free-market capitalism."[37]

5.2 The Racial Wealth Gap

The functioning of free markets does not vary based on the race or ethnicity of market participants. Williams describes many striking examples showing that ethnic minorities prosper in free markets, despite the existence of racial discrimination. On that basis he argues that even in the worst circumstances of racial exploitation and oppression "gross racial discrimination alone has never been sufficient to prevent blacks

---

[35] Devine, *The Enduring Tension*, p 205.

[36] Lucas, R. E. Jr. (2004, May 1). The Industrial Revolution: Past and Future. 2003 *Annual Report Essay.* https://www.minneapolisfed.org/article/2004/the-industrial-revolution-past-and-future.

[37] Ibid. p 200.

from earning a living and bettering themselves by working as skilled or unskilled craftsmen and business owners, accumulating considerable wealth."[38] A similar result is arrived at by other economists such as Higgs.[39]

But the benefits of free markets in promoting prosperity for ethnic minorities are of little interest to those concerned about the racial wealth gap. The idea of substantive equality has in recent decades come to coalesce around personal identity characteristics such as race, sex or gender, by reference to which the gap in economic outcomes between different groups is measured. The racial wealth gap has in that way come to occupy such a dominant position in the policy discourse as to render economic progress almost irrelevant in policy debates about justice and fairness. Wealth is said not to be equally or fairly distributed among the population on racial or other demographic lines, and the desire to resolve that through the quick fix of wealth transfers overrides other more gradual approaches such as investing in education and training skills.

The rationale for downplaying the importance of skills training in the inequality debates is that the value of such skills cannot be easily measured, and unmeasurable qualities are of little interest to those who wish to measure wealth gaps. Attempts to highlight the value of human capital, which may be measured at least by proxy, are objected to on grounds that the terminology of "capital" which is also used to refer to finance and physical property is dehumanising if used to refer to skills and talents.[40] Yet dismissing factors such as education and skills from a discussion of inequality, or accounting for them only as a measure of a "gap" rather than by reference to their substantive value, paradoxically diverts attention from the very factors that would help to reduce inequality. For example, comparing whether all schools have the same number of playing fields becomes more important than the quality of

---

[38] Williams, W. E. (2011). *Race and Economics: How Much Can Be Blamed on Discrimination?* Hoover Institution Press, p 28.

[39] Higgs, R. (1977). *Competition and Coercion: Blacks in the American Economy, 1865–1914*. Cambridge University Press.

[40] For example Piketty defines capital as "the sum total of nonhuman assets that can be owned and exchanged on some market": Piketty, T. (2014). *Capital in the Twenty First Century*. Belknap Press, p 46.

education in each school. Similarly whether one person has less income than another is deemed to be more important than whether they have enough for their daily provision. The preoccupation with measuring gaps pulls policy in the opposite direction from that which it should pursue, and diverts resources to areas which make no long-term difference to quality of life.

Understanding inequality is not simply a matter of measuring gaps in money or finance, which are the factors normally highlighted in the analysis of wealth inequality. Even worse, the easiest measure of wealth inequality is selected, so that the studies focus on income to the exclusion of other sources of wealth, and narrow down the measure of income even further to income tax returns. This is the error made by Piketty. As Boudreaux points out, this preoccupation with income inequality is narrowly concerned with monetary inequality and derives its policy proposals based entirely on "differences in people's monetary portfolios".[41] Focusing on the wealth gap in that narrow sense then overshadows improvements in the overall quality of life and rising living standards for humanity in general. As Eberstadt points out, this gives a skewed picture of inequality:

> Whatever may be said about economic inequalities in our epoch, material forces are quite obviously not working relentlessly and universally to increase differences in living standards across humanity today. From the standpoint of length of life and years of education, indeed, the human condition is incontestably more equal today than it has ever been before.[42]

The evidence relating to rising levels of consumption and quality of life advancement even among the poorest communities is excluded altogether from accounts of inequality which focus on income gaps, especially those which devote resources to matching the wealth gap to racism

[41] Boudreaux, D. J. (2017). Get Real: A Review of Thomas Piketty's Capital in the 21st Century. In Delsol, J.-P., Lecaussin, N. and Martin, E. (Eds). (2017). *Anti-Piketty: Capital for the 21st Century*. Cato Institute, p 187.

[42] Eberstadt, N. (2017). Longevity, Education, and the Huge New Worldwide Increases in Equality. In *Anti-Piketty: Capital for the 21st Century*, p 27.

and discrimination. By leaving rising prosperity entirely out of the analysis, a misleading picture is created of the extent to which capitalism improves living standards. The undisputed trend under free market capitalism is for the rich to get richer, and for the poor *also* to get richer. The egalitarian complaint has never been that the poor are *not* getting richer; rather their complaint is that the poor continue to be "left behind" by the rich who are also getting richer. In other words, egalitarians are concerned that the rate of wealth increase in capitalism is unfair as it does not catch the poor up with the rich fast enough. That concern relates not to poverty alleviation, but simply to the wealth gap or rather the speed at which the wealth gap falls over time.

It is not so much that egalitarian perspectives ignore rising prosperity, but that they consider it to be irrelevant if it goes along with a rising gap between rich and poor. The unfairness, for the socialist, lies in the gap itself. Thus they have no reason to focus on factors which do not pertain to the gap. For example Piketty, in arguing that capitalism leads to rising and unsustainable levels of inequality, focuses on wealth inequality measured by income tax data and attaches little significance to the weaknesses of relying on tax returns as a useful indicator of overall wealth. He disregards other measures of wealth such as consumption, and takes no account of the rising level of prosperity over time. Piketty identifies capitalism itself as the driving force behind wealth inequality, arguing that economic growth is beneficial only to the wealthy and super-wealthy. On that basis Piketty argues that the rate of return on capital exceeds the rate of economic growth, which means that inequality will continue to grow unless the state intervenes in markets to restore equality.

The preoccupation with the wealth gap overlooks the fact that state interventions designed to correct inequality also influence incentives in ways that may be undesirable. As Tanner aptly remarks, "[Piketty] seems to believe that 'confiscatory taxes' (his term) can be imposed without changing incentives or discouraging innovation and wealth creation. Piketty's solutions would undoubtedly yield a more equal society, but also a remarkably poorer society."[43] Piketty's discussion of demand and supply therefore focuses entirely on the redistributive implications, and

[43] Tanner, M. *Piketty Gets it Wrong.*

emphasises demand while ignoring supply in explaining how markets set prices. He emphasises shifts in demand on the premise that understanding demand helps the government to fix prices correctly and distribute goods fairly, while saying little about the factors that drive shifts in supply. Thus he concludes that "If the supply of any good is insufficient, and its price is too high, then demand for that good should decrease, which would lead to a decline in its price."[44]

Piketty's critique of capitalism as a driver of inequality also presumes returns to capital in free markets to be automatic: capital investments passively yield financial returns at a fixed rate. This approach follows the model of Solow, in which changes in technology, not additions to capital, are the primary drivers of growth.[45] By contrast, Mises observes that without sufficient capital the knowledge of technology in poor countries far exceeds the ability of these countries to put this knowledge into practice; more capital investment is therefore required. It is also important to highlight the role of productive activity in economic growth. As Holcombe argues, "capital does not just earn a rate of return, but has to be employed in productive activity by its owner… capital has value only because it provides a flow of income to its owners, and it only provides that flow if the owners employ it productively".[46]

Would it be worthwhile to limit economic growth and prosperity in order to advance racial wealth equality? Some egalitarian economists do consider that a poorer society would be a price worth paying for a more equal society. Atkinson, for example, argues that it may be better to have a smaller economic "cake" more equally distributed than a larger cake with more unequal distribution.[47] Piketty's argument also implies that it matters little how prosperous people are if there is a gap between levels of income. In other words he highlights the *income gap* between rich and poor, paying little regard to evidence of social mobility or the improving

---

[44] Piketty, *Capital*, p 6. "Confusing a shift in the demand curve with movement along the demand curve was an interesting start to a treatise on economics": Palmer, T. G. Foreword. In *Anti-Piketty*, p xii.

[45] See for example Solow, R. M. (1962). Technical Progress, Capital Formation, and Economic Growth. *The American Economic Review*, 52(2), 76.

[46] Holcombe, R. Capital, Returns, and Risk: A Critique of Thomas Piketty's Capital in the 21st Century. In *Anti-Piketty*, p 205.

[47] Atkinson, A. (2015). *Inequality: What Can Be Done?* Harvard University Press.

quality of life, based on indicators such as greater access to education and health, experienced by all members of society. It is not the alleviation of poverty or how to improve material conditions that concerns him, but the income gap.[48] Piketty's concern is that even if the capitalist investment does promote economic growth, without state intervention capitalists will seize too much of the benefit for themselves, which would mean that the poor are no better off—they are after all still faced with inequality. This would imply that capitalists accumulate private wealth faster than they produce wealth to sustain the types of economic growth from which all society benefits. Against that, Sinn argues that "Such a conclusion would only be warranted if the savings of an economy could be set equal to the economy's capital income, so the rate of economic growth is the same as the interest rate. But this is not the case. Rather, savings are consistently smaller than the sum of all capital income. The wealthy consume substantial parts of their income. … Thus, the growth rate of wealth lies significantly below the interest rate; the fact that the interest rate exceeds the rate of economic growth in no way implies that wealth grows faster than the economy."[49]

Economic progress is the most reliable path proven to reduce inequality. While income inequality may be rising in countries with high incomes at the top end of the scale, recent decades have seen a worldwide reduction in global poverty.

> In 1990, 47 percent of the world population lived on less than a dollar a day. Twenty years later, 22 percent still shared that terrible lot, surviving on less than $1.25 per day (the equivalent of $1.00 in 1990). Viewed more positively, 700 million people were lifted out of extreme poverty.[50]

Capitalism has reduced the inequality of material conditions and led to an increase in education, health and life expectancy around the world.[51] As Delsol observes, "the gap in consumption between the rich and poor

---

48 Delsol et al., *Anti-Piketty*.

49 Sinn, H.-W. Piketty's World Formula. In *Anti-Piketty*, p 215.

50 Delsol, J.-P. (2017). The Great Process of Equalization of Conditions. In *Antipiketty*, p 8.

51 Boudreaux, D. J. (2017). Get Real: A Review of Thomas Piketty's Capital in the 21st Century. In *Anti-Piketty*, p 187.

has recently decreased like nothing before thanks to the unprecedented rise in exchanges and innovations. Consumption inequality in food and basic services has never been as low."[52] Similarly Boudreaux observes that

> If we follow the advice of Adam Smith and examine people's ability to consume, we discover that nearly everyone in market economies is growing richer. We discover also that the real economic differences separating the rich from the middle classes and the poor are shrinking. Reckoned in standards of living – in ability to consume – capitalism is creating an ever-more egalitarian society.[53]

Dorn therefore argues that "Economic history has shown that the plight of the poor is more likely to improve by increasing economic freedom and growth, rather than by reducing the return to capital" through measures such as confiscatory taxes.[54]

Those concerned with measuring wealth gaps fall into these errors not so much from a failure to understand how markets work, but because how markets work is taken to be irrelevant. Regardless of how well markets function, there will always be income gaps as human diversity guarantees that everyone will never have equal amounts of wealth. To egalitarians, this is sufficient to condemn free markets as unjust. For example when Darity and Mullen argue that the racial wealth gap should be closed by making financial payments to individuals they are concerned only with identifying the quickest and most effective ways of achieving that goal through various publicly funded social welfare schemes designed to redistribute wealth.[55] Little thought is given to the broader economic implications of such schemes, as they are presumed to have no adverse implications that merit our attention.

This preoccupation with the gap is unjustified. Social mobility ensures that fortunes are not fixed over time. "The rich" is not a closed group

---

[52] Delsol, J.-P. *The Great Process of Equalization of Conditions*, p 7.

[53] Boudreaux, D. J. *Get Real: A Review of Thomas Piketty's Capital in the 21st Century*, p 188.

[54] Dorn, J. Piketty's Plan for Equality Would Reduce Personal Freedom and Undermine Growth. In *Anti-Piketty*, p 236.

[55] Darity, W. A. and Mullen, K. (2020). *From Here to Equality: Reparations for Black Americans in the 21st Century*. University of North Carolina Press.

with fixed members who exist on the other side of a chasm unbridgeable by outsiders to the group. Instead, "the rich" encompasses a group whose members vary from person to person, or indeed vary over the course of life of the same person whose fortunes may rise and fall: "even among the wealthiest, mobility is high. Of the Americans who were in the top 1 percent of the wealthiest people in the world in 1987, only 24 percent were still in that group in 2007, 20 years later."[56] The presumption that the rich are a sealed and immutable or impermeable group leads in turn to an inordinate concern with who is in and who is out and their relative numbers in proportion to each other, with the out group often referred to as the 99 percent. As Delsol observes, "the stratification in deciles from the poorest to the wealthiest ignores the central fact that deciles are porous."[57]

Delsol also points out that often it is not social stratification in itself that presents problems of unfairness, but the inability of people to move from one class to another due to collusion between the wealthy and government. Social mobility is itself an important element in social perceptions of fairness, as people are concerned not by varying fortunes per se but by whether they are able to improve their own fortunes through their own efforts. It is not the presence of the rich that people resent, but the impression that they themselves are unable to improve their own conditions despite their best efforts. As Delsol explains:

> Yes, the wealth of some may be unbearable, conceited and arrogant. But the question is less about whether such gaps are morally justified, even if this may be relevant, than about reflecting on the impact of such gaps and their influence on economic and social conditions.[58]

Social mobility and the potential to improve one's own fortunes is also important in understanding trends in wealth accumulation over time, including factors such as retirement spending, inheritance taxes, fragmentation of estates among various heirs, and the "shirtsleeves to shirtsleeves in three generations" principle which sees family fortunes rise

[56] Lecaussin, N. The Sociology of Piketty's Anti-Rich Stance. In *Antipiketty,* p 42.
[57] Delsol, J.-P. The Great Process of Equalization of Conditions. In *Antipiketty*, p 11.
[58] Ibid. p 14.

and wane.[59] All these factors create a society that is generally accepted to be fair in the sense that each person's choices and conduct have an influence on his life outcomes. That is in fact the original authentic meaning of equal opportunities, an ideal which has now been reduced to a phrase concerned purely with measuring attainment gaps and wealth disparities.

It might be said that egalitarians are not always concerned with gaps per se, but only with *unacceptable* gaps. This is sometimes expressed in the sentiment that there is "too much" inequality. This does not avoid the difficulty of deciding how much of a gap is acceptable, how much inequality is too much, and what is to be done when some feel that even the smallest measure of inequality is inherently too much. Attempts are sometimes made to resolve this by reference to arbitrary indicators, for instance by specifying a particular multiple of wealth that is fair or at least socially acceptable: the CEO should not earn more than 100 times the wage of the average worker. This, however, is inevitably unsatisfactory. There is no principled reason to regard a multiple of 100 as more unacceptable than a multiple of, say, 90, and it is in that sense a matter of gauging in each case whether people generally feel in some intuitive sense that the encroachment upon their liberty has gone "too far."

While it is conceivable that such issues could be resolved by democratic vote, for instance by a majority view on the multiple of wealth which is acceptable, it leaves the underlying moral concerns unaddressed. As discussed in Chapter 4, the process of democratic decision-making does not ascertain in a principled or ethical sense what is right or just, but simply ascertains what a majority would want. This leaves the case open to a potential tyranny of the majority, with little scope to defend individual rights if the majority should choose to abrogate those rights. Thus a principled response to inequality concerns must take account of individual liberty and property rights.

[59] Jaffe, D. (2019, January 28). The 'Shirtsleeves-To-Shirtsleeves' Curse: How Family Wealth Can Survive It. *Forbes*. www.forbes.com/sites/dennisjaffe/2019/01/28/the-shirtsleeves-to-shirtsleeves-curse-how-family-wealth-can-survive-it/?sh=4cbc35476c8d. "The 'shirtsleeves' curse refers to the very real danger of declining family wealth across generations. Hearing it triggers fear in family leaders, for it not only asserts that family fortunes dissipate over generations, but also that the cause of failure lies with their heirs. It implies that the second and third generations of a family are lazy and unmotivated and use up the fruits of their elders' hard work".

5.3 The Causes of Economic Growth

Egalitarian perspectives, as has been shown by the discussion so far, are not concerned with the factors which drive productivity and wealth creation. Nor are egalitarians concerned with how misguided attempts to close the wealth gap might undermine productivity. The discussion so far has shown that egalitarians are concerned not with the causes of inequality, but with closing the wealth gap. There is little reason for egalitarians to be concerned with the causes of inequality since their goal is to eradicate inequality regardless of how it came about. They presume, applying the Rawlsian heuristic of the veil of ignorance, that human beings naturally desire to have material equality. But this presumption is untrue. Comparing one's material conditions with others, and desiring to have everyone's position equalised, may be human nature in the sense that envy is a natural human trait. But envy is not a vice to which everyone aspires. In reality, inequality is endemic in nature as people do not naturally exhibit uniform talents, skills, choices or life outcomes. The desire to improve one's own conditions or the conditions of one's family or community is not driven by comparison of one's conditions with others, but by self-fulfilment and the sentiment that it is meaningful to improve one's own conditions and the conditions of one's family, dependants or community. The egalitarian insistence that wealth inequality is an evil that requires to be corrected, and that it can be corrected by equalising life outcomes, is therefore one that requires substantiation rather than being taken as axiomatic.

For similar reasons, it matters little to egalitarians whether inequality is in fact effectively reduced by wealth transfers, in other words whether wealth transfers actually *work*. If the point of redistribution is simply to do something to plug the wealth gap then redistributive strategies constitute a self-fulfilling goal: redistribution reduces inequality and therefore justifies itself with no reason to question whether it *works* in improving quality of life. The process of redistribution is the goal. The effectiveness of redistributive measures is irrelevant in the sense that so long as a wealth gap persists that is in no way taken to be indicative that redistributive measures have failed—on the contrary, it is taken as evidence that the injustice persists and therefore more measures are needed to correct the wealth gap. The task of redressing inequality is in that sense a Sisyphean effort.

Understanding the egalitarian worldview helps to explain why decades of failed redistribution policies do not cause egalitarians to reconsider whether such schemes are the wrong approach; failed schemes only give rise to stronger arguments that wealth transfers should be expanded and enforced more stringently. If we accept the premise that inequality is self-evidently wrong then any measures that would reduce inequality are by the same token self-evidently worth implementing. It would follow from these presumptions that the problem of inequality should be addressed by ensuring that people live more equal lives to the fullest extent possible. The restorative justice debate conducted by egalitarians among themselves is therefore concerned with identifying the types of redistributive measures that would most effectively close the wealth gap, rather than being concerned in any way with the causes of inequality.

Yet the causes of inequality often have no necessary connection to injustice. For example if a person has no income because he freely chooses not to work, that is not an injustice for which reparations or retribution would be an appropriate response. Moreover there are many causes of inequality including environmental, social and cultural factors. The view that inequality is presumptive evidence of injustice precludes a clear understanding of the influence of these factors. Because the causes of things matter, any theory of justice which regards causation as irrelevant risks producing only more injustice.

If inequality is not explained by historical legacies of discrimination, then it is important to understand what the causes of inequality are. In evaluating the causal links between historical legacies and contemporary economic outcomes, we may also observe that it is unlikely to be the case that discrimination today is worse than it was in the historical era when slavery and colonialism were rooted not only in people's conduct but also in law and official policy. If it is claimed that the economic fortunes of marginalised races have declined since then (a matter which may itself be contested), some other explanation must be sought for why this is the case. Critical race theories assert that persistent economic underperformance in itself is evidence of "systemic legacies" but this merely reasserts the claim in dispute without establishing the causal link that is being questioned.[60]

That the causes of things matter should be clear to anyone with a goal he wishes to pursue, as that is the only rational basis on which we can ascertain the appropriate steps to take towards that goal. As Mises explains:

> Man is in a position to act because he has the ability to discover causal relations which determine change and becoming in the universe. Acting requires and presupposes the category of causality. Only a man who sees the world in the light of causality is fitted to act… In a world without causality and regularity of phenomena there would be no field for human reasoning and human action. Such a world would be a chaos in which man would be at a loss to find any orientation and guidance.[61]

This does not mean that we always know all the precise causes of social phenomena, that we can identify and measure all the factors that pertain or that we can isolate all the influential factors some of which may have been random chance events. It means that human action depends on "ability to influence the cause": it is not enough simply to understand in a theoretical sense what might be the potential causes of things, but it is necessary to focus on those causes in relation to which we are able to take action.[62] This means that:

> Even when he knows the causal relation involved, man cannot act if he is not in a position to influence the cause. The archetype of causality research was: where and how must I interfere in order to divert the course of events from the way it would go in the absence of my interference in a direction which better suits my wishes?[63]

In other words, "in order to act, man must know the causal relationship between events, processes, or states of affairs. And only as far as he

---

[60] See for example Kendi, I. X. (2019). *How to Be an Antiracist*. Penguin Books.

[61] Mises, *Human Action*, p 22.

[62] Ibid.

[63] Ibid.

knows this relationship, can his action attain the ends sought."[64] It does not suffice to observe that a social phenomenon exists. It is necessary to understand the factors responsible for its existence, and the extent to which those factors can be avoided or replicated as the case may require.

It is therefore important to emphasise causality in the racial inequality debates. The debates tend to focus attention on describing problems and proposing preferred solutions with little attempt to consider whether the proposed solutions would in fact alleviate the problem or yield the desired outcome. This is especially the case in relation to arguments that take the form "I have suffered harm and therefore demand compensation." In the law of tort, for example, questions of causation are important. Compensation is payable by the person who, having a duty of care, breached that duty and thereby caused harm. The harm must be attributable to the breach of duty, and not merely coincidentally or tangentially related to that breach. The claim is not simply brought against whoever happens to be standing in the vicinity on grounds that he can afford to pay.

Understanding the causal links between historical events and economic disparities also highlights the importance of distinguishing between factors often referred to as "lived experiences" and objective evidence of causation. As Williams emphasises, it is not enough to show that racism *exists* or that people have experienced discrimination. To understand the causes of economic inequality we must go further than observing social trends. The converse is also true: the claim that there is no evidence of a causal connection does not amount to a claim that historical exploitation *did not exist* or that racial discrimination today *does not exist*. Nor does the absence of a causal connection between historical injustice and economic outcomes deny that historical injustices occurred, but questions whether current economic outcomes are attributable to those injustices. Ascertaining what once *existed* or now *exists* is the easy part. Establishing causal relations is more difficult.

64 Ibid. p 23.

Sternberg identifies the causes of things in the economic sense as causes on which we can base decisions and take steps to achieve the desired economic goal. As she expresses it, in understanding the causes of things "All effects require the coming together of a jointly sufficient set of antecedent conditions. What counts as the cause of an effect is usually a function of the relative distinctiveness and manageability of the various elements of the causal set."[65] When people declare that the reason for their economic failure lies in events that transpired in the eighteenth or nineteenth century, they are not referring to the cause of their failure in this sense. They have simply failed to take seriously the need to establish the causal links between the events with which they are concerned. In distinguishing relevant causal factors from all the potential events that might conceivably have contributed to an outcome, Sternberg draws upon Richard Wright's "NESS (necessary element of a sufficient set) account of natural (scientific, 'actual', 'factual') causation [which] is usually acknowledged to be a more satisfactory and comprehensive account than the traditional sine qua non ('but for') account."[66] In the context of understanding inequality the "but for" causation analysis would run for example as follows: I would have been economically successful in life, but for racial discrimination, or were it not for racism I would have been (more) economically successful. In the NESS account of causation, the search is for something more than a correlation, something that is causally relevant and constitutes a causal contribution to the outcome.

Following this approach racism could be seen as a necessary element in the set of factors that account for economic outcomes, in that it may not be the sole cause but may be one of the causal factors. As Higgs observed, it cannot be proved that racism is not a factor influencing life outcomes, nor can all the personal or coincidental factors that influence life outcomes ever be comprehensively identified by social science methodology.[67] Some of the causes of poverty are difficult to prove,

[65] Sternberg, *Defining Capitalism*, p 389.

[66] Wright, R. W. (2011). 'The NESS Account of Natural Causation: A Response to Criticisms'. In Goldberg, R. (Ed.). (2011). *Perspectives on Causation.* Hart Publishing, Chapter 14, p 1. http://ssrn.com/abstract=1918405.

[67] Higgs, R. (1977). *Competition and Coercion.*

for example, cultural and behavioural factors such as the proportion of people in work. Such factors are also complex and are in turn influenced by many different factors. Government incentives, for example, influence the choice of whether to work, for example, disincentivising work by payment of higher welfare benefits. Therefore all causes of life outcomes may not be conclusively identified or measured, but the point is that the existence of different causes should be acknowledged before attributing all economic outcomes uncritically to discrimination.

Yet no attempt is made in the racial justice debates to address the lack of any causal connection between discrimination and poverty highlighted for example by Williams,[68] nor to acknowledge the evidence that the causes of poverty lie principally in factors such as low levels of human capital, health, and education.[69] Either discrimination is viewed as the only feasible cause of inequality, or else the causes of inequality are regarded as irrelevant. Rather than directing attention to causation, critical race theories simply make comparative claims about wealth "gaps" which presume that all humans would be expected to achieve equal outcomes in the absence of discrimination. In other words the concern for such theories is not what causes poverty, or indeed what causes success, but what explains the difference between two outcomes that they would otherwise have expected to be equal. This assertion that the racial wealth gap is caused by discrimination is readily disproved by evidence of ethnic groups who have succeeded economically despite suffering the same (or worse) racial discrimination. Given the diversity of human nature, and a variety of cultural and other factors, the expectation that outcomes would be expected to be equal in the absence of discrimination lacks any rational foundation.

---

68 Williams, *Race & Economics.*

69 Chakraborty, S. and Das, M. (2005). Mortality, Human Capital and Persistent Inequality. *Journal of Economic Growth*, 10, 159.

5.4 Free Markets, Productivity and Redistribution

Wealth must be created, not simply redistributed. Lucas highlights the importance of productivity, cautioning against the tendency to presume that prosperity is achieved through redistribution. Since the Industrial Revolution global prosperity has been achieved not through wealth redistribution but through an exponential growth in productivity. Lucas highlights the rise in productivity in the period between 1960 and 2000:

> total world production has grown much faster than population, from $6.5 trillion in 1960 to $31 trillion in 2000...That is, world production was nearly multiplied by five over this 40-year period, growing at an annual rate of 4 percent. Production per person—real income—thus grew at 2.3 percent per year, which is to say that the living standard of the average world citizen more than doubled.[70]

But egalitarians are concerned that this rate of growth has not been equal, and that growth which fails to manifest equally in all times and places must thereupon be redistributed. Lucas acknowledges that growth does not occur at equal rates in all locations:

> At the end of the period, as at the beginning, the degree of inequality is enormous. The poorest countries in 1990 have per capita incomes of around $1,000 per year compared to the U.S. average of $18,000: a factor of 18. This degree of inequality between the richest and poorest societies is without precedent in human history, as is the growth in population and living standards in the postwar period.[71]

Lucas's point is that the disparity between rich and poor must be seen alongside the rise in the material conditions of all. The unprecedented level of growth since the Industrial Revolution cannot be dissociated from the rise in global prosperity, because when the world was on the

70 Lucas, *The Industrial Revolution.*

71 Ibid.

whole much poorer the differences between countries were less marked. As Lucas explains:

> up to 1800 or maybe 1750, no society had experienced sustained growth in per capita income. (Eighteenth century population growth also averaged one-third of 1 percent, the same as production growth.) That is, up to about two centuries ago, per capita incomes in all societies were stagnated at around $400 to $800 per year.[72]

His point is that nations were historically more equal, but they were also all much poorer. The industrial revolution that lifted all nations out of poverty and raised living standards across the globe also exacerbated inequality between those at the vanguard of the revolution and those trailing behind.[73] The rise in productivity and growth has therefore come with a notable gap between the most productive and least productive countries. This leads some people to disregard the growth in productivity in order to focus on redistributing wealth from rich to poor countries. But as highlighted in previous chapters, there is no evidence that redistributive schemes such as foreign aid help poor countries to grow or catch up with richer countries, in the absence of productivity. This is precisely Lucas's point about the importance of productivity.

The argument here is not that economic progress offers a good justification for ignoring economic inequality, nor that all social problems caused by poverty and deprivation will be solved by markets with no need for any element of what Adam Smith called "beneficence."[74] The claim is not that nobody needs to care about the plight of the poor, but rather that state redistribution of wealth is not the best way for society to improve material conditions for the poor in the long run. Nor do we argue that markets work perfectly well, that human action is always rational and fully informed, or that longer term market coordination raises no shorter-term concerns about inequality. We do not treat free markets as presumptively perfect or efficient, nor do we depict markets as

[72] Ibid.

[73] "If the living standard in traditional economies was low, it was at least fairly equally low across various societies … inequality is a product of the industrial revolution": Ibid.

[74] Devine, *The Enduring Tension*, p 205.

the best solution for all social and moral concerns, for the simple reason that life is not all about market exchange. Free markets are not responsible for the totality of life experiences. A defence of free markets also recognises the boundaries of what ought to be achieved through markets. In a healthy society there is also a role for friendship, family, community and other voluntary societies in improving the quality of life for as many people as possible. As Casey argues:

> The limited, although potent, scope of libertarianism is not intended to deny the importance of love, community, discipline, order, learning or any of the other values that are essential to human flourishing. Libertarians can cherish these values as much as anyone else but, however much they cherish them, they reject any and all attempts to produce them by force, coercion or intimidation.[75]

Thus defenders of free markets do not claim that markets are the sole priority in life. On the contrary, it is supporters of state welfare who contend that the state ought properly to be responsible for all life outcomes and therefore denigrate the role of self-reliance, family and community. State welfarism has tended to create the impression that private charity is not necessary as tax contributions will serve the same function more effectively, ignoring the fact that charity and mutual support have historically played a greater role than the state in lifting marginalised communities out of poverty. For example Williams observes that during colonial days in the US "New Orleans had the largest population of free blacks in the Deep South" who "owned some $2 million worth of property and dominated skilled crafts" and "created privately supported benevolent societies, schools, and orphanages to assist their impoverished brethren".[76]

Similarly, it is also true that economic measures do not capture all the aspects of fairness in society that those who are concerned about

[75] Casey, G. (2012). *Libertarian Anarchy: Against the State*. Continuum Books, p 54.

[76] Williams, *Race & Economics*, p 16.

inequality might consider important. For example Lucas focuses on economic success, measured by production: "By a country's average real income, I mean simply its gross domestic product (GDP) in constant dollars divided by its population. Although I will touch on other aspects of society, my focus will be on economic success, as measured by population and production."[77] This approach undoubtedly masks many measures that egalitarians consider to be important in the economics of distribution such as wealth distribution between households or between different identity groups such as race or sex.[78] However, the point Lucas makes is precisely that it would be a mistake to divert attention away from productivity, in order to address these types of distributive measures. He argues that "Of the tendencies that are harmful to sound economics, the most seductive, and in my opinion the most poisonous, is to focus on questions of distribution."[79] His point is not that there should be no concern for the poor, but that productivity and growth offer a more sustainable and effective way to increase the well-being of the poor:

> [inequality] seems to us a terrible wrong, justifying direct corrective action, and perhaps some actions of this kind can and should be taken. But of the vast increase in the well-being of hundreds of millions of people that has occurred in the 200-year course of the industrial revolution to date, virtually none of it can be attributed to the direct redistribution of resources from rich to poor. The potential for improving the lives of poor people by finding different ways of distributing current production is nothing compared to the apparently limitless potential of increasing production.[80]

---

[77] Lucas, *The Industrial Revolution.*

[78] See for example Salverda, W., Nolan, B. and Smeeding, T. M. (2009). *The Oxford Handbook of Economic Inequality*. Oxford University Press.

[79] Lucas, *The Industrial Revolution.*

[80] Ibid.

References

Atkinson, A. (2015). *Inequality: What Can Be Done?* Harvard University Press.

Banerjee, A., & Duflo, E. (2011). *Poor Economics: The Surprising Truth about Life on Less Than $1 a Day*. Penguin Books.

Bauer, P. (2000). *From Subsistence to Exchange and Other Essays*. Princeton University Press.

Block, W. (2019). *Property Rights: The Argument for Privatization*. Palgrave Macmillan.

Casey, G. (2012). *Libertarian Anarchy: Against the State*. Continuum Books.

Chakraborty, S., & Das, M. (2005). Mortality, Human Capital and Persistent Inequality. *Journal of Economic Growth, 10*, 159.

Cooter, R. D. (2006). An Escape from Poverty: Developing Productive Organization. *Southwestern Journal of Law and Trade in the Americas, XII*(2), 186.

Darity, W. A., & Mullen, K. (2020). *From Here to Equality: Reparations for Black Americans in the 21st Century*. University of North Carolina Press.

Delsol, J-P., Lecaussin, N., & Martin, E. (Eds.). (2017). *Anti-Piketty: Capital for the 21st Century.* Cato Institute.

Devine, D. J. (2021). *The Enduring Tension: Capitalism and the Moral Order.* Encounter Books.

Easterly, W. (2006). *The White Man's Burden: Why the West's Efforts to Aid the Rest Have Done So Much Ill and So Little Good*. Oxford University Press.

Epstein, R. A. (2018). Meeting the Fundamental Objections to Classical Liberalism. In M. T. Henderson (Ed.), *2018* (p. 280). Cambridge University Press.

Goldberg, R. (Ed.). (2011). *Perspectives on Causation*. Hart Publishing.

Gordon, D. (2000). Development as Freedom by Amartya Sen. *The Quarterly Journal of Austrian Economics, 3*(1), 89.

Hay, D. (1984). Equality, The Third World and Economic Delusion. *Transformation, 1*(2).

Hayek, F. A. (1945). The Use of Knowledge in Society. *American Economic Review, 35*(4), 519.

Hayek, F. A. (1960). *The Constitution of Liberty*. University of Chicago Press.

Henry, J. (2014, December 30). Thomas Sowell on the Root Causes of Income Inequality. *World*. https://wng.org/sift/thomas-sowell-on-the-root-causes-of-income-inequality-1617252316

Higgs, R. (1977). *Competition and Coercion: Blacks in the American Economy, 1865–1914*. Cambridge University Press.

Jaffe, D. (2019, January 28). The 'Shirtsleeves-To-Shirtsleeves' Curse: How Family Wealth Can Survive It. *Forbes*. www.forbes.com/sites/dennisjaffe/2019/01/28/the-shirtsleeves-to-shirtsleeves-curse-how-family-wealth-can-survive-it/?sh=4cbc35476c8d

Kendi, I. X. (2019). *How to Be an Antiracist*. Penguin Books.

Locke, J. (1980). *Second Treatise of Government*. In C. B. Macpherson (Ed.). Hackett Publishing.

Lucas, R. E. Jr. (2004, May 1). *The Industrial Revolution: Past and Future*. 2003 Annual Report Essay https://www.minneapolisfed.org/article/2004/the-industrial-revolution-past-and-future

Mises, L. v. (1962). *Socialism: An Economic and Sociological Analysis*. Yale University Press (first published 1951).

Mises, L. v. (2012). *Human Action: A Treatise on Economics*. Martino Publishing.

Piketty, T. (2014). *Capital in the Twenty First Century*. Belknap Press.

Pinker, S. (2018). *Enlightenment Now: The Case for Reason, Science*. Random House.

Roy, T. (2020). *The Economic History of India 1857–2010*. Oxford University Press.

Salverda, W., Nolan, B., & Smeeding, T. M. (2009). *The Oxford Handbook of Economic Inequality*. Oxford University Press.

Sen, A. (1999). *Development as Freedom*. Alfred Knopf.

Solow, R. M. (1962). Technical Progress, Capital Formation, and Economic Growth. *The American Economic Review, 52*(2), 76.

Sowell, T. (2014). *Basic Economics: A Common Sense Guide to the Economy*. Basic Books.

Sternberg, E. (2015). Defining Capitalism. *Economic Affairs, 35*(3), 380.

Waldron, J. (2002). Redressing Historic Injustice. *The University of Toronto Law Journal, 52*(1), 135.

Williams, W. E. (2011). *Race and Economics: How Much Can Be Blamed on Discrimination?* Hoover Institution Press.

6
Conclusion

The discussion in this book has been concerned primarily with the normative foundations of debates surrounding redressing historical injustice, in particular the meaning of justice and the importance of property rights for individual liberty. The book has argued that the causal links between historical injustice and contemporary wealth distribution are weak, and that the historical events with which racial justice debates are preoccupied cannot be regarded as a robust explanation for prevailing economic inequality. The arguments linking economic inequality with historical injustice treat the connection between racial exploitation and economic inequality as self-evident, rather than as a claim requiring substantiation. It is easy to find that connection being *asserted* by those who support paying reparations, but to assert is not to prove. This concluding chapter considers some of the policy implications of the foregoing analysis. We focus on the financial implications of state interventions designed to promote economic equality, and on the implications for the legitimacy of the state. As Nozick argues, "What persons may and may not do to one another limits what they may do through the apparatus of a state, or do to establish such an apparatus. The

D. Gordon and W. Njoya, *Redressing Historical Injustice*, Palgrave Studies in Classical Liberalism,
https://doi.org/10.1007/978-3-031-26584-6_6

moral prohibitions it is permissible to enforce are the source of whatever legitimacy the state's fundamental coercive power has."[1]

The role of the state in redistributing wealth is highly contested. In the context of redressing historical injustice the key issue is whether race-based social welfare payments can be justified. Such race-based payments are defended on grounds that they are necessary to ensure substantive equality for all races. But as Williams points out, the pursuit of equal racial outcomes is fundamentally a proposal to redistribute wealth and therefore has overriding financial implications.[2] For example the claim that the historical experience of black people is somehow exceptional compared to the historical experience of other racial groups, which we discussed in Chapter 3, is advanced in order to justify payment of reparations from the public purse. As a purely practical matter it is not feasible for all forms of historical injustice to be granted financial compensation funded by taxes, so the argument that black people alone of all who have suffered in history are entitled to compensation is an important part of the justification for paying different forms of compensation loosely described as reparations. The political significance of the historical injustice debates is ultimately explicable more by reference to their financial implications than by reference to ethical concerns. Therefore, although the book has been concerned with ethical and normative arguments, it is appropriate to conclude with some observations about the financial implications and the role of the state in raising and distributing reparations payments.

An example of these financial implications is seen in proposals for racial and cultural segregation, which is said to benefit specific racial groups by facilitating targeted support and providing them with dedicated space in which to develop cultural responses to their peculiar life challenges. The controversial aspect of this idea lies not in the suggestion that an ethnic community may wish to follow a separate path,

---

[1] Nozick. *Anarchy, State and Utopia*, p 6.

[2] Williams, W. E. (2011). *Race and Economics: How Much Can Be Blamed on Discrimination?* Hoover Institution Press, p 15: "The importance of recognizing that political power and/or social benevolence is not a necessary condition for socioeconomic progress of an ethnic group is not only an important intellectual exercise but also has practical importance, because all activities require resource expenditure."

which is their choice should that be their preference, but whether they are entitled to expect the public to pay for that choice. For example, in Canada the implementation of the United Nations Declaration on the Rights of Indigenous People "essentially provides that Indigenous people, amongst other things, own the land and resources, have the right to self-government and to their own distinct political, legal, economic, social and cultural institutions and educational systems, and that the federal government shall pay for all of it."[3] State protection for minority cultures is then put in issue not purely as a matter of valuing or protecting the culture, as is often claimed in the social justice discourse, but in relation to the legitimacy of paying for such special protection through public funds. It could be argued that "there is no reason to suppose that present-day liberal democracies owe their cultural minorities anything more than that same degree of tolerance and respect that they owe their cultural majorities."[4] Therefore the policy debate is primarily about justifying the allocation of public funds, rather than debating the appropriate priority of cultural heritage.

The main challenge that arises is that proponents of wealth redistribution often do not concern themselves with the long-term financial implications of their proposals, and consider it cruel for others to ask how these schemes are to be funded. Egalitarians often regard tax revenues as a store of wealth to be allocated to whatever ends society may desire, and in that light they presuppose the existence of a "reserve fund" of assets to be redistributed: "The idea underlying all interventionist policies is that the higher income and wealth of the more affluent part of the population is a fund which can be freely used for the improvement of the conditions of the less prosperous. The essence of the interventionist policy is to take from one group to give to another. It is confiscation and distribution".[5] Yet such interventionist policies risk depleting that very

[3] Pardy, B. (2020, September 18). Thirteen Things That Can't Be Said About Aboriginal Law and Policy in Canada. *C2C Journal*. https://c2cjournal.ca/2020/09/thirteen-things-that-cant-be-said-about-aboriginal-law-and-policy-in-canada/ (emphasis added).

[4] Conway, D. (2004). *In Defence of the Realm: The Place of Nations in Classical Liberalism*. Ashgate, pp 51–52.

[5] Mises, L. v. (2012). *Human Action: A Treatise on Economics*. Martino Publishing.

store of funds: "An essential point in the social philosophy of interventionism is the existence of an inexhaustible fund which can be squeezed forever. The whole system of interventionism collapses when this function is drained off: The Santa Claus principle liquidates itself".[6] Public policy involves difficult choices between conflicting priorities not only because the underlying normative and policy goals are in conflict but also because there is no magic reserve fund from which all financial demands can be satisfied.

An important point often overlooked in the policy debates is that wealth does not just exist in nature, or spring forth without effort or creative input, so that all that remains is for the state to redistribute it. Businesses do not run themselves, automatically yielding profits.[7] Instead, wealth must be created and produced, and the processes by which that occurs and incentives driving productivity are important. There is no "right" to a share of other people's property. As Block asks: "How is it possible for both the rightful owner (the one who earned the money through voluntary market activity), as well as for the recipients of all these programs, to have a right to this wealth?"[8] Appropriate constraints on state interventions ought therefore to be based not on the demands of equality nor even on correcting market failures but on the principle of self-ownership, namely based on the concept of ownership as "prior claims that individuals acquire through natural rights. In particular, the state, or other agency that establishes the legal limits of property, is not free to take over income or wealth as it sees fit."[9]

---

[6] Ibid.

[7] For example in Piketty's account, "the risky, entrepreneurial element in business formation eventually recedes in importance until the business naturally evolves toward its logical destination—that of a perpetual cash machine that regularly spits out rents…In his world, capitalism is a system of profits; in the real world, it's a system of profit and loss" Boudreaux, D. J. Get Real: A Review of Thomas Piketty's Capital in the 21st Century. In *Anti-Piketty*, p 190.

[8] Block, W. (2019). *Property Rights: The Argument for Privatization.* Palgrave Macmillan, p 23.

[9] Gordon, D. (2017). *An Austro-Libertarian View Vol. I: Economics, Philosophy, Law.* Ludwig von Mises Institute, p 378, discussing the distinction between Thomas Nagel's account of property and the libertarian conception.

6.1 State Interventions and Mixed Economies

Many egalitarians emphasise that they do not seek the perfect equalisation or endless and limitless redistribution of wealth, but merely seek targeted state interventions to ameliorate the material conditions of those whose economic fortunes lag behind others. If liberty is our highest priority we may choose to tolerate a higher incidence of inequality in upholding economic freedom, but if reducing inequality is our highest priority we may choose to tolerate encroaching upon freedom in order to achieve more equality. The extent to which there is a trade-off between freedom and equality is therefore central to evaluating the policy implications of wealth redistribution whose aim is to resolve the racial wealth gap. Socialists who are keen not to be depicted as communists or Marxists are very quick to emphasise that they support a mixed economy rather than state ownership of the means of production.

For example Roemer proposes a version of market socialism which incorporates market features while prioritising equality.[10] For instance he suggests that firms in a market socialist order would be independent of the state and would not be subject to arbitrary state interference: instead they would be subject to publicly controlled institutions whose independence would be constitutionally guaranteed. It is true that all liberal market economies are interventionist to some degree, and are thus often described as a mixed system rather than as full-scale socialist. In Roemer's view socialists may promote equality of opportunity in relation to specific aspects of society: "(1) self-realization and welfare, (2) political influence, and (3) social status".[11] In this model the actual level of self-realisation is less significant than whether everyone has an equal opportunity to pursue these goal. This emphasis on equal opportunities is favoured by many people, who would favour wealth redistribution linked to equalising opportunity and would not be concerned about the implications for property rights. Thus for example Roemer is critical of the principle of self-ownership on grounds that "Libertarians use

[10] Roemer, J. (1994). *A Future for Socialism.* Harvard University Press.

[11] Ibid., p. 11.

the postulate of self-ownership to deduce the injustice of redistributive taxation".[12] Self-ownership would therefore be rejected in this form of market socialism.

Other socialists have also suggested ways to reconceptualise socialism to incorporate free market elements. For example Rorty argues that socialism need not involve a centrally planned economy, and may instead consist of efforts to achieve "humanistic values."[13] Absent a market-based price system socialist planners would struggle to determine which resources should be directed to the consumer goods they wish to produce, which leads some socialists to envisage a socialist system that uses market pricing.[14] There are many other examples of economic models incorporating mixed socialist and capitalist features.[15]

Banerjee and Duflo make the point that welfare interventions may have mixed implications exhibiting both successes and failures, the implication being that state intervention may or may not be beneficial and therefore each situation should be evaluated on its own facts. For example interventions may fail at the macro level while still exhibiting effectiveness at the micro level.[16] These types of arguments cause many observers to suppose that there is nothing much to choose between different economic models, and mixed models can be adopted with beneficial elements from different approaches.

While it is true that state interventions can be shown to be beneficial in specific situations, with positive outcomes for the people who benefit, interventionist policies which seem to have positive outcomes at the micro level may yet inadvertently harm disadvantaged groups or even have deleterious social welfare implications, despite having provable benefits for individual candidates who benefit personally from preferential treatment. The question is then whether those who benefit personally

---

[12] Ibid., p 16.

[13] Rorty, R. (1999). *Philosophy and Social Hope*. Penguin Books.

[14] See for example Lange, O. (1965). *Problems of Political Economy of Socialism.* Peoples Publishing House.

[15] Ikeda, S. (1997). *The Dynamics of the Mixed Economy: Toward a Theory of Interventionism.* Routledge.

[16] Banerjee, A. and Duflo, E. (2011). *Poor Economics: The Surprising Truth about Life on Less Than $1 a Day*. Penguin Books.

from poverty-reduction or preferential-treatment measures at the micro level would have been likely to benefit from any measures regardless of the nature of the policy and are likely also to do equally well without any interventionist policies—the question being one of causation and whether those who succeed would likely have found alternative ways to succeed if the path they followed had not been available. This analysis is also relevant in evaluating the benefits to be derived from reparations. It cannot be argued that *nobody* would benefit from reparations or other redistributive policies such as social welfare or affirmative action; but the moral justification for redistributive policies may still be questioned given that even a deleterious public policy intervention with longer term harmful effects may well produce benefits for an identifiable person or subset of people. In addition, Mises argues that these types of mixed "third way" state interventionism which aim to combine features of capitalism and socialism lead inevitably to socialism. He illustrates this with the example of price controls in, say, the milk market. The direct result of a price cap on milk is to create a milk shortage, which is then resolved by imposing a further series of price caps on other products related to milk production in an attempt to resolve the shortage. That further set of controls is designed to increase the quantity of milk, but it in turn creates further shortages in the affected product markets. Should the planners continue along the path of price regulation to resolve those further shortages, they soon arrive at a system in which the government sets all prices: namely socialism.[17]

6.2 The New Equity

This book has argued that policies designed to address racial inequality through various forms of wealth redistribution are both ineffective in meeting their stated goals, and unjust in their implications for individual rights and liberties. Although the argument is sometimes advanced that reparations claims are analogous to compensation for theft, injury or

[17] Mises, L. v. (1952). *The Middle of the Road Leads to Socialism.* In Planning for Freedom. Libertarian Press.

other events analogous to crimes, the book has argued that these claims offer a weak basis for wealth redistribution as the facts on which they rely occurred centuries ago and their perpetrators are no longer with us. But not all proponents of race-based financial claims to public support ground their claim on historical legacies of exploitation. Some proponents of race-based claims argue that regardless of the causes of inequality justice requires that wealth in society be redistributed along racial lines to produce material equality between all racial groups. This is the essential principle behind the concept of "equity."

Proponents of equity, including financial equity, see the wealth gap as an automatic ground for wealth redistribution. They treat the causes of inequality as irrelevant and justify the case for redistribution purely on the egalitarian grounds that people should have equal amounts of wealth to the greatest extent possible as a basic requirement of justice. The arguments advanced in support of that position are similar to those used to justify the case for a universal basic income. The supporters of financial equity argue that rather than being concerned with redressing historical injustice, a more persuasive basis for wealth transfers is simply that the wealth gap ought to be eradicated. Thus for example many demands for "land justice" are soon transmuted into a preference for monetary compensation to reflect the value of the land claimed to have been lost. The sense of grievance is ultimately expressed as a financial claim, so that the historical injustice arguments serve the purpose not of establishing a claim to property but a claim for financial support from the state.

The case for financial equity seems superficially plausible to those who regard wealth gaps as self-evidently wrong. But the moral basis of equity is put in doubt by the double standards entailed in selecting certain races to be the beneficiaries of racial equity and excluding other groups based on their race. This suggests that the reparations arguments are not as deeply rooted in moral justice as may at first glance be thought—if the claim truly had a significant moral component we would expect to hear the same arguments being advanced in relation to all historic injustices, not just those suffered by black people or those committed by Western nations. The debate surrounding historic injustice in practice does not attempt to cover all historical grievances but is linked to very specific historic events, especially those involving the British Empire and the historical subjection of non-white races. Thus the translation of this grievance into a financial claim cannot be said to reflect principles of justice.

Ultimately the equalisation of wealth through financial equity does not resolve any of the questions about legacies of racial injustice. It merely exacerbates them. The debate about redressing historical injustice is therefore not so much about injustice in general, but about racial humiliation and subjugation—precisely the sort of claim for which money and property transfers not only cannot be an appropriate answer but are likely to exacerbate the very humiliation of which complaint is made. After all, nothing could be more humiliating than the idea that one race subsists off the largesse of another.

Nor do measures such as targeted benefits for specific races produce net benefits for welfare recipients. One paradox of the case for reparations is that by supporting special wealth allocations for specified races or cultures it relies more heavily on segregation than the historical forms of segregation to which it is opposed, as its claims for financial support are linked to a separate non-market path for specified racial groups.[18] As Widdowson argues in relation to targeted welfare benefits for native communities in Canada, institutionalised forms of segregation which aim to protect specific cultures from the hardships of market participation by offering welfare payments tend unfortunately to encourage a culture of welfare-dependency which in turn leads to rising rates of social isolation, poverty, educational failure, violence and suicide.[19] Wealth transfers such as those prioritised by reparations do not address such tragic outcomes and seem entirely unconcerned about the psychic effects of dependency. Instead they continue simplistically to suppose that such social ills will magically cease to be a problem if the welfare budget is further increased, a solution popularly known as "throw more of other people's money at the problem".

---

[18] As Clarence Thomas remarked in the Supreme Court hearing on the lawfulness of racial preferences in university admissions, "I don't put much stock in that because I've heard similar arguments in favor of segregation, too." Sneed, T. (2022, October 31). Supreme Court Hears Arguments on College Affirmative Action Cases. *CNN*. https://edition.cnn.com/politics/live-news/supreme-court-affirmative-action-oral-arguments/index.html.

[19] Widdowson, F. (2019). *Separate but Unequal: How Parallelist Ideology Conceals Indigenous Dependency*. University of Ottawa Press.

At one level it could be said that it does not matter if poverty alleviation schemes do not work, as they are intended to be nothing more than aspirational; it is after all useful to have social schemes which reflect a signal of the goals which society intends to pursue regardless of whether there is a realistic prospect of achieving those goals. Nevertheless, honesty matters too. Policy schemes ought to match the goals which it is hoped realistically to achieve, not simply aspirations which in theory would be a good ideal to which society might aspire.

A further concern with such interventions is that they produce unintended effects. This is precisely what makes it important not to evaluate such interventions based on their intentions, but instead on their effects. For example, Williams shows some of the ways in which laws intended to regulate labour markets in order to help disadvantaged racial minorities end up hurting their purported beneficiaries: "restrictive laws harm blacks equally, whether they were written with the explicit intent—as in the past—to eliminate black competition or written—as in our time—with such benign goals as protecting public health, safety and welfare, and preventing exploitation of workers."[20] For example legislation designed to create better working opportunities for black workers indirectly contributed "as a major factor in reducing work opportunities for blacks."[21] The clearest illustration of this is federal minimum wage laws in the US which were originally intended to prevent the South from having a perceived competitive advantage occasioned by a lower wage bill.[22] Similarly, "equal pay for equal work" laws in apartheid South Africa may have equalised wages but only at the expense of making it no longer worthwhile for black workers to be hired: a racist employer who might previously have hired black workers simply because it would be cheaper to do so, now had no incentive to hire them at all.[23]

Rather than repealing laws which produce these types of harmful effects, the general tendency is to respond to deleterious outcomes by

---

[20] Williams, *Race & Economics*, p 29.

[21] Ibid., p 32.

[22] Ibid., p 33: quoting a commissioner of labor statistics: "A contractor from a Southern State secured a contract to build a Government marine hospital…he brought with him an entire outfit of Negro laborers from the South".

[23] Ibid., p 49.

enacting further legislation to attempt to reverse those effects.[24] Williams gives the example of occupational licencing laws which were originally introduced to keep black people out of specified trades such as hairdressing or plumbing and entrance tests which were originally designed deliberately to have a disparate impact on black applicants. Rather than abolish these intrusive measures, which price tradesmen out of the reach of lower income earners, huge amounts of effort have instead been expended to enforce antidiscrimination legislation to ensure that the tests are "fair" and do not indirectly discriminate against any race. Yet, as Williams shows, better alternatives can be found to open up the market for these trades and facilitate information disclosure, rather than trying to achieve safety standards through tighter and more costly policing of entry restrictions. This tendency to compound legislative failures with yet more disastrous legislation explains the burgeoning corpus of human rights legislation, antidiscrimination laws based on disparate impact or indirect discrimination, as well as the more recent legislative initiatives based on "anti-racism" and "equity." Human rights codes and employment equity laws are supplemented and enhanced with even more race-based measures to protect specified ethnic groups through targeted affirmative action measures.

Williams shows that problems relating to poverty and low income cannot be fixed through legislation. What then should be done to resolve intractable economic problems? There is no quick fix. The political pressure to "do something quickly" results in market solutions being rejected on grounds that they would take too long to yield results, but the quick interventionist solutions which are instead adopted simply do not work. For example, while being more highly skilled might attract a higher wage and consistently rising income levels, becoming skilled requires a considerable investment of time. As Williams observes, "The real problem is that workers are not so much underpaid as they are under-skilled. And the real task is to help those people become skilled."[25] The lack of a quick fix for the challenges of economic progress sometimes causes people to despair, imagining that it would take centuries to build up the skills and

---

[24] For discussion see Leoni, B. (1961). *Freedom and the Law*. D. Van Nostrand Company.

[25] Williams, *Race & Economics*, p 58.

institutions that lead to economic success and that state interventions would be quicker and better. But although there is no quick fix, neither is there cause for despair. There is no need to reinvent the wheel, and it does not take the same investment to reinvent what is already known as it did to invent it at the outset. Further, economic growth is exponential rather than incremental, and information and knowledge sharing in the digital age enables much faster progress than was heretofore possible.

Nor should there be an inordinate concern with relative speeds of progress: if some advance faster than others, that is not automatically unfair nor does it call for state intervention. Deaton argues that it is in the nature of progress that it must begin somewhere, and it ought not to be surprising if there is a time lag between the emergence and the spread of progress.[26] Similarly Lucas observes that "Of course, the industrial revolution did not affect all parts of the world uniformly, nor is it doing so today."[27] These economists highlight an important point: that "life is better now than at almost any time in history" so although "the world is hugely unequal" the improvement in living standards, education, health and life expectancy are causes for hope rather than despair.[28]

6.3 Implications for Economic Development

A further set of questions arises concerning the demands of justice in relation to inequality between nations. The claim for post-colonial reparations is based on the simple observation that former colonial powers are rich while their former colonies are still poor. This is a matter of concern to egalitarians who regard all inequalities as putatively unjust, but it poses philosophical and practical difficulties for proponents of distributive justice who desire to restrict their welfare schemes to operate within

[26] Angus Deaton. (2013). *The Great Escape: Health, Wealth, and the Origins of Inequality.* Princeton University Press.

[27] Lucas, R. R. Jr. (2004, May 1). The Industrial Revolution: Past and Future. *2003 Annual Report Essay.* https://www.minneapolisfed.org/article/2004/the-industrial-revolution-past-and-future.

[28] Deaton, *The Great Escape*, p 1.

their own borders. Even supposing it were to be agreed to promote redistributive justice within a nation, the question of redistributing wealth between richer and poorer nations is a different proposition altogether. The aim of eradicating global poverty through efforts such as declaring a "war on poverty" are more aspirational than effective, and if the attempt is made to extend this to the global level further ethical concerns arise in relation to neglecting the poor in one's own country in a bid to alleviate poverty in other countries. Gordon highlights the inconsistencies and contradictions, one might even say hypocrisies, buried in this iteration of distributive justice:

> Almost all political philosophers, and most economists, favor income redistribution to the poor. But do any good arguments justify this? Is it that we wish to eliminate or alleviate poverty? But in that case, why do we give aid to the poor in our own country rather than to much more poverty stricken inhabitants of the third world?[29]

Egalitarians have great difficulty in responding to these questions and approach them in different ways. While Rawls did not outline his theory of distributive justice in a global sense, many of his followers have extended the demands of justice to include international wealth redistribution.[30] Nagel for example would not extend welfare schemes beyond national boundaries but others would extend redistributive interventions to encompass the entire globe.[31] As discussed in Chapter 3, there is no evidence that foreign aid lifts poor countries out of poverty. Banerjee and Duflo are right to note that large sweeping arguments on whether aid does, or does not, work in improving the fortunes of poor countries often amount simply to speculation on a grand scale. We can speculate on the factors that probably do or do not help in particular circumstances, but generalisations about foreign aid as a path to global prosperity are unlikely to clarify the issues at stake. Further, in the context of policy debates, the issue is not merely what works, but also what justifies the

---

[29] Gordon, D. (1999, April 1). The Master Doubter. *Mises Review*.

[30] Rawls, J. (2001). *The Law of Peoples*. Harvard University Press.

[31] Nagel, T. (2010). The Problem of Global Justice. In *Secular Philosophy and the Religious Temperament: Essays 2002–2008*. Oxford University Press.

priority accorded to it in public spending. Not only does foreign aid fail to eradicate poverty, but the "fungibility of aid money" may lead to worse outcomes for example where it "frees up government resources to be spent on something bad, like the army."[32] Thus the issue is not simply what has or has not worked to lift poor countries out of poverty, but also the legal and philosophical justifications offered for particular policies—after all a scheme might "work" in achieving the desired goal, but this does not mean it is ethically justifiable.

Based on the variations in the outcomes of foreign aid Easterly concludes that "aid cannot achieve the end of poverty. Only home-grown development based on the dynamism of individuals and firms in free markets can do that."[33] The spontaneous nature of free markets means that facilitating economic growth in poor countries is not a simple matter of instructing poor countries to have free markets. Hence Easterly observes that "free markets work, but free-market reforms often don't".[34] Rather, "people everywhere have to explore with piecemeal, experimental steps how to move toward free markets".[35] Easterly is right to caution that "you can't plan a market" and that the attempts by organisations such as the IMF and World Bank to tie free market reforms to "structural adjustment" programmes have failed spectacularly partly due to the reliance on "shock therapy" to jolt developing countries into top-down comprehensive reforms instead of facilitating markets from the ground up. Free market reforms implemented in the context of "poor institutions that failed to prevent public corruption and private looting" failed, and "Most African countries that received intensive treatment from structural adjustment have had negative or zero growth".[36]

Easterly, with first-hand knowledge of failed pro-market reforms implemented by the World Bank in Africa, observes that there is no "simple recipe" to make markets work in jurisdictions where there are no established markets: "no simple recipe exists, only a confusing welter

---

[32] Easterly, W. (2006). *The White Man's Burden: Why the West's Efforts to Aid the Rest Have Done So Much Ill and So Little Good*. Oxford University Press, p 325.

[33] Ibid., p 322.

[34] Ibid., p 53.

[35] Ibid., p 54.

[36] Ibid., p 59.

of bottom-up social institutions and norms essential for markets. These evolve slowly on their own from the actions of many agents; the Western outsiders and Planners don't have a clue how to create these norms and institutions."[37] Central planners cannot create or direct markets, and this is true for markets in one's own or any other jurisdiction. This applies in the same way to questions of global justice: "So the West cannot design a comprehensive reform for a poor country that creates benevolent laws and good institutions to make markets work."[38]

Nevertheless, the fact that markets arise spontaneously and not by deliberate design or mandate does not mean we cannot ascertain ex post what has worked in prosperous countries and learn valuable lessons from that. While institutions cannot simply be transplanted from one jurisdiction to another, it is nevertheless possible to learn from successful institutions and adapt them to different contexts where they might be helpful. It is one thing to say that the West cannot impose private property rights on developing countries, and quite another to say that nobody knows what makes markets work or that developing countries need not protect private property rights if that is not their culture. As shown in Chapter 3, property rights are essential for economic progress and the reality is that the protection of private property is one striking feature of cultures associated with economic growth. The lesson to be derived from a comparative analysis is not that nobody knows the path to prosperity that would work for all countries, but rather that each country must be free and would be well advised to follow the path that has worked for others through its own reforms.

6.4 Stateless Justice and Anarchy

In *Anarchy, State and Utopia* Nozick highlights the fundamental principle that "individuals have rights, and there are things no person or group may do to them (without violating their rights). So strong and far-reaching are those rights that they raise the question of what, if anything,

[37] Ibid., p 67.

[38] Ibid., p 88.

the state and its officials may do. How much room do individual rights leave for the state?"[39]

The reparations debate has exposed a widespread expectation that the state has power to direct taxes to redressing historical injustice as it deems fit, with California for example proposing to pay descendants of slaves $569 billion to cover "housing discrimination", an amount greater than the annual cost of running public schools, hospitals and prisons in California.[40] Few question the ethical basis of the claim, as the public debate has confined itself to distinguishing which black residents will qualify, which black residents will not and how the whole scheme will be paid for. There is also a widespread expectation that subject only to fulfilling the requirements of democratic voting processes, the state has the power to seize property as it deems fit. South Africa for example has passed legislation to permit expropriation without compensation. These developments, which happen in liberal market democracies and not in communist states, call into question the principles highlighted by Nozick concerning "the nature of the state and its legitimate functions."[41] As the discussion in this book has shown, reparations claims go far beyond the minimal state defended by Nozick, and beyond the case he makes for rectification in cases of unjust acquisition of property.

In evaluating the role of the state there are significant philosophical differences between classical liberal and libertarian perspectives. The classical liberal view generally defends the allocation of tax revenues towards a limited range of public purposes, and in principle would treat reparations claims as part of the social welfare function of the state within prescribed limits. The libertarian view is more radical, and would call into question the redistributive functions of the state. A strict libertarian perspective would go even further, to question the role of the state in its entirety. Libertarianism in this sense is "a radical political view which holds that individual liberty, understood as the absence of interference

[39] Nozick, R. (1974). *Anarchy, State and Utopia*. Blackwell Publishing, p ix.

[40] Lee, K. (2022, December 1). California Panel Sizes Up Reparations for Black Citizens: The State is Undertaking the Nation's Most Ambitious Effort So Far to Compensate for the Economic Legacy of Slavery and Racism. *New York Times*. https://www.nytimes.com/2022/12/01/business/economy/california-black-reparations.html.

[41] Nozick. *Anarchy, State and Utopia*, p ix.

with a person's body and rightfully acquired property, is a moral absolute or near-absolute, and that the only governmental activities consistent with that liberty are (if any) those necessary to protect individuals from aggression by others."[42] Libertarians in that sense "combine a deep scepticism of political authority with a belief in the moral significance of private property, the efficiency and morality of free markets, the primacy of negative liberty, the importance of individualism, and the power of spontaneous order."[43] The question then is what the implications of that position would be in light of the political developments associated with the social justice movement, such as racial preferences and financial equity. As Block explains:

> If the sole justification for the limited state is to protect the person and property of the citizen, then these entitlements must be seen as a contradiction or violation of that principle. The point is, if we are to undertake a thorough moral analysis of entitlements, we must not constrict the scope of our deliberations merely to the recipients. Even on the unwarranted assumption that the people who receive these monies actually benefit from them, the transfers cannot be morally sanctioned because they violate the rights of those who made the contributions.[44]

This book has drawn upon a wide range of classical liberal views in the property rights debates, and many of the philosophers whose ideas we have discussed would see an important role for taxation and the welfare state in defined circumstances to meet goals such as education and health. Adam Smith regarded taxation as justified in pursuit of public goals, and many classical liberal perspectives take the position that taxation is only justified if strictly limited to a bare minimum; while they do not go so far as to question or reject any role for the state, they nevertheless question whether government interventions are the most appropriate response to economic inequality. Kaufman for example observes that

---

[42] Zwolinski, M. and Ferguson, B. (Eds.). (2022). *The Routledge Companion to Libertarianism.* Routledge, p 2.

[43] Ibid., p 3.

[44] Block, *Property Rights*, pp 24, 25.

state intervention in the use of private property is inherent in the power of the state, and sets out to explore the appropriate limits on that power:

> Taking the power away from government is no more possible than doing away with government itself. Government's *dominium eminens*, supreme lordship, shall always be with us, like the poor. We have the first recorded instance about 870 BC when Jezebel uses Phoenician law to acquire Naboth's vineyard for Ahab (1 Kings 21).[45]

Kaufman argues that in some cases state intervention may yield a benefit to the public in a utilitarian sense: "Eminent domain's excuse for being will always be making us, as a community, richer".[46] There are no doubt decisions taken by the state that have a beneficial outcome for society in a utilitarian sense, and Kaufman takes a pragmatic approach in observing that unless we wish to "liberate ourselves from this government power" the best we can do is to consider some ways to make it "a lighter burden on our liberties…less demanding on the fruits of our labors."[47] He also poses a question which is essential for the rule of law: "How can [government interventions] be fairer and thus create greater confidence in our laws and those who use them?"[48]

Many classical liberals would argue along similar lines as Kaufman, seeing state intervention as being sometimes justified, but highlighting the need for caution concerning its potentially harmful effects. They would regard state interventions that limit the rights of ownership as an issue that requires striking the right balance, and would regard such intervention as a last resort after first taking into account private benevolence and charity, eliminating artificial barriers to trade and market participation, and distinguishing between poverty or deprivation and relative inequality. Some supporters of state interventions do not necessarily deny that free markets yield prosperity more effectively than the alternatives,

[45] Kaufman, W. (2010). How Fair is Market Value? An Appraiser's Report of Temptations, Deficiencies, and Distortions in the Condemnation Process. In Benson, B. L. (Ed). *Property Rights: Eminent Domain and Regulatory Takings Re-Examined*. Palgrave Macmillan, p 77.

[46] Ibid.

[47] Ibid.

[48] Ibid.

but argue that law has an important role to play in speeding up market processes, correcting market failures, and generally redirecting market outcomes towards a more equal distribution. In that sense such critiques would not see coercive law as a threat to the market, but as a facilitator designed to correct market weaknesses or failures.[49] For example Moller defends property rights and free markets from a Smithian and Lockean perspective but proposes moral limits on the payment of reparations while remaining in principle open to the view that the state has a role to play in wealth redistribution as part of its social welfare function.[50]

Other classical liberals would not regard any state interventions as justified. For example Say regarded taxes as theft, and clearly under a view of taxation as theft no amount of tax is justifiable regardless of its limits. The anarchist debate on whether we need a state to protect property rights in modern liberal democracies is outside the confines of the inquiry in this book, as that would require a philosophical inquiry of a different character than that which was embarked upon here. But the cause for hope through free markets is relevant also in evaluating both anarchist perspectives as well as the perception that without state interventions ethnic minorities cannot prosper. Rothbardian libertarianism, for example, rejects altogether the validity of state interventions designed to reallocate wealth through measures such as taxation, and also rejects a role for the state in creating the institutions of law and law enforcement.

One implication of distinguishing between legislation and principles of natural law is that principles of natural law, as expressed in the common law, do not require state-created institutions to define and adjudicate them. This distinction between the natural law or common law on the one hand, and the state on the other, means that law based on the principles of self-ownership and property would not require a state for the peaceful resolution of disputes.[51] For example Casey argues that "the fundamental cultural institutions of human society — language, law,

[49] Deakin, S. (2002). Commentary in Epstein, R. A. (2002). *Equal Opportunity or More Opportunity: The Good Thing About Discrimination.* Civitas. http://www.civitas.org.uk/pdf/cs18.pdf.

[50] Moller, D. (2019). *Governing Least: A New England Libertarianism.* Oxford University Press.

[51] Gordon, D. (2012, October 24). Libertarian Anarchy. *Mises Daily Articles.* https://mises.org/library/libertarian-anarchy.

logic, and morals, are all of them the outcome of a spontaneous evolutionary process which is the creation of no one or no group's design but which is nonetheless rational.[52] In Chapter 3 an example was given of communities who spontaneously respect private property in conditions where private property is banned by the state, showing that the state is not required for private property rights to be upheld.[53]

The state is said to be necessary in order to uphold the rule of law. As Block explains the role of the state:

> For the limited government, free enterprise-oriented classical liberal, there is only one type of entitlement the citizen may properly receive from the state: security of his person and property. This entitlement entails an army to protect him from foreign despots, a police force to shield him from domestic villains, and a court system to determine who is and who is not an initiator of violence against another person or his property. Any and all other entitlements are illegitimate—at least from the perspective of this economic philosophy.[54]

Yet even this bare minimum of state functions is disregarded when the state fails to secure the rights to liberty and property. This issue becomes even more pressing as courts increasingly adopt the principles of critical race theories, endorsing the concepts of "systemic racism" and privileging certain litigants above others purely on grounds of their race.[55] In enforcing contested critical race theories courts are deviating from the common law understanding of entitlements towards statutorily created entitlements whose content is ideologically malleable. The

---

[52] Casey, G. (2012). *Libertarian Anarchy*, p 93.

[53] Easterly. *The White Man's Burden*, pp 93–94, describing the "Miracle in Xiaogang".

[54] Block. *Property Rights*, p 19.

[55] For example the Washington State Supreme Court recently stated: "This court has stated, unequivocally, that we owe a duty to increase access to justice, reduce and eradicate racism and prejudice, and continue to develop our legal system into one that serves the ends of justice… Whether explicit or implicit, purposeful or unconscious, racial bias has no place in a system of justice." The court's notion of "eradicating racism" in this case entailed taking the race of the litigants into account in deciding whether attacking the credibility of a witness undermines the fairness of the hearing. The court held that is not unfair to question the credibility of the witness if the witness is white, but if the witness is black questioning her credibility merits a retrial. https://www.courts.wa.gov/opinions/pdf/976724.pdf.

growing perception that legislatures can create any entitlements desired by a majority of voters leads not to the protection of private property rights but to expropriation. As can be seen in the example of South Africa where the law upholds expropriation without compensation, often the state does not protect the property rights of the citizens: on the contrary, the threat to the property rights of citizens comes from the state.

As discussed in Chapter 4, the rule of law must mean something more than blindly following legislative edicts. It should involve also a normative evaluation of whether the law is just. In this book we have argued that any rule which violates principles of justice is incompatible with the rule of law. We have defended the classical ideal of justice based on equality before the law, individual liberty and self-ownership. Any institution, including an institution of the state, which violates these principles with impunity cannot claim to be upholding the rule of law. In a time when the meaning of justice has been revised to enable the state to redistribute wealth between citizens based purely on their racial or ethnic identity, we must question whether any state which adheres to this race-based allocation of rights is fulfilling the functions for which its very existence is said to be justified.

References

Banerjee, A., & Duflo, E. (2011). *Poor Economics: The Surprising Truth about Life on Less Than $1 a Day*. Penguin Books.

Benson, B. L. (Ed). (2010). *Property Rights: Eminent Domain and Regulatory Takings Re-Examined*. Palgrave Macmillan.

Block, W. (2019). *Property Rights: The Argument for Privatization.* Palgrave Macmillan.

Casey, G. (2012). *Libertarian Anarchy: Against the State*. Continuum Books.

Conway, D. (2004). *In Defence of the Realm: The Place of Nations in Classical Liberalism.* Ashgate.

Deaton, A. (2013). *The Great Escape: Health, Wealth, and the Origins of Inequality*. Princeton University Press.

Delsol, J.-P., Lecaussin, N., & Martin, E. (Eds.). (2017). *Anti-Piketty: Capital for the 21st Century.* Cato Institute.

Easterly, W. (2006). *The White Man's Burden: Why the West's Efforts to Aid the Rest Have Done So Much Ill and So Little Good*. Oxford University Press.

Epstein, R.A. (2002). *Equal Opportunity or More Opportunity: The Good Thing About Discrimination.* Civitas. http://www.civitas.org.uk/pdf/cs18.pdf

Friedman, M. D. (2015). *Libertarian Philosophy in the Real World: The Politics of Natural Rights*. Bloomsbury Academic.

Furedi, F. (2004). *Where Have All the Intellectuals Gone?* Continuum Books.

Gordon, D. (1999, April 1). The Master Doubter. *Mises Review.*

Gordon, D. (2012, October 24). Libertarian Anarchy. https://mises.org/library/libertarian-anarchy

Gordon, D. (2017). *An Austro-libertarian View* (Vols. I, II, and III). Ludwig von Mises Institute.

Ikeda, S. (1997). *The Dynamics of the Mixed Economy: Toward a Theory of Interventionism.* Routlege.

Lange, O. (1965). *Problems of Political Economy of Socialism.* Peoples Publishing House.

Lee, K. (2022, December 1). California Panel Sizes Up Reparations for Black Citizens: The State is Undertaking the Nation's Most Ambitious Effort So Far to Compensate for the Economic Legacy of Slavery and Racism. *New York Times*. https://www.nytimes.com/2022/12/01/business/economy/california-black-reparations.html

Leoni, B. 1961. *Freedom and the Law*. D. Van Nostrand Company.

Lucas, R. E. Jr. (2004, May 1). *The Industrial Revolution: Past and Future*. 2003 Annual Report Essay. https://www.minneapolisfed.org/article/2004/the-industrial-revolution-past-and-future

Maritain, J. (1961). *On The Use of Philosophy: Three Essays*. Princeton University Press.

Mises, L. v. (1952). The Middle of the Road Leads to Socialism. In:*Planning for Freedom.* Libertarian Press.

Mises, L. v. (2012). *Human Action: A Treatise on Economics*. Martino Publishing.

Moller, D. (2019). *Governing Least: A New England Libertarianism.* Oxford University Press.

Nagel, T. (2010). The Problem of Global Justice. In: *Secular Philosophy and the Religious Temperament: Essays 2002–2008*. Oxford University Press.

Nozick, R. (1974). *Anarchy, State and Utopia.* Blackwell Publishing.

Pardy, B. (2020, September 18). Thirteen Things That Can't Be Said About Aboriginal Law and Policy in Canada. *C2C Journal*. https://c2cjournal.ca/2020/09/thirteen-things-that-cant-be-said-about-aboriginal-law-and-policy-in-canada/

Rawls, J. (2001). *The Law of Peoples*. Harvard University Press.

Roemer, J. (1994). *A Future For Socialism*. Harvard University Press.

Rorty, R. (1999). *Philosophy and Social Hope*. Penguin Books.

Shaw, W. H. (2003). They Stole Our Land: Debating the Expropriation of White Farms in Zimbabwe. *The Journal of Modern African Studies, 41*(1), 75.

Sneed, T. (2022, October 31). Supreme Court Hears Arguments on College Affirmative Action Cases. *CNN*. https://edition.cnn.com/politics/live-news/supreme-court-affirmative-action-oral-arguments/index.html

Widdowson, F. (2019). *Separate but Unequal: How Parallelist Ideology Conceals Indigenous Dependency*. University of Ottawa Press.

Williams, W. E. (2011). *Race and Economics: How Much Can Be Blamed on Discrimination?* Hoover Institution Press.

Zwolinski, M., & Ferguson, B. (Eds.). (2022). *The Routledge Companion to Libertarianism*. Routledge.

Bibliography

Alchian, A. A. (2007). Private Property. In D. R. Henderson (Ed.), *The Concise Encyclopedia of Economics.* Liberty Fund.

Atkinson, A. (2015). *Inequality: What Can Be Done?* Harvard University Press.

Baradaran, M. (2020). Closing The Racial Wealth Gap. *New York University Law Review Online, 95*(1), 57.

Baudin, L. (1962). *A Socialist Empire: The Incas of Peru.* Duke University Press.

Bauer, P. (2000). *From Subsistence to Exchange and Other Essays.* Princeton University Press.

Bean, J. (2009). Race and Liberty in America: The Essential Reader The Independent Institute.

Bell, D. (Ed.). (2019). *Empire, Race and Global Justice.* Cambridge University Press.

Bell, R. (2020, May 9). The Unintended Consequences of Promising Black Americans Reparations. *Journal of Higher Education Theory and Practice, 20*(4), 11. https://ssrn.com/abstract=3597158

Benson, B. L. (Ed). (2010). *Property Rights: Eminent Domain and Regulatory Takings Re-Examined.* Palgrave Macmillan.

Bingham, T. (2007). The Rule of Law. *Cambridge Law Journal, 66*(1), 67.

D. Gordon and W. Njoya, *Redressing Historical Injustice*, Palgrave Studies in Classical Liberalism, https://doi.org/10.1007/978-3-031-26584-6

Bingham, T. (2010). *The Rule of Law*. Allen Lane.
Black, J. (2011). *A Brief History of Slavery*. Robinson Press.
Banerjee, A., & Duflo, E. (2011). *Poor Economics: The Surprising Truth about Life on Less Than $1 a Day*. Penguin Books.
Block, W. (2019). *Property Rights: The Argument for Privatization.* Palgrave Macmillan.
Block, W., & Epstein, R. A. (2005). Debate on Eminent Domain. *NYU Journal of Law & Liberty, 1*(3), 1148.
Brenkert, G. G. (1998). Self-Ownership, Freedom, and Autonomy. *The Journal of Ethics, 2*(1), 27.
Casey, G. (2012). *Libertarian Anarchy: Against the State*. Continuum Books.
Chakraborty, S., & Das, M. (2005). Mortality, Human Capital and Persistent Inequality. *Journal of Economic Growth, 10*, 159.
Cohen, G. A. (1995). *Self-Ownership, Freedom, and Equality*. Cambridge University Press.
Cooter, R. D. (2006). An Escape from Poverty: Developing Productive Organization. *Southwestern Journal of Law and Trade in the Americas, XII*(2), 186.
Darity, W. A., & Mullen, K. (2020). *From Here to Equality: Reparations for Black Americans in the 21st Century*. University of North Carolina Press.
Deaton, A. (2013). *The Great Escape: Health, Wealth, and the Origins of Inequality*. Princeton University Press.
Delsol, J.-P., Lecaussin, N., & Martin, E. (Eds.). (2017). *Anti-Piketty: Capital for the 21st Century.* Cato Institute.
Deist, J. (2021, June 3). *A Libertarian Approach to Disputed Land Titles. Mises Wire*. https://mises.org/wire/libertarian-approach-disputed-land-titles
Devine, D. J. (2021). *The Enduring Tension: Capitalism and the Moral Order.* Encounter Books.
Epstein, R. A. (2022, June 22). California's Reparations Overreach. *Defining Ideas*. https://www.hoover.org/research/californias-reparations-overreach
Epstein, R. A. (2011). *Design for Liberty: Private Property, Public Administration, and the Rule of Law*. Harvard University Press.
Epstein, R. A. (2002). *Equal Opportunity or More Opportunity: The Good Thing About Discrimination.* Civitas. http://www.civitas.org.uk/pdf/cs18.pdf
Epstein, R. A. (1989). The Utilitarian Foundations of Natural Law. *Harvard Journal of Law and Public Policy, 12*, 711.
Easterly, W. (2006). *The White Man's Burden: Why the West's Efforts to Aid the Rest Have Done So Much Ill and So Little Good*. Oxford University Press.

Ferreira, F. H. G., & Ravallion, M. (2009). Poverty and Inequality: The Global Context. In W. Salverda, B. Nolan, & T. M. Smeeding (Eds.), *The Oxford Handbook of Economic Inequality.* Oxford University Press.

Finnis, J. (1980). *Natural Law and Natural Rights*. Oxford University Press.

Friedman, M. D. (2015). *Libertarian Philosophy in the Real World: The Politics of Natural Rights*. Bloomsbury Academic.

Flew, A. (2009). Justice: Real or Social? *Social Philosophy & Policy*, 151.

Flew, A. (1986). Enforced Equality—Or Justice? *Journal of Libertarian Studies, 8*(1), 31.

Forrester, K. (2019). Reparations, History and the Origins of Global Justice. In D. Bell (Ed.), *Empire, Race and Global Justice*. Cambridge University Press.

Furedi, F. (2004). *Where Have All the Intellectuals Gone?* Continuum Books.

Gilley, B. (2018). The Case for Colonialism. *Academic Questions, 31*, 167.

Gordon, D. (2019, November 15). Yes, Taxation Is Theft. *Mises Wire*. https://mises.org/wire/yes-taxation-theft

Gordon, D. (2012, August 9). Waldron's Rule of Law. *Mises Daily Articles*. https://mises.org/library/waldrons-rule-law

Gordon, D. (2021, February 19). Are There Any Limits to Natural Rights? *Friday Philosophy*. https://mises.org/library/are-there-any-limits-natural-rights

Gordon, D. (2020, February 21). Individual Responsibility and Guilt. *Mises Wire*. https://mises.org/wire/individual-responsibility-and-guilt

Gordon, D. (2017). An Austro-libertarian View (Vols. I, II and III). Ludwig von Mises Institute.

Gordon, D. (2009, September 25). Private Property's Philosopher. *The Mises Review, 5*(1). https://mises.org/library/private-propertys-philosopher

Gordon, D. (2000). Development as Freedom by Amartya Sen. *The Quarterly Journal of Austrian Economics, 3*(1), 89.

Gordon, D., & Njoya, W. (2023). Response to Symposiasts. *Cosmos and Taxis, 11*(1), 31.

Harris, J. W. (1996). *Property and Justice*. Oxford University Press.

Hay, D. (1984). Equality, the Third World and Economic Delusion. *Transformation, 1*(2).

Hayek, F. A. (1945). The Use of Knowledge in Society. *American Economic Review, 35*(4), 519.

Hayek, F. A. (1960). *The Constitution of Liberty*. University of Chicago Press.

Henderson, M. T. (Ed.). (2018). *The Cambridge Handbook of Classical Liberal Thought.* Cambridge University Press.

Higgs, R. (1977). *Competition and Coercion: Blacks in the American Economy, 1865–1914*. Cambridge University Press.

Kay, J. (2003). *The Truth about Markets—Why Some Nations Are Rich but Most Remain Poor*. Harper Collins.

Kim, J. (2019, December 1). Black Reparations for Twentieth Century Federal Housing Discrimination: The Construction of White Wealth and the Effects of Denied Black Homeownership. *Boston University Public Interest Law Journal, 29*(135). https://ssrn.com/abstract=3615775

Kukathas, C. (2019). Libertarianism Without Self-ownership. *Social Philosophy and Policy, 36*(2), 71.

Kurrild-Klitgaard, P. (2000). Self-Ownership and Consent. *Journal of Libertarian Studies, 15*(1), 43.

Leoni, B. (1961). *Freedom and the Law*. D. Van Nostrand Company.

Lewis, H. D. (1948). Collective Responsibility. *Philosophy, 23*(84), 3.

Locke, J. (1980). *Second Treatise of Government* (C. B. Macpherson, Ed.). Hackett Publishing.

Lucas, R. E. Jr. (2004, May 1). *The Industrial Revolution: Past and Future*. 2003 Annual Report Essay. https://www.minneapolisfed.org/article/2004/the-industrial-revolution-past-and-future

Maritain, J. (1961). *On The Use of Philosophy: Three Essays*. Princeton University Press.

McCloskey, D. (2015). 'How Piketty Misses the Point' (July 2015 vol 37:4) Cato Policy Report 5. https://www.cato.org/sites/cato.org/files/serials/files/policy-report/2015/7/cpr-v37n4-1.pdf

Mises, L. v. (2012). *Human Action: A Treatise on Economics*. Martino Publishing.

Mises, L. v. (1962). *Socialism: An Economic and Sociological Analysis*. Yale University Press (First published 1951).

Mises, L. v. (1952). The Middle of the Road Leads to Socialism. In *Planning for Freedom*. Libertarian Press.

Mises, L. v. (2005). *Liberalism: The Classical Tradition* (B. B. Greaves, Ed.). Liberty Fund (Original work published 1927).

Muhammad, P. M. (2020). The Trans-Atlantic Slave Trade's African Elephant in the International Courtroom: African Nations Owe Blacks of the Diaspora Reparations. *UC Davis Journal of International Law & Policy, 27*(1), 81. https://ssrn.com/abstract=3863452

Moller, D. (2019). *Governing Least: A New England Libertarianism*. Oxford University Press.

Murphy, L., & Nagel, T. (2002). *The Myth of Ownership: Taxes and Justice*. Oxford University Press.

Njoya, W. (Ed.). (2023). Symposium on Economic Freedom and Social Justice: The Classical Ideal of Equality in Contexts of Racial Diversity. *Cosmos + Taxis: Studies in Emergent Order and Organization, 11*(1).

Njoya, W. (2021). *Economic Freedom and Social Justice: The Classical Ideal of Equality in Contexts of Racial Diversity*. Palgrave Macmillan.

Njoya, W. (2021). A Critique of Equality Legislation. *Journal of Libertarian Studies, 25*(1), 272.

Nozick, R. (1974). *Anarchy, State and Utopia*. Blackwell Publishing.

Olsthoorn, J. (2019). Self-Ownership and Despotism: Locke on Property in the Person, Divine Dominium of Human Life, and Rights-Forfeiture. *Social Philosophy and Policy, 36*(2), 242.

Palmer, T. G. (Ed.). (2012). *After the Welfare State: Politicians Stole Your Future*. Jameson Books.

Pardy, B. (2020, September 18). Thirteen Things That Can't Be Said About Aboriginal Law and Policy in Canada. *C2C Journal*. https://c2cjournal.ca/2020/09/thirteen-things-that-cant-be-said-about-aboriginal-law-and-policy-in-canada/

Perry, A. (2020). *Know Your Price: Valuing Black Lives and Property in America's Black Cities*. Brookings Institution Press.

Piketty, T. (2014). *Capital in the Twenty First Century*. Belknap Press.

Pinker, S. (2018). *Enlightenment Now: The Case for Reason, Science, Humanism and Progress*. Random House.

Posner, E. A., & Vermeule, A. (2003). Reparations for Slavery and Other Historical Injustices. *Columbia Law Review, 103*, 689.

Rothbard, M. N. (2002). *The Ethics of Liberty*. New York University Press (original publication 1982).

Roemer, J. (1994). *A Future for Socialism*. Harvard University Press.

Rothbard, M. N. (1995). *An Austrian Perspective on the History of Economic Thought*. Edward Elgar.

Roy, T. (2020). *The Economic History of India 1857–2010*. Oxford University Press.

Salverda, W., Nolan, B., & Smeeding, T. M. (2009). *The Oxford Handbook of Economic Inequality*. Oxford University Press.

Shaw, W. H. (2003). They Stole Our Land: Debating the Expropriation of White Farms in Zimbabwe. *The Journal of Modern African Studies, 41*(1), 75.

Sternberg, E. (2015). Defining Capitalism. *Economic Affairs, 35*(3), 380.

Sen, A. (1999). *Development as Freedom.* Alfred Knopf.

Sherwin, E. (2004). Reparations and Unjust Enrichment. *Boston University Law Review, 84*(5), 1443.

Sowell, T. (1999). *The Quest for Cosmic Justice.* Touchstone.

Sowell, T. (1993). *Is Reality Optional? and Other Essays.* Hoover Institution Press.

Sowell, T. (2013). *Intellectuals and Race.* Basic Books.

Smith, A., Raphael, D. D., & Macfie, A. L. (1982). *The Theory of Moral Sentiments.* Liberty Classics.

Thomas, D. A. (1996). Adverse Possession: Acquiring Title to Stolen Personal Property. *Probate & Property, 10*, 12.

Waldron, J. (2012). *The Rule of Law and the Measure of Property.* Cambridge University Press.

Waldron, J. (2002). *God, Locke and Equality: Christian Foundations of John Locke's Political Thought*. Cambridge University Press.

Waldron, J. (2002). Redressing Historic Injustice. *The University of Toronto Law Journal, 52*(1), 135.

Waldron, J. (1990). *The Law.* Routledge.

Widdowson, F. (2019). *Separate but Unequal: How Parallelist Ideology Conceals Indigenous Dependency.* University of Ottawa Press.

Williams, W. E. (2011). *Race and Economics: How Much Can Be Blamed on Discrimination?* Hoover Institution Press.

Wright, R. W. (2001). Once More into the Bramble Bush: Duty, Causal Contribution, and the Extent of Legal Responsibility. *Vanderbilt Law Review, 54*(3). http://ssrn.com/abstract=254875

Wright, R. W. (2011). The NESS Account of Natural Causation: A Response to Criticisms. In R. Goldberg (Ed.), *Perspectives on Causation.* Hart Publishing. http://ssrn.com/abstract=1918405.

Zwolinski, M., & Ferguson, B. (Eds.). (2022). *The Routledge Companion to Libertarianism.*

Index

D. Gordon and W. Njoya, *Redressing Historical Injustice*, Palgrave Studies in Classical Liberalism, https://doi.org/10.1007/978-3-031-26584-6

P

R

S

GPSR Compliance
The European Union's (EU) General Product Safety Regulation (GPSR) is a set of rules that requires consumer products to be safe and our obligations to ensure this.

If you have any concerns about our products, you can contact us on

ProductSafety@springernature.com

In case Publisher is established outside the EU, the EU authorized representative is:

Springer Nature Customer Service Center GmbH
Europaplatz 3
69115 Heidelberg, Germany

www.ingramcontent.com/pod-product-compliance
Lightning Source LLC
Chambersburg PA
CBHW062143200726
48454CB00005BB/366
* 9 7 8 3 0 3 1 2 6 5 8 3 9 *